I0866656

Rambling with Rukka

Rambling with Rukka

A Moving Memoir

Rukmini Srinivas and
Lakshmi Srinivas

RUPA

Published by
Rupa Publications India Pvt. Ltd 2024
7/16, Ansari Road, Daryaganj
New Delhi 110002

Sales centres:
Bengaluru Chennai Hyderabad
Jaipur Kathmandu Kolkata
Mumbai Prayagraj

Copyright © Rukmini Srinivas and Lakshmi Srinivas 2024
Images courtesy: Authors' archives unless stated otherwise

The views and opinions expressed in this book are the authors' own and the facts are as reported by them which have been verified to the extent possible, and the publishers are not in any way liable for the same.

All rights reserved.
No part of this publication may be reproduced, transmitted, or stored in a retrieval system, in any form or by any means, electronic, mechanical, photocopying, recording or otherwise, without the prior permission of the publisher.

P-ISBN: 978-93-5702-522-5
E-ISBN: 978-93-5702-523-2

First impression 2024

10 9 8 7 6 5 4 3 2 1

The moral right of the author has been asserted.

This book is sold subject to the condition that it shall not, by way of trade or otherwise, be lent, resold, hired out, or otherwise circulated, without the publisher's prior consent, in any form of binding or cover other than that in which it is published.

For Chamu

Contents

Preface
by Rukmini Srinivas

I called my friend Krishna in Bangalore. Answering the phone, he promptly said, 'Hello, Mrs Srinivas, but isn't it a bit late in the evening for you to call? What time is it in Boston?' Krishna and I would occasionally call one another in this way, the time difference between Bangalore and Boston made it either too early or too late for one of us. On this occasion as we continued talking about this and that, I interjected, 'As usual, I'm rambling, Krishna.' He responded, 'I love your ramblings, continue to ramble! What are you doing these days?' It was comforting to know that friends like Krishna liked my stories and that encouraged me to write this second book of memoirs.

My father meticulously kept a record of family events and happenings in a diary. The same diary served as an accounts book for monthly family expenditure. My husband Chamu also kept a diary for his work, and I found it to be a very scholarly piece of writing. Maybe my father's and Chamu's habits influenced me to keep a record of what has been happening in my life. These days, my diary not only has many doctor's appointments that I have to remember, but also has a record of visits from friends and family.

My daughters kept me updated on the reception of my food memoir *Tiffin*. The encouraging reviews for the book had me scribbling notes for another volume on happy memories of the years gone by. Unfortunately, my scribblings became fewer and fewer as my eyes weakened. My family was upset that my pleasures of reading and writing had to come to a halt. Lakshmi offered to write and document my stories. She prodded me to retell some of the stories I had told her and her sister Tulasi years ago. That started me off on my journey into the past, into my childhood, my early adulthood and beyond. The book took shape through the conversations and interactions Lakshmi and I have been having over the past few years.

Our collaboration has had its own challenges. In my rambling stories, I tend to go back and forth in time. Some memories are clearer than others. In thinking about one experience, often others come into focus. Through our lengthy conversations over several months, I recalled details that I would otherwise have not thought about. Sometimes the stories would develop through my desire to tell Lakshmi about certain events and situations. It must not have been easy for her to draw stories from my, sometimes disconnected, memories of happenings from half a century ago.

I was at times frustrated with myself for being unable to write and for the way the narration seemed to be in fits and starts and not flowing smoothly. At times, I would feel exasperated. But Lakshmi would joke about it like her father used to and that would lift my spirits. She would ask me questions about my experiences and the incidents in my life and encourage me to elaborate on them. Some of the stories in the book are what I have told my family, including Chamu, and my friends, years ago, but others came about in conversations with Lakshmi that I wouldn't have thought to include. I did feel cheered talking about the bygone days, my old friends and family, and connecting to places and people through these retellings.

So, this volume simply chronicles the past from personal memories. I have tried to stay faithful to my observations and the events in my life as I remember them.

Introduction
by Lakshmi Srinivas

It was only after I left home for college in the United States that I came to know my mother as a storyteller. In the days before email, I would wait impatiently for the blue airmail envelopes that would arrive every few weeks. Painstakingly written in my mother's precise hand, the rambling letters were brimful with news of family and friends, our dachshund Cherokee, updates on the garden, happenings in Bangalore and recipes for me to try out. I devoured them in my homesickness. It is difficult to say when this book began, but I think it may have begun with those letters ages ago.

When my father passed away in 1999, my sister and I persuaded my mother to spend at least a few months of the year with us in the Boston area. For the next several years, my mother travelled between Boston and Bangalore, timing her trips to avoid the snowy New England winters. When international travel became difficult, she somewhat reluctantly moved to the United States leaving behind her friends, her home and the city where she had lived happily with my father for three decades. She was in her late 70s when her life was uprooted in this way, or rather transplanted, as she continued with her interests—reading, gardening, cooking and teaching. The vegetarian cooking classes she held in Cambridge became hugely popular and she went on to host a cooking show on local television, making new friends along the way. It was at this time that she started her first book, a food memoir. *Tiffin: Memories and Recipes of Indian Vegetarian Food* was written in a leafy New England suburb, far away from the settings of her childhood and adult life which feature vividly in it.

While working on *Tiffin* my mother spent long hours at her computer, sometimes writing into the early hours of the morning. My sister and I were not used to seeing her immersed in this way. In our family, my father would be the one with his books and papers, and my mother would always be in a whirlwind of activities—managing the household, driving us around, cooking and shopping for the family, all in addition to her teaching duties.

Delighted, yet somewhat surprised by the enthusiasm with which her first book was received, my mother explained that she owed her storytelling skills to the conversations she had with her father from the time she was five. A man of routine, upon coming home from work late in the afternoon, he would have a bath and change his clothes. Then, after a cup of tea, he would settle down to ask my mother and her sisters about their day at school. My mother would then faithfully recount the events of the day. When she was older, she and her father would read together and talk about their favourite books. As he grew hard of hearing, these conversations became all the more important as she would patiently, and with a raised voice, chat with him—allowing him to be part of her life.

In 2018, my mother was engaged in drafting a follow-up to *Tiffin,* a memoir without recipes this time. Our collaboration began when I offered to help put down her stories on paper.

Over the next couple of years, many afternoons and evenings were spent in storytelling and sharing memories. I looked forward to these sessions and to my mother's stories from what seemed an endless trove. She would embark on one of her rambling tales, vividly recounting the days gone by, and I would document the anecdotes, interrupting with questions, asking for elaboration or offer suggestions of stories to include. That is how our collaboration grew. We looked at old photographs which yielded even more tales. My sister would sometimes stop by to see if we were making progress, and she would give her suggestions for anecdotes. My mother's remarkable memory and wide knowledge never failed us.

There were frequent interruptions due to her health, which was indifferent at the time, my work, and the general intrusions of our lives. During a snowstorm in New England, when it was impossible for us to meet, we talked over the phone and hoped that the electricity wouldn't go off. We took our writing to Cape Cod on the Atlantic, a place my mother loves and an easy escape during the pandemic. A good day would involve some writing, a stroll or a drive. A visit to the farmers' market would recall her mother's kitchen garden in Tanjore, and the thrift stores with their collection of random objects prompted memories of the lessons in thrift learnt as a schoolgirl in Poona (now Pune).

My mother's family was a typical middle-class South Indian Brahmin family, and fairly traditional. My grandmother cooked vegetarian food, and Hindu festivals were celebrated at home. My mother and her sisters learnt South Indian classical music or dance. But the family was unusual in other ways. Though neither of my mother's parents had a university education, or perhaps because of it, they wanted all eight daughters to receive a college degree and be independent. This was uncommon for women of their class and background in those days. My grandfather spared no expense on his daughters' education, earning ridicule and criticism from kinsfolk. He made sure his daughters were enrolled in the best convent schools run by British Protestants, even though some of these schools charged double fees for Indian students in those days.

Convent schools had other advantages. They accepted students who moved from state to state and schooled them for the central Senior Cambridge examinations. This meant greater geographical mobility thereafter.

My mother and her sisters grew up juggling many cultures. My grandfather's job in the Southern Command of the military meant he was frequently transferred, and the family moved with him. My grandmother could speak and understand several languages—she had picked up a little Hindi, a few words of Urdu in Quetta, and Marathi when the family lived in Poona. She spoke Tamil fluently and could understand Malayalam. My mother and her sisters spoke Tamil and English at home, Marathi and Hindi with friends, and were taught the Queen's English at school.

At school, my mother learnt the piano. Reciting the Lord's prayer was a daily ritual at her school assembly, and she fondly remembers the hymns she sang in the choir. On Christmas Eve, she and her friends would go carolling in the neighbourhood. Though not a bookish child, preferring to ride around the neighbourhood on her bicycle, my mother grew up on Jane Austen, Thomas Hardy, William Shakespeare and the English poets. My grandfather's Anglophilia extended to a taste for English biscuits, Polson's butter and Scottish marmalade. Cakes and chocolates from the famous Italian confectionery Monginis in Bombay (now Mumbai) were for very special occasions. They were the same Monginis brothers one of whom was a fascist and proud supporter of Benito Mussolini. The extended family of more orthodox relatives frowned upon this upbringing—they warned my grandfather that nothing good would come of girls growing up in this way.

A favourite pastime for my mother and her sisters was putting on plays and musical dramas for family and friends. Stories from Hindu mythology and folktales as well as children's stories, such as Cinderella or Sleeping Beauty, were all part of the repertoire. This love for performance has stayed with my mother—she is a natural. An excellent mimic, she would amuse my father with her imitations and he would wickedly egg her on. She was deep in rehearsals for a college play the first time my father called on her, and had he not called again they would most likely not have met.

Learning of her interest in theatre and in performance made me view the faded photographs of her school and college amateur dramatics differently. When she was 10, my mother announced she wanted to be an actress—clearly out of the question for girls from respectable middle-class families at the time. Nearly 5 feet 8 inches in her late teens, she was unusually tall for a South Indian woman of her generation. She was also rail thin like a fashion model, all through her 20s, prompting people to ask concernedly if she suffered from tuberculosis. Those who knew her compared her charismatic good looks to the Bombay film star Nargis, who was cast in a mould different from the feminine beauties who typically became film heroines. Yet, my mother's leanness, her height and angular features meant she often played the male lead or the villain in school plays and in performances at home. Perhaps, this casting played over into her life, for my mother felt she was more of a son than a daughter to her father.

Unlike many women of her class and generation in their 20s who had marriage on their minds or were preoccupied with managing a household, my mother had decided not to marry. She felt responsible to help her father who had her six younger sisters to educate. In 1952, when she received a master's degree in Human Geography from Madras University, she was among the first batch of women geographers in independent India. Soon after, she was appointed as a lecturer at Queen Mary's College, which allowed her to continue teaching and living in Madras—an overnight train ride from her parents. But fate intervened in the shape of my father. They were married in 1955 in a simple ceremony on the terrace of my grandparents' home in Tanjore, and my mother left with him for Baroda that very night.

My interest in my mother as a woman of her generation has certainly shaped the stories, along with some of my own interests in urban life and the natural world. Yet, the stories are my mother's, from her life and experiences, and are all narrated in her voice. They centre around the people, events and happenings that shaped her world. Many revisit her childhood and young adulthood in pre-Independence India, others tell of her life with my anthropologist father and of her experiences as an educator in Delhi and Bangalore. A number of stories delve into the chance meetings and occurrences that became consequential for the way her life unfolded, including our family's rather sudden move to Bangalore in the 1970s.

Moving to Bangalore to start a research centre for social sciences fulfilled a cherished dream for my father. I never realized it at the time, but for my parents, Bangalore was like coming home in many ways. It was closer to my father's family in Mysore and to my mother's mother and sisters in Madras. My father knew Bangalore from his childhood days and my mother was born there. Language and culture were not alien, unlike in Delhi.

In Bangalore, my mother joined the Geography unit at the newly-established Institute for Social and Economic Change. She was the only woman researcher, driving all over the city and its outskirts in her black Fiat. A skilled driver, she has navigated the California freeways and the congested roads in Delhi. She could reverse down a street with speed and, on a couple of occasions, when her car caught fire, she had the presence of mind to jump out, rather like a stunt driver in an action film, I thought. Few women were seen driving cars in Bangalore in those days and she attracted hecklers and shouts of 'Lady Driver'. Even so, driving around Bangalore was a pleasure, as my mother recounts. My father's teasing name for her was '*thiruhaltippi*' in Tamil, or 'one who likes to roam around'. It is true she loved to wander, frequently getting lost and enjoying it. She insists that she discovered much of Bangalore this way.

Wandering through memories with my mother has been a journey full of surprises and we often ended up in all sorts of unlikely places. A recollection of her days as a college student led to a story about her orthodox aunt's ritual-ridden existence in the 'village of flowers' outside Madras; retelling the story of our move from Delhi to Bangalore involved an encounter with an astrologer who made predictions by measuring one's shadow; and my mother's search for property in Bangalore is a story as full of twists and turns as the roads she travelled in the city.

Writing this book with my mother has made me see her in a different light. When my sister and I were children, my mother was the disciplinarian in the family, appearing rather stern. I never realized how charismatic she is—drawing people to her—or how gentle. I've also been struck by her unquestioning acceptance of what life brought her and her ability to find contentment. My father would remark on her 'simple faith', perhaps a bit enviously as he felt it eluded him. It may have been this faith that played a role in the way my mother approached a life that brimmed with new experiences and adventures, sudden moves and changes which she adapted to, finding a place for herself wherever my father's work and chance took them.

The stories in the book are not neatly laid out in chapters because that is not how the book flowed—they evolved from letters, scattered conversations, shared experiences, photographs and, of course, memories. Readers of her first book, *Tiffin*, may find some characters and events central to her life make an appearance here.

Never a planner, my mother has intuitively found her way through life—for better or for worse. Her love of wandering and discovery gives this book its sense of unfolding.

CHILDHOOD AND COLLEGE DAYS

Life with My Parents and the Family Atmosphere

I was born and raised in a middle-class South Indian family. My father's ancestors owned agricultural land in the village of Thirukkarugavur, located in the fertile deltaic plains of the tributaries of the Kaveri. My paternal grandfather, the eldest male of the joint family, managed the agricultural operations of the family's lands in the village of Velur nearby. My father once told me that his father, being the eldest sibling, was responsible for the welfare of the family and so he had to reluctantly stop his formal education while he was still in secondary school. He encouraged his younger brother to study to become an engineer, and the family's pride when his brother rose to become chief engineer of the Mettur Dam was never underplayed.

When my father's parents passed on, he missed their nurturing care and the family dynamics changed. He decided to leave home and joined the Military Accounts Department, setting aside his admission to a science seat at the prestigious Presidency College in Madras. As a young man, he was posted to Quetta and soon after he married Sahayavalli, my mother, then a 13-year-old from Madurai.

I was born in May of 1927 in the Gosha Hospital in Tasker Town in Bangalore. Tasker Town was near the bustling Shivaji Nagar area. Years later, in 1976, when I had moved to Bangalore and was living in the Cantonment, I located the hospital much to my delight.

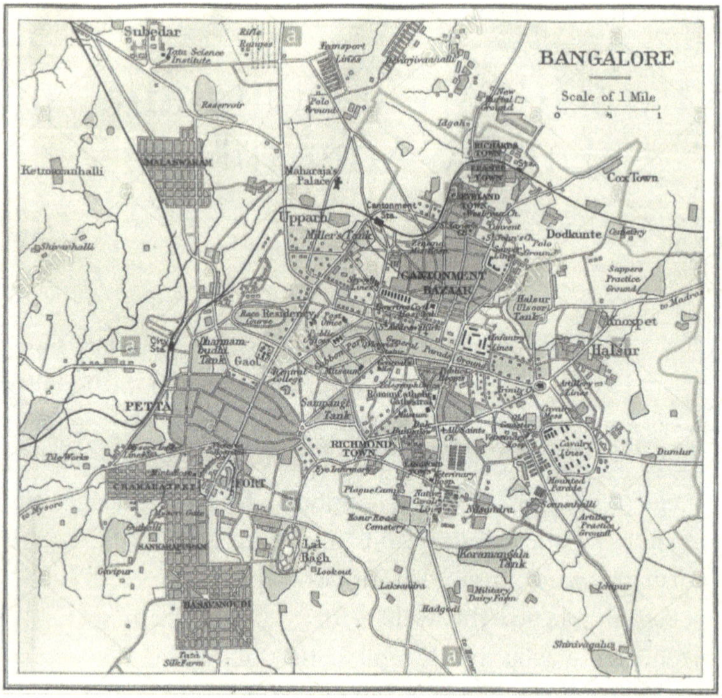

Bangalore Cantonment and Petta, 1924

At the time of my birth, my parents lived in Cox Town in north Bangalore. If we do place some value on memories, especially of childhood, I daresay I remember surprisingly quite a bit of my parents' Cox Town home where I lived for the first four years of my life. The house was set back and surrounded by a low compound wall. It had an expansive front garden. I remember a large front yard with shrubs and trees all around the perimeter of the lot. It was a single-storey house with a portico and a generous front verandah. Right in front of the verandah was a little fountain.

I am told I was born underweight unlike my older siblings—my sister and brother—who were chubby and fair 10-pounders. The doctors warned my mother that I might not survive into adulthood. If I remember rightly, I was massaged with cod liver oil and left in my pram in the sunny garden of our home. Perhaps it was my child's mind that made the garden feel endless.

There was an *amla* (gooseberry) tree under which I lay, soaking up the sun from morning to afternoon. I remember my mother gardening nearby. I also fondly remember Deval Thatha, an elderly neighbour from across the street who used to sit on the garden bench next to the pram and hum and sing to me. That was the kind of lullaby I grew up with. When in later years I asked my mother if my memory, as a two-year-old, of Deval Thatha was correct, she said, 'Oh yes, he was a widower with no children and spent a lot of time with us. He was very fond of your father and me and he was an excellent gardener.' Deval Thatha would gift us flowers and vegetables from his garden. He would stick a flower in my pram almost every day.

Paul Fernandes' sketch 'Old Bungalow'

As I grew and explored my surroundings, I remember a long, trellised passageway that led from the main house to the kitchen. We were a smallish family then—just my parents, elder brother, sister and myself. My sister, six years older to me, went to the Bishop Cotton Girls' School and would be away most weekdays. My brother was about two years my senior and we would spend much of our time together with our mother at home. My mother always had dogs and I remember a photograph of her with a white shaggy dog. In the evenings, my father and mother would go for walks in the neighbourhood. Bangalore was truly a garden city in those days and every home had a patch of a garden. My mother told me that her life in Bangalore was as pleasant as she could remember.

Over the next decade, our small family grew until we were nine—one brother and eight sisters. My father (Appa) had a nine-to-five job working in the Defence Services, Military Accounts Department of the Southern Command. Not having a university education did not make much of a difference in Appa's life. He surrounded himself with books ranging from Tamil classics to tomes on philosophy, social history, travel, bird watching and much more. Simply put, he was well-read with an abiding interest in ideas. He enjoyed Indian and Western classical music, and English literature, particularly reading Shakespeare and the English poets.

Though Appa had grown up in a Brahmin family and was a vegetarian, he had developed a taste for different foods. His breakfast was invariably Quaker Oats. When he had toast, it was with Polson's butter, imported from England in those days, rather than the homemade butter my mother made, which he liked with South Indian food. Another favourite of Appa's was marmite with hot buttered toast.

When Appa took us to his office canteen, I remember ordering mushroom soup and Welsh rarebit with cheese. In Bombay we would go to Monginis, where he would get us

Appa and Amma

marzipan and chocolates. After he retired in Tanjore, I would take him bread and cakes from Spencer's in Madras.

Appa was disciplined and meticulous. He kept a record of family events and happenings in a diary. The same diary served as an accounts book for monthly family expenditure. He believed in planning, even on a day-to-day basis. And given his modest income and our large family, he had to plan and prepare a budget. He and my mother would carefully budget monthly household expenses together.

As Appa was the sole breadwinner for the family, some corners had to be cut. Unlike his colleagues, he did not buy a car. Instead, he bought us all bicycles that we could use to travel across town—to school and back. But he was insistent that we develop a reading habit. We had a small library at home and that became a lending library for children in the neighbourhood.

Education was very important to my parents, and they had grand plans of educating all their daughters to the university level. We were enrolled in the best private schools. While many of our school friends talked about having private tutors, Appa neither believed in private tutors nor could he have afforded them. He would sit with us every evening while we did our homework and help us if needed. He closely monitored our performance at school and frequently visited the school to talk to our teachers about our progress or lack thereof. But it was not just book learning that my parents wanted us to excel in.

My mother was a trained vocalist in Carnatic music. In Poona she also learnt Hindustani music. Both she and my father wished to expose us to the arts: music, dance and theatre. We attended musical evenings by classical singers Abdul Karim Khan and Hirabai Barodekar, both favourites of my mother. These were public performances that anyone could attend, and they were free.

At home, we were tutored in music and dance. Our teachers, maestros of the time, would come home a few times a week and my mother would make sure we practised every evening. My eldest sister played the violin and reached a professional level; I was the vocalist of the family and learnt classical South Indian music; my younger sister Sarasa played the sitar; and Leelu, the youngest of us at that time, learnt to play the tabla. Some of my younger sisters learnt Bharatanatyam for many years and became proficient enough to give public dance performances.

At home, we formed a mini orchestral group. On occasions, we would entertain friends and visitors. Sometimes, we would get together with children our age from other families in the neighbourhood and give impromptu performances. I remember, immediately after India's independence, we formed a group that met every weekend and sang Gandhiji's favourite songs. I was asked to sing 'Lead Kindly Light' and my sister Kamala played the Hindu bhajan 'Vaishnava Jana To' on her violin, with Sarasa and Leelu accompanying her. Other friends would join in. The friendships we developed in this way lasted for decades.

Amateur dramatics at home. Rukka (centre) with a sari-clad Sarasa and cousin Gowri.

Summer holidays brought a respite from routines of the school year. When we lived in Poona, we would go to Bombay for our holidays. My cousin, Chandru, who was a student at the Sir J.J. School of Art, would come to receive us at the Dadar station in a hired 'Victoria', as the iconic horse-drawn carriages were known. I remember once, on the way home, he halted the Victoria suddenly. The first time we asked why, he mysteriously said, 'Wait and see', and looked up at the balcony in front of us. We joined the gathering crowd on the street and waited. Then, following his gaze, we saw an apparition in a white sari walk across the balcony. And all the people who had gathered on the street threw flowers onto the balcony. Chandru asked, 'Did you recognize her?' and added, 'That was Nargis!' Though we only had a very brief glimpse of the passing figure, I was very excited to see my favourite Bombay film star—whom I was thought to resemble in my circle of relatives and friends.

We sisters had our other interests and ways of entertaining ourselves. In Jabalpur, Sarasa, who was closest in age to me, and I would play hopscotch outside in the courtyard. We also spent a lot of time playing board games—carrom, and snakes and ladders—in a study adjoining the living room. The study was also where we did our homework. It was a dark room with overgrown shrubbery outside the window. There was no ceiling fan in the study, but it was cool even in summer. The family radio was housed in the study. On weekend afternoons, Sarasa and I would religiously listen to the programme of popular music and film songs—*Aap ki Pharmaish* (By your request)—transmitted from Radio Ceylon, hoping that our requests, sent by postcard, would be played.

We were fans of film music and ghazals that spoke of jilted heroines pining for their lovers, of heroes who awaited their beloved, and of unrequited love and longing. We would drool over the songs of K.L. Saigal, K.C. Dey, Manna Dey and Kanan Bala. As we had heard the songs countless times, we would sing along. Laying our heads on the table next to the radio and enjoying the music, we were transported to a fantasy world. That is when I dreamt of becoming an actress. Kamala was star-struck and collected movie posters, and had a little album of stamp-sized photos of Hollywood stars that she had saved from chocolate wrappers. In school, Sarasa and I would trade our duplicate stamps for ones Kamala did not have so that she could complete her album.

Rukka with radio

My mother was a homemaker in every sense of the word. She was a stay-at-home mother who always seemed to be juggling a variety of chores around the house as she managed a growing family. Her kitchen was an 'open house' with friends stopping by to savour her hospitality. The youngest of five, she was married off while still in school. She had started a life with her husband, my father, when she was barely 15 years old, in faraway Quetta (in present-day Pakistan)—a world away from her hometown of Madurai in the heart of South India.

My mother, very quickly, had to learn how to keep house. In Indian homes, recipes were handed down orally and techniques of cooking were learnt simply through watching and participating in a domestic setting. But my mother had lost her mother when she was just four years old. She was looked after in Madurai by her maternal uncle, a prominent lawyer, and his wife. So, after marriage, my mother had to learn how to cook and care for her family all on her own and without any guidance. She turned out to be an excellent cook and her repertoire included North and South Indian food as well as food from Maharashtra, all of which she learnt how to prepare during our time living in Poona.

As with many families in India who are vegetarian, cooking in our family began with fresh vegetables and spices. The vegetable seller who would come by the house every day would supply green chillies, ginger, lemon, fresh coriander and seasonal greens, like amaranthus, fenugreek leaves, dill and colocasia leaves. My mother grew some vegetables at home and also grew green chillies and coriander. *Ponnaganni kerai* (purslane) was easy to grow and my mother always had a plentiful supply that she would share with neighbours.

As we lived in rented homes in Poona in the 1930s and 1940s, my mother was not at liberty to use the garden space. Not having a garden plot did not hamper her from indulging in her passion for gardening. My earliest memories of Amma's kitchen garden are of long and rectangular wooden trough-like boxes, arranged in the sun-drenched spacious deck adjoining the kitchen, in which she grew vegetables, herbs and flowers.

In the morning even before we dressed for school, my sister Sarasa and I would dash out as soon as the back door was opened, to pluck tender brinjals, beans, 'lady's fingers' and green chillies. Sarasa would compete with me and hastily pluck the not-as-yet-ready tender vegetables, yanking the plants out with the roots! Being the younger sibling, she would get away with it and Amma would gently dig another small pit and replant them.

Amma not only had a green thumb, but she also believed that talking to plants, singing to them and gently stripping the dry and wilted leaves and flowers encouraged the well-being of plants and contributed to their healthy growth. I remember decades later, when Chamu, my husband, and I lived in Delhi, we visited the Pusa Agricultural Institute where research was being conducted on the benefits of music to enhance healthy growth and productivity in plants. Amma was not a 'formal' researcher, but she had a sensitivity to plants which they seemed to respond to.

When we did have a garden, my mother planted two *moringa* (in Tamil, *murungakai*) saplings in a corner of the compound near the garage. Moringa is now considered a superfood, rich in antioxidants, vitamins and fibre, but growing up it was simply a part of our diet. My mother's moringa plants were young and did not yield their characteristic drumsticks, the long pods that could grow to 18 inches in length. My father—who was also very fond of the flavour and taste of moringa—would buy a few pods in season whenever he went to the market and Amma would cook them as sambar with lentils or as *aviyal* (a mixed vegetable dish with ground coconut and yoghurt). The moringa leaves, when cooked, were delicious. One dish that Amma made with the moringa leaves was an elaborate spicy dumpling with a ground chana dal batter. Red chillies and other spices were added, and the dumplings were steamed. As a special treat for my sister and me, she would sprinkle powdered jaggery on fried moringa leaves when they were hot and mix it up, and we would enjoy this crunchy snack. After retirement, my father built his own house in Tanjore and my mother planted several moringa trees in the large garden. She would spread a reed mat under the tree and the creamy white flowers that fell would be collected and added to any kind of vegetable she cooked for lunch. The taste of moringa leaves from my childhood is an indelible memory. I did not know the health benefits of moringa at the time, but I became so addicted to eating the leaves and the bean pods that I planted saplings in every house I lived in.

In Poona, when my sisters and I returned home from school late in the afternoon, mouth-watering aromas would greet us. My mother would have prepared tiffin. Some days we would come home to steaming idlis with delicately flavoured coconut chutney, another day it would be paper-thin *dosai*, which we would eat with *molahapudi*, or *uppuma* made with semolina, peas, onions and tomatoes. We would devour these and other delicious treats. Sometimes my mother would use moringa leaves to make savoury *vadai* with ground chickpea batter, or spicy pancakes called *adai*.

The vegetables we harvested in the morning would be served for dinner in the form of a delicious sambar that accompanied steamed rice and soft wheat chapattis. Rice mixed with yoghurt (set at home) was always the last course. Amma cooked greens in a variety of ways. We now hear of protein intake being essential for a vegetarian diet—we ate our protein as dals and beans that were cooked and added to greens. The addition of tomatoes, sautéed onions and tamarind water, as well as shredded ground coconut, would transform the taste of spinach and other greens.

Cooking in our house was mostly done once a day. We had no refrigerator, so we followed an indigenous cooling method of dunking the pots of cooked food in cool water to keep food from getting spoilt. Some greens were cooked dry and this would also help keep them from spoiling. The pots my mother used for cooking were made from heavy stoneware called *kalchetty*. They enhanced the flavours of the food. The stoneware would heat up slowly and retain heat, altering the pace of cooking, and that, as I learnt later, was what gave the food its special taste.

My parents soon decided to have a live-in cook to relieve my mother of some of the kitchen chores. But with her love for and interest in cooking, Amma continued to spend many hours trying out new recipes—not from recipe books, but from her memory and recollection of the appearance and taste of the food she might have eaten years ago. She told me often that 'taste' in food was not something you easily forgot. The memory storehouse of the food eaten long ago would help, she would say.

Summer Activities

Poona, 1937

Summer was a busy time in our family. Some summers we would go to Bombay, to my uncle's home. My father's younger brother would lovingly plan for a vacation in Matheran, one of the 'hill stations' not far from Bombay. Hill stations, both in India and Africa, got their name from the British colonial officials' practice of using these small towns at higher elevations to escape the summer heat. We girls loved it in Matheran. For us it meant not only cooler weather but also long pony rides and playing in the wading pools.

But my memory goes back to summer holidays in Poona. I and my two younger sisters closest in age to me, would look forward to two months of waking up late, not having to rush to school and no exams to study for. In the summer of 1937, my father's youngest sister, Annam Athai, visited us for a couple of months with her daughter. Athai lived in a small village in Tanjore district and this was her daughter's first visit to our home. Many outings were planned: to the Bund Garden, Parvati Hill, the sacred city of Nasik and the Karla Caves.

The couple of months of scorching sunshine before the monsoons set in were precious, and my mother and her friends would make full use of them. As I remember, the rooftop terrace in our home where my sisters and the landlady's granddaughter Kusum used to play hopscotch was an expansive space with cement flooring. My mother would dry clothes there and use the hot sun to make her herbal hair oils with hibiscus and amla. One advantage of this terrace was that there were no overhanging trees, like in our neighbour's house. The terrace was flooded with sunlight from dawn to nearly dusk.

Annam Athai was a great cook, and her specialty was making papads or *appalam*, as we called them. Early one Sunday morning, Sarasa and I woke up to a flurry of kitchen activity. Soon my mother's friends—Vaini, the landlord's daughter-in-law who lived on the first floor; Mrs Bhusnurmath, the young bride from next door; and Alamelu, the adult daughter of my mother's friend down the road—all trooped in one by one, carrying bags. Sarasa and I were curious, and we peered into the kitchen to find Athai vigorously pounding a big ball of dough in a stone mortar with a tall wooden pestle.

Athai was short and squat, with an animal energy about her. She wore a nine-yard sari the traditional way, as my mother did, and her curly hair would be wound back in a big bun at the nape of her neck. She was tough and was used to heavy-duty kitchen work. With her sari's *pallu* tucked into her waist to allow freedom of movement, she assumed charge of working the dough. From time to time, she used the ends of her pallu to wipe her sweaty hands and face.

My mother said we could watch, but not touch anything. We also had to stand at a distance to avoid any accidents. We had heard stories of relatives who had had their fingers crushed by the heavy mortar. The stiff ball of dough was a mix of rice flour and urad flour. There was a bowl of, what we later learnt, was pure castor oil that Athai would, at intervals, smear over the dough and continue pounding till it became more elastic. Towards the end, a few cumin seeds would be thrown in and the dough would be taken out on a banana leaf. Our three neighbours pinched off small balls of dough, which they rolled into flat discs. Each had a rolling pin and a flat, round wooden or stone board. When all the dough was rolled out, the discs were stacked on a tray and taken to the terrace where my mother and Parvatibai laid out wicker mats on which thick bedsheets were spread. At that time, Sarasa and I were told, 'If you want to help, you can lay each disc next to another, flat on the cloth, leaving a little space in-between and see that the crows are kept away.' We were thrilled to help and spent several hours in the hot sun. By midday, my aunt came up to the terrace to turn the discs over. After a couple of hours, she returned to collect them. By then, the discs were wrinkled and shrunk, with the edges turning in. She flattened them out with her hands, piled them up, tied them in the sheet and took them down.

This was an elaborate three-day operation. The next morning, the whole process was repeated with the wicker mats, sheets and discs being spread out to dry. Sarasa and I were not able to resist stealing a few of the half-dried appalams, which were chewy and delicious. On the third day, the appalams were bone dry and ready to be stored. The metal storing bins were airtight and very light. The women who participated in the making collected their share.

A few varieties of appalams were made: one with just salt and jeera; another with garlic, green chillies and coriander paste kneaded into the flour; and a third with the juice of boiled tomatoes, carefully strained, which would give it a pink tinge. Another variety was *sago vadaam*, made either from sago powder or boiled sago that would be added to the rice flour and then spooned into small *vadaam* or wafers to be dried.

Homemade appalams were a treat and a perfect snack. They could be roasted over hot embers or fried. I remember seeing Athai snacking on crisp fried appalam in the afternoon and offering them to us.

The heat of the sun was not to be wasted and prompted a range of activities. Our friend Ramakrishna Apte lived down the street in Saraswath Colony. Rama's father, Sheoram Apte, was a wholesale contractor for vegetables at Poona's Somwarpeth Market. Over the years, our families became good friends and Rama used to have lunch with us over many weekends and school holidays. Mr Sheoram, in appreciation of my mother treating Rama like one of her own, would send baskets of fresh, tender okra, long and thin purple brinjals and *gowarphali* (cluster beans). Faced with this bounty, more than what she could cook immediately, my mother would decide to dry them in the sun. Each of the vegetables had to be processed somewhat differently before they were dried on the terrace. Sarasa and I would help in washing all the okra in big basins of water, draining them and wiping each one dry with a cotton towel. My mother would then cut them into inch-long pieces and set them aside. The brinjals would also be washed, dried and cut into small cubes, and the gowarphali would be boiled al dente in salt water and turmeric and then drained. Once again, the reed mats would be placed on the terrace and covered with old cotton sheets. Rama, Sarasa and I would sometimes help excitedly with the mats and sheets and Amma would uniformly scatter vegetables, one variety at a time, on each of those sheets. Parvatibai's daughter, Kusum, and her friend would keep watch to ensure no birds or squirrels came near. By mid-afternoon, Amma would go and gently roll the vegetables over with her hand, so that they would be uniformly exposed to the bright, hot sun. Later, around five in the evening, she would, with Parvati's help, tie the sheets into bundles. These bundles were then brought down to the kitchen where they would be stored for the night. For the next three or four days the process would be repeated till they were really dry. The dried vegetables would be stored in metal biscuit tins and used for making *vettai khozhumbu*—a delicious spicy stew prepared with tamarind sauce that is often made in South Indian households. Vettai khozhumbu somehow tastes better during the rainy season and the winter. I think it gives that much-needed warmth to the body.

There was never a dull moment in my mother's kitchen. The summer also found her making fruit juices, mainly lime juice. Apte would bring us baskets of fresh juicy limes, and Sarasa and I would enthusiastically squeeze the limes using a fruit squeezer made of glass. The juice would be boiled with sugar and a pinch of salt. Jars of this lime juice would be kept in the sun for months. Once the lime juice concentrate was ready, a little cardamom powder and crushed ginger would be added to make refreshing drinks.

My mother's kitchen was also a place for a variety of health-related activities unrelated to food. A regular Saturday morning routine included the 'oil bath' for all four of us sisters. Our convent school was very particular that we did not come to school with oily, greasy hair and encouraged students to wear their hair short. So, to make up for the five days of school, our heads and hair would be drenched with medicated hair oil, our bodies massaged with warm sesame oil and my mother would give each one of us an elaborate 'head bath' on weekends. I remember those were the times we used neither shampoo for the hair nor soap for the body. Shikakai powder—made from a long, dried pod of the Shikakai tree—was mixed with a tablespoon of water to form a thin, runny paste that would be rubbed into the scalp to clean it and remove the oil from the hair, leaving the hair soft and glossy. Sometimes, milled moong bean flour and turmeric powder was mixed into the paste and this would also be used as a body scrub. Later, I learnt that turmeric was not only an ingredient for healing but also a depilatory.

The herbal hair oil that Amma made was stored in a large stoneware jar and generally lasted a whole year. I neither remember the exact proportion nor do I remember all the ingredients, but the oils that she used were a combination of sesame oil and unscented castor oil into which hibiscus flowers and leaves, leaves of the henna or mardani plant (*Lawsonia inermis*), curry leaves and a variety of twigs, roots and flowers were thrown in and kept in the sun for several weeks.

Our neighbour, Kamalam Aunty, was very aware of her light-skinned good looks and spent much time during the day looking after herself. My mother once gifted her a bottle of the hair oil. Although Kamalam Aunty was certain that her black tresses grew longer and healthier after using the oil, in order to camouflage the herbal smell, she used to add a few drops of rose-scented Parisian perfume that was available in Bombay.

Jabalpur, 1941

My thoughts move from Poona to Jabalpur, where my father was posted in 1941 and where I first tasted *amsat*—thin sheets of dried mango pulp and juice that are delicious, tangy and sweet. Amsat was both a dessert and snack for Sarasa and I. Making it was a long and laborious process, and another summer event. Every summer, Narayana, our cook in Jabalpur, would go to the fruit *mandi* in Gol Bazaar and return with baskets of extra-ripe mangoes. These mangoes were not the hybrid variety. They were definitely juicier, and you couldn't slice them. As my husband Chamu used to joke, they had to be eaten in the bathroom as it was such a messy affair!

Our home in Jabalpur had a large, airy *aangan* (courtyard) open to the sky with a 12-ft-wide paved verandah that wrapped around it on all sides. Amsat-making would commence early in the morning in the courtyard, with Narayana dunking a whole basket full of mangoes in a huge tub of water and rinsing them. Sarasa and I would join to help him and following Narayana's example, we would pick up each fruit and roll it between our palms lightly. The stem end would be plucked off, making an opening. Then the mango would be squeezed till all the juice and pulp came out. It was a delicate operation, as the skin had to be kept intact. The mango stone or seed had a lot of juicy pulp attached, so it would be kept aside in another big tub. After squeezing the skins, the stones were taken out and squeezed.

Narayana would churn all the pulp and juice to mix it up. He would then taste it. If it was not sweet enough, he would add a little powdered jaggery. He was an innovative cook and would sometimes add a little cardamom powder for flavour. The pulp and juice would be poured and spread thinly on the big metal trays that he rented from the *halwai*'s (confectioner) store. These trays would be kept in the sun, and to keep the birds and squirrels away Narayana would place sticks attached with black pieces of cloth around the trays. In the evening, the trays would be stacked in the kitchen and brought to the courtyard every morning for the next week to dry fully. The dried pulp would be scored with a knife and the strips would be rolled on sticks, like lollipops. The rest would be cut and kept for storing. The amsat was a chewy, tangy, sweet and addictive snack for us.

My father's stern expression belied his zest for life. He had a wide circle of friends—both men and women—from different walks of life. In Jabalpur, he and his friends would look forward to the summer when he would enthusiastically arrange for *poori*, *rabadi* and *amras* parties. Sarasa and I would also look forward to these parties when, for a few hours, our home would be bustling with about 50 to 80 guests, many of them my father's colleagues and bridge friends; their wives, husbands and a few neighbours close to my parents would also be invited. Kamala's friends at the women's club and my mother's friend, Mrs Ghosh, from the nearby Gol Bazaar orphanage would never fail to come for these parties. There was a lot of talking and more eating.

Poori and amras was a traditional and delicious combination. But the specialty of these parties was the rabadi, an out-of-this-world caramelized milk pudding, slow-cooked in huge vats with a generous mix of raisins, almonds, *paruppu* (a kind of dal), pistachios and whole cardamom pods. My father loved rabadi. The halwais of Mandla were his good friends because he was a regular customer every summer.

Rabadi needed milk that was high in fat, so buffalo milk was perfect for it. In fact, measuring the fat content in milk was a year-round preoccupation for my father. In those days in Jabalpur, milk vendors would go door to door. I remember Pannalal, who would come by on a bicycle, carrying two cans of buffalo milk for our family. At six o'clock in the morning, he would be on our front verandah and call out to Narayana, '*Bhaiyya, aao, degree dalo* (Bring your lactometer and check the fat content of the milk)!' This was a daily ritual.

The journey to Mandla to get the rabadi would take us through teak forests. For this journey, my father would hire a jeep and I accompanied him on several occasions. There was no way of conveying our arrival on a particular day to the halwai except by my father's handwritten postcard in English. When we arrived, the halwai would produce the four kerosene tins filled with rabadi. The jeep would then take us and our delicious cargo back home to Jabalpur.

Once home, Narayana would very efficiently unload the kerosene tins (each had a wooden handlebar across the top for transportation) and line them up in a zinc sheet tub, half filled with cold water. This worked like magic to keep the rabadi fresh till lunch the following day.

The courtyard was, once again, the centre of activity—the space for food and fun! One side of the verandah that surrounded the courtyard opened out onto a medium-sized kitchen from where Narayana, together with the neighbour's cook and household help, would produce puffy pooris of wheat flour and the amras made with mango pulp mixed with sugar, ground almond, cardamom and saffron in milk. It was chilled in a big vat containing ice.

In summer, there would be a daily supply of ice from the ice factory in Jabalpur. It would be covered with sawdust and a gunny sack wrapped over it. Sarasa and I would stand near the front door watching the young men haul blocks of ice on their bent backs from the *tonga*.

While Narayana was busy in the kitchen, frying pooris with the help of the neighbour's cook, our neighbour's household help, Govind, would help in making the amras. Several baskets of overripe mangoes would be washed. The stems would be deftly clipped off and then each mango was rolled between the palms of their hands to loosen the pulp, following which the juice was squeezed out. The mango stone would be dropped in another basket lined with muslin cloth. The secret of extracting all the pulp was in the brisk pressing and rolling of the mangoes. And as with making amsat, the mango stones in the muslin cloth were squeezed to extract as much of the juice and pulp as possible. Sarasa and I would sit on our haunches with folded newspapers in our hands, swinging them back and forth to keep the flies away.

The making of amras took several hours, but the lunch would be ready on time. My mother would be hovering in the kitchen, but she really wouldn't have much to do. Narayana would be in total command. The frying of the pooris smelt heavenly! And he would borrow huge metal trays from the local halwai to prevent the pooris from being stacked and flattened. Part of the pleasure of eating a poori was putting your finger in, breaking the surface and letting the steam out. Narayana would knead the wheat flour for quite some time before he smeared oil on it and set it aside before rolling out each poori to fry. The smell of pooris being fried in a mixture of ghee and oil is lost nowadays. We talk of frying mediums like hydrogenated oils but when I was growing up, we were only familiar with pure oil, ghee or butter.

I would describe rabadi as food fit for the gods. Milk and sugar in the right proportion, cooked slowly for several hours thickened the milk solids to a consistency that was creamy with a delicate caramel flavour that left you longing for more. There could be no better combination than a well-made poori, a rich caramel rabadi, and silky smooth, sweet and sour amras.

Those were pre-plastic days, and I remember the pooris being served on dried wide teak leaves, and the rabadi and amras in clay pots. After the meal, Narayana would collect the pots in a big basket and sitting in the aangan he would smash the pots on the granite stone floor. The broken clay would be dumped under the trees in the garden.

Tanjore, 1947

My father retired and moved to Tanjore in 1947. Although Tanjore was not defined by summer and winter, as it was hot all year round, there was a rainy season. So once again, activities like making pickles or the sun-drying of vegetables were confined to the months before the rains.

Every time my aunt visited, preparations for making pickle would commence. Favourites were raw mango, lime or lemon, bitter lemon and lime and green peppercorns with fresh ginger root. My aunt would enthusiastically help, but I overheard her telling my mother, '*Manni* (brother's wife), you make the pickles because my hands are not good for pickle-making.' Somehow, in a few weeks' time, the pickles my aunt prepared would develop mould and maggots. Annam Athai was as puzzled as anyone else, 'I don't know whether it is because my body is heaty; I try to be careful but it hasn't worked till now.' I don't know if there is any truth to this, but my mother's pickles would last for years and grow tastier with time. After I married Chamu, there was one type of pickle that gained my mother much praise from his family. There is a variety of miniature mango that is made into *vadu maanga* pickle—tiny whole mangoes, smeared with a little castor oil, dunked in salt and turmeric powder and kept in a porcelain jar with a tight lid. Over time, the baby mangoes shrivel but remain crisp and have a distinctive flavour. In our home, rice mixed with curd and this pickle was a favourite of ours. It also helps in battling nausea, as I noticed, and so has been a favourite with pregnant women. It was also a favourite of my brother-in-law, Parthasarathy (Pachu), who would remind me every summer to get him his share from Tanjore.

A Tanjore specialty was a dehydrated pickle made from a locally grown variety of miniature green bell pepper. The procedure for making it was quite elaborate as I remember from watching my mother. These miniature green peppers would be soaked in a slurry of thick, slightly sour curd with salt, ground fenugreek seeds, ground turmeric root and asafoetida powder mixed in a stoneware jar. This mixture would be stirred with a wooden ladle. My mother was very particular that she attended to this pickle only after her bath. After about three to four days of soaking, the chillies would be spread out on a reed mat on the terrace in the sun. They would be ready in about four days. This dehydrated pickle was deep-fried and acted as a delicious accompaniment to curd rice.

The sun was our solar cooker and in Tanjore, too, we used its heat to dehydrate vegetables. Whenever I would go to the *sante* or farmers' market, which was held every Sunday in Tanjore, I would come back with a whole lot of tender brinjals in season or *kothaivaranga* (cluster beans) and green *shundaikai* (known as 'turkey berry' in the West). My mother would sometimes ask me to get a red pumpkin. I thought it unusual that she would slice and dry the pumpkin, but I found it to be delicious. She would use my favourite dried and cubed baby brinjal for making *vettai kozhumbu.* Dehydrated neem flowers are a specialty of the South. In the summer, the neem trees in my parents' garden would hardly have any leaves, for they would be covered in blooms. Mats would be spread under the trees and the flowers shed in the morning and early afternoon would be collected and dried on bamboo winnows. These dried flowers, which have a slightly bitter taste, are a delicacy and used for making rasam. These days, friends from India send us these dried flowers.

'John', from Shanghai

Sarasa and I would be waiting for John on the doorstep of our house in Poona. And sure enough, at the stroke of 12 on a Sunday afternoon, the clear 'Srrrk...' would ring in our ears and we would excitedly rush out of the gate into the street to greet him.

The first time John came with his silk fabrics was in 1935 and every summer thereafter, he was a visitor till 1939, when our family moved to Madras. John was from a village near Shanghai. He told us his name was John probably thinking we wouldn't be able to pronounce his Chinese name. His English was faltering but he spoke Hindi fluently. He once hinted to my mother that he had left a family in the Khasi Hills. It now occurs to me that he might have married into one of the Khasi tribes.

After greeting John, we would rush indoors to find our mother. Leaning his bicycle against the wall, John would effortlessly bring a huge khaki-coloured canvas bundle out onto the side verandah, where he would set about untying the bundle and very carefully arrange his silk wares on the mat.

John was a master salesman, plying his silks from house to house. He knew exactly what my mother would like for her four daughters and he would tell her where each piece of silk came from. My mother would end up buying silk by the yard. The fabric was of various textures; she would buy the thicker ones for our long skirts and the lighter ones for our blouses. While some of the fabric was plain and of pastel shades, there were others that were dramatically coloured—golden yellow, maroonish-red or velvety black—and very often printed with gold dragons, contrasting coloured flowers or other motifs. If my mother asked John to bring more of a particular kind of silk she liked, he would always say 'next time'—but his stock would be entirely different the next year.

John did not believe in bargaining; he would quote a price and that was final. He operated on trust. If my mother said she did not have the money at home, John would say that it was no problem and agree to come another day to collect his money.

For Sarasa and I, John's visit was an event but not because of the silk that would be made into dresses for us. We were enchanted by the little stick dolls he made out of rice flour. Sitting on the doorstep, he would take some white dough from a double-lined box and, in a few minutes, fashion a doll on a Popsicle stick. He had a little paintbox with some brushes of different kinds. He would very deftly colour the figure and add details of the clothes, the hairdo and hair accessories. The decoration was quite elaborate, with gold paint as well as black paint for the hair and so on. The dolls were not for sale. They were gifts to us children and my mother would display them in her *Navarathri Kolu* arrangement. We would treasure them till the day would come when we found them with all of their hair eaten off by ants.

Navarathri Kolu Festival

Women's worlds did not revolve around the kitchen and cooking food alone. The many festivals in a year gave them an opportunity to socialize with family and friends in the community. On these occasions, the women in our neighbourhood came into their own.

The nine-day Navarathri celebration, usually in October, is one of the highlights of the Hindu calendar. Navarathri is celebrated differently in different parts of India and it represents the battle between good and evil, and the triumph of the cosmic forces of good on Vijayadashami (the tenth day). On the ninth day is Ayudha Pooja (the worship of tools), which is when Goddess Saraswati is worshipped. The celebrations include visiting temples, rituals of worship, chanting prayers and singing devotional songs as well as telling and listening to mythological stories, stories from the Puranas and so on. The festival is an occasion for families to come together and a social occasion for communities, as friends, neighbours and relatives welcome one another into their homes.

In Poona's Saraswat Colony, at our South Indian friends' homes, Navarathri Kolu was a lavish celebration and preparations started weeks, if not months, before. One of the main rooms in the house was set aside for the arrangement and display of the kolu. Trunkloads of religious figurines along with *bommai* (dolls) and figures that represented everyday life were unwrapped and assembled every year. The dolls and figurines, made of wood, clay or porcelain, would be arranged on a pedestal with an odd number of wooden steps—odd numbers being auspicious. In my friend Kamali's house, I remember there were seven to nine tiers of wooden steps from the ceiling to the floor. Each step could be dismantled and stacked away for the rest of the year, then fixed back into place for the festival.

In our family, Navarathri was a low-key celebration with the exception of the Saraswati Pooja—the day when all our books and musical instruments would be placed reverently before Goddess Saraswati, the patron of knowledge and the arts. The Michaelmas holiday at our school, St Helena's, would be spent in helping our mother prepare and arrange for the bommai kolu (dolls' festival) that lasted for nine days. We looked forward excitedly to these activities. Annam Athai would visit us from her village in Tanjore district every year during Navarathri and participate enthusiastically in the preparations. I remember her telling us that the celebration of the festival in the form of arrangement of dolls, once started, should go on from one year to the next unless there was a tragedy in the family.

Weeks in advance, our gardener, Dhondu, would help in taking down the heavy trunks of dolls and display items from the topmost shelves in the storeroom. Four black metal trunks contained treasures: wooden, porcelain and glass dolls from England; clay dolls; and many more artefacts, some being miniature musical instruments—violin, harmonium and flute—all wrapped very carefully in tissue paper. They were packed in different sections in the trunk in thematic fashion to facilitate the arrangement for the next year's festival.

In our house, the kolu arrangement had five to seven steps, and as with kolu arrangements generally, the steps would be arranged in a pyramidal shape: with the tiers becoming shorter as they went higher. Dhondu and his son Keshav helped in erecting the steps. We would all happily work together—sit and dust and wipe the dolls—and then help our mother in arranging them after covering the steps with white bedsheets. This was before plastic took over people's lives.

Every house had its own arrangement of dolls and deities, wherein family aesthetics, tastes and interests would find expression in the kolu. In our house, each step was devoted to a theme and followed a pattern. Given our family's interest in music, one theme was a *pattu kacheri* (musical concert) with miniature singers and musicians, musical instruments and even an audience. The detail was remarkable, even down to the tuft of hair on the musician's head. Other themes included a grocer's store with a fat storekeeper (with sacks of grain and lentils around him) placed next to figures of women shoppers; textile shops with little folded cloth pieces; miniature figurines in wood or clay of women doing household chores (cooking, pounding rice, making appalam); and so on, with a full accompaniment of miniature kitchen utensils. I remember a classroom theme with tiny books, figures of students sitting at desks, a teacher in front of the blackboard and, not to forget, the ruler in the teacher's hand. Though the kolu festival was mainly for women and girls, I remember that my male cousins once had a display of a cricket match, which was unusual and interesting.

The toys and figurines were collected over decades from different parts of India and the UK. Friends who travelled would bring back gifts of local crafts and I remember my Bombay uncle returning from Europe with porcelain figurines of blue and pink angels with gold wings that found their way into the kolu. A centrepiece of attraction among the imported angels and dolls was 'Shanghai John's' rice flour and plasticine dolls that he had made for Sarasa and me.

In our house, the arrangement of the kolu followed a pattern. In the middle of each step, dividing the right and left sides, a deity would be placed. Ganesha was on the lowest step; Vishnu with Lakshmi; and Rama, Shiva, Durga and Krishna were placed on ascending steps. On Ayudha Pooja day, much time would be spent in decorating the floor with elaborate *kolam* made of rice flour, over which teak wood planks would be placed covered with a silk shawl. This kolam was a smaller version of the kolam that would be drawn on the threshold of the front door of every Hindu household with ground rice flour. The idea, as my mother said, was to feed the ants, though I've seen birds and squirrels eat the rice flour kolam. Mice too, probably.

The majestic figure of Saraswati—goddess of knowledge, learning and the arts—would be placed ceremoniously over the shawl. Books, writing materials, musical instruments and my father's old Remington typewriter were arranged around the Goddess's figure. Being weak in mathematics, I would place my math books at the feet of the goddess hoping to fare better in the coming year. A special oil lamp with wicks would be lit; a coconut would be cracked open and arranged with betel leaves and bananas. Incense and camphor would be lit for the *aarathi*.

For the kolu display, we children set about enthusiastically to create local attractions and landscapes: Parvati Hill, the local zoo and the Yerawada Central Jail, where Gandhiji was imprisoned, often featured in our kolu. Over a bed of straw we fashioned a mud hillock, gradually patting in the mud. On the summit we placed a miniature temple of painted wood. To make the hill look natural, we added little pebbles here and there, scattered mustard seeds and watered them. Mustard was the obvious choice as the seeds sprouted in a short period of time. Before dashing off to school, one of us would sprinkle the hillock with water. In two or three days, the hillock would be covered in little stalks of green and leaf buds.

Living in Poona, how could one forget the Bund Garden? It was part of my weekly bicycle ride with my father. To recreate a miniature Bund Garden in the kolu, we planted twigs and leaves and miniature shrubbery randomly after covering part of the floor with soil. At one end, I embedded a small saucer with water representing a pool. I was keen to show the Mulamutha River and the bridge across it with the Yeravada Jail on the other side, and was disappointed at not being able to create the bridge. My cousin Chandru, five or six years older than me, who became an artist and later started an advertising company, advised me on creating the river out of plasticine and painting it blue (which we did). The gardens, the zoo with little animals and birds, and the river were placed on the floor at the foot of the kolu steps.

My mother being an avid gardener had a couple of garden scenes for the kolu. One was a garden with potted plants. Over the years, she had collected miniature potted plants of colourful flowering shrubs and creepers, some made of porcelain, some of clay, others of crepe paper and wires. Sarasa and I helped Amma in making the wire and paper pots and flowers. You could see the white of the jasmine, the red of the hibiscus, the bluebells, a creeper which grew in Poona with tubular blue flowers, and roses as well as miniature trees. My mother arranged the garden scene with great care and an eye for detail. The other scene she developed was a farm. I think she wanted to show paddy cultivation. So, the mustard seeds were planted well in advance on a bed of soil. A miniature figure of two bullocks, yoked with a ploughshare, and the farmer behind ploughing the furrows, with another figure a few inches away sowing the seeds, completed the scene. The whole room was lit up with colourful Christmas lights and these added to the air of festivity and joy.

Part of the excitement for us children in the neighbourhood was visiting the homes of our neighbours and relatives, meeting friends and family and dressing in festive clothing. Returning from school, my sisters and I would change into a rather grand silk *pavaade* (long skirt) and put on some jewellery. With our hair in neat plaits, we would do the rounds visiting our South Indian neighbours in Saraswat Colony. Our school friend and neighbour, Shabnam, would come to our home and we would all set out together. I remember running into friends and neighbours on the street. The conversation would often be about an exceptional kolu in someone's home and the food that was offered. It was a lot of fun!

Women came into their own at these festivals. As we entered people's homes, the strains of South Indian devotional music played on gramophones, the women and children would welcome us in. The kolu display was the centre of attraction. As the evening progressed, visitors would be invited to sing. Children were encouraged and persuaded to sing whatever songs they knew. While some children who had learnt South Indian music would sing confidently to the accompaniment of the harmonium, others would stand around awkwardly. My friend Kamali's mother would say, 'You don't have to sing just South Indian music, sing anything you know.' Women would encourage children to recite 'portry' or nursery rhymes and would make suggestions like 'Twinkle Twinkle Little Star'. Hymns learnt at convent school would also find their way into the kolu festival!

As dusk fell, aarathi would be performed in each home and guests would be given *sundal* as *prasadam* before leaving. On different days, the sundal would be made of peas, peanuts, lentils or chickpeas, garnished with green chillies, mustard seeds, curry leaves, sometimes with coconut. We would come home with an odd collection of prasadam from different homes and sometimes with a sweet made using banana, coconut and jaggery.

Some Indian families living outside India celebrate Navarathri with an elaborate kolu festival. I was invited to a kolu display near Boston, where I now live. Some of the toys had been brought from India: the famous Channapatna wooden toys, Tanjore dolls, chettiar bommai made of clay, all carefully transported and displayed along with porcelain dolls from the UK and toys bought in the United States, most likely made in China!

Dr Sabnis' Home Remedies

These days, when I have so many doctors attending to my health, my thoughts turn to the doctors I have known over the years—the ones who have treated me and my family and who became my friends.

Poona's Saraswath Colony was a well-laid-out middle class residential locality of professionals—doctors, engineers, college professors and the like. Our doctor's clinic was just around the corner from the entrance to the colony and Dr Sabnis, a general physician and a retired army doctor, was a household name among the residents. I remember him as being very tall, lean and wiry with high cheekbones, sunken cheeks and deep-set eyes with arched greying eyebrows. His lips were two horizontal thin lines. He had a generous grey mustache and a broad square jaw. I had imagined all retirees to be elderly with greying hair but surprisingly, Dr Sabnis had a crop of jet-black hair, parted in the middle.

The first time I met Dr Sabnis was when my father walked me to his clinic. His strong guttural voice was intimidating and I did not like him one bit. Over time, with the frequency and regularity of my visits, I grew fond of him and would stop over at his clinic to say hello even when I was well. This became a habit. We developed a friendship, and he would gently tease me. The moment I entered, he would welcome me with 'Don't tell me you are not well again! I saw you only last week.'

My childhood affliction was bronchitis and whenever the weather was damp or cold, I would miss a few days of school every month. My mother would effectively stave off the worsening of the wheezing and congestion by giving me a warm chest fomentation. Dr Sabnis would greet me with 'Come, let me listen to what your lungs have to tell me,' following which he would disappear into an anteroom to wash his hands with carbolic soap, which filled the air with a strong unmistakable tar smell. Those were the times before hand sanitizers made their way into our daily lives. 'Yes, now jump up,' Dr Sabnis would instruct, and I would follow the routine of climbing up onto the wooden table covered with a blue Rexine cloth. He would start by taking my temperature and then instruct me, 'Now cough, open your mouth wide and say "aahhhh",' as he pressed the back of my tongue with a flat, metal 'shoe horn' kind of instrument. It hurt.

Antibiotics were not prescribed as easily in those days as they are now. Dr Sabnis compounded his medicines and potions. In a well-lit side room, there were shelves of labelled glass bottles, containing liquids, powders, granules and pastes—white, orange, brown, cream and some speckled. Mortars and pestles, and glass funnels of varying sizes, ounce glasses and smaller glass bottles (into which he would pour the medicines he had made) lined the shelves. Before handing the bottle of freshly compounded medicine to me, he took out his black Waterman pen from the inner pocket of his jacket and filled in clear instructions on a label, which he then proceeded to paste onto the bottle. He would then hand me a roll of thick white cotton drill rolled into a cylinder and a jar of white paste that smelt strongly of menthol and eucalyptus oil, adding, 'Your mother knows what to do with this.' And she certainly did. She would cut the drill to the size of my chest, spread a thin layer of the paste on one side, warm up the drill on a skillet and gently place it on my chest. The antiphlogistine paste helped clear the inflammation and congestion in my lungs, and I looked forward to this soothing treatment.

Dr Sabnis' moves were deliberate and unhurried. I would wait patiently looking around at his framed certificates, quite a few of them in fact, hanging on the wall. There were also large, coloured posters of the human anatomy and enlarged posters of the heart, lungs, intestines, upper and lower limbs, the circulatory system and more. He once asked me, 'Would you like to be a doctor? You seem to be interested.' I am not imagining the distant past when I say that I left behind a friend in Dr Sabnis when I left Poona for Madras to pursue my graduate and postgraduate education at Queen Mary's College.

The Village LMP

Readers of my first book, *Tiffin*, may find some parts of this story overlapping with anecdotes about my uncle, Dr Chitappa, that they came across in the book. But Dr Chitappa was so much a part of our lives that I feel I cannot leave him out when writing about my life.

I think I've always been interested in healing, be it my mother's home remedies or the medicine practised by doctors. Doctor Chitappa, my father's youngest brother, opted to be a physician in Tanjore district, where his duties took him to villages near and far. Besides seeing patients in his clinic, he would do rounds on his bicycle or by *maatu vandi* (bullock cart), known as the 'bandy', an Anglicized version of the Tamil '*vandi*', meaning vehicle. Dr Chitappa was an LMP—a Licentiate in Medical Practice. He loved his profession so much that he did a lot of free service in rural areas and small towns. His patients would often attempt to express their gratitude with a coconut or a sheaf of bananas.

During my summer holidays, I would sometimes visit Chitappa in the villages where he was posted at the time. Those villages seemed far away from civilization, with no electricity, no piped water and only mud roads. I saw an open well for the first time in one of those villages.

Whenever I visited him, I would accompany Chitappa on his rounds to his patients' homes. He would set off after closing his dispensary in the evening, carrying his medical kit with his stethoscope, thermometer, ounce glass, syringes, bandages and dressing, spirit and tincture iodine, blood pressure monitor and eucalyptus oil (what villagers called *Nilgiri thailam* as eucalyptus grew in the Nilgiri Hills).

Rukka with Dr Chitappa

Very often, we travelled through paddy fields or coconut groves and came upon groups of villagers, men and women, walking home at the end of the day. At dusk, without any street lighting, the only source of light would be the one or two kerosene lanterns hanging on the sides of the maatu vandi. Those rides on rough terrain were rather frightening. The maatu vandi used to rock from side to side on the rough tracks and the lanterns would swing along with the movement of the cart, casting eerie shadows. I would try to keep my balance by moving from one side of the cart to the other and sometimes end up bumping my head in the attempt.

Once when Chitappa went for an emergency visit to a patient's house, I got to witness a childbirth in the village—my very first such experience. It was in the afternoon on a weekend and Chitappa had made some delicious masala vadai on his small kerosene stove. We were just sitting down to eat when Selvan, the male nurse from the hospital, interrupted us to say there was a message from the colony of scavengers and sweepers—a woman had gone into labour and was in difficulty. Chitappa immediately shut off the stove, covered the food and changed into his work clothes—trousers and a shirt. He did not want me to stay alone in the house, so he told me to get ready to accompany him. Without much delay, we collected Chitappa's medical kit, his stethoscope and a duffel bag with a couple of pails, mugs, towels, soaps, disinfectant and two flashlights. The hospital midwife joined us on our journey across the paddy fields and down the dusty country lanes. We reached the 'Harijan colony', as it was called in those days, around sundown. Inside one of the huts was a woman, twisting and turning in pain, lying on a reed mat on the floor. I sat and fanned her with a palm-frond fan and stroked her hair, while Chitappa and the midwife delivered the baby by the light of the two flashlights. With folded hands, the grateful and happy family gifted Chitappa a coconut, some bananas and betel leaves—a gift of a *tambulam*—to mark the auspicious occasion of the birth.

I had several unforgettable experiences while at my uncle's dispensary. I would clock in with him every working day. In fact, he made me his ledger keeper. I took my duties very seriously. I kept a log of the patients who would come to the dispensary and painstakingly entered my uncle's diagnosis for each patient against their name.

One day, a man came in barefoot and limping, and complained of pain in the heel and sole of his right foot. The dispensary attendant washed his feet and rubbed them generously with spirit. Then, on the examination table, my uncle examined his leg and found that he had big blisters. Of course, Chitappa knew immediately what the problem was. He took out a lancet and cut through each one of the blisters, then took what looked like a long stick and dipped it in the bottle of spirit. Then, even before he took it to the blister, there was something wriggling up through the skin. Chitappa placed the stick, so that he could wind it around the wriggling worm that thrust itself out through the blister. As he did, he explained to me that the procedure had to be done very slowly and carefully, so as not to snap the worm, as it would then disappear back into the body and reappear elsewhere. He then sent the patient home and resumed the process a few days later. After the worm was gradually extracted, the blister was cleaned and bandaged. In some villages, infections due to the particular parasite had escalated to become endemic. I later came to know that it was the Guinea worm, which spread through stagnant water.

Years later, in Madras, when I was at the university, I sprained my ankle on a field trip. The orthopaedic surgeon, Dr Thaimanaswamy, at the Madras General Hospital, asked me, 'By the way, are you a medical student?' I had asked him several searching questions while he was attending to me. I looked up at him questioningly and he said, 'You have the hands of a surgeon.' I did regret that I did not pursue medicine.

Lessons in Thrift

Living in Boston, I find myself frequently thinking about my childhood days in Poona and Jabalpur—a different world from eight decades ago. Especially when it comes to buying and owning things, and notions of waste and thrift, these are different eras.

My father abhorred waste and would always impress upon us the importance of conserving resources. This meant constant instruction about turning off taps, switching off lights, serving oneself just enough food so that nothing was wasted on the plate, and so on. Appa would be particular about using the last bit of shoe polish in the tin and believed in conserving soap by making sure it was dry and put away after a bath. I remember him at home with a towel over his shoulder. And when the towel frayed after use, he would cut it into smaller lengths for use as rags, or to polish shoes. Socks that developed holes were sent for darning and were not thrown away. Worn out shoes were always repaired or resoled.

During the war years, in the late 1930s, the taps would run dry for several hours in Poona. All household vessels, pots and pans and every bucket would be used to store water. If we children left the water tap dripping, Appa would point out to us that water was being wasted. He would place buckets under taps at all times. Conserving water also meant limiting our baths to one bucket each. My father would carefully mix hot and cold water in buckets for each of us to have our bath.

My mother was also a very careful homemaker. In her kitchen, there was a big cistern where she would collect the water used for washing vegetables, rice, grains and lentils. After the vegetables and grains were washed, the same water would be collected and used to water plants in her garden.

Like many other middle-class men and women of their generation, being thrifty was a way of life for my parents. We sisters all wore hand-me-downs. My younger sister, Leelu, once lamented that she never got to wear new clothes or shoes. Not entirely true, but that was how she felt given the number of hand-me-down clothes she was given. My mother had a few good saris; my father, a few shirts and trousers. In those days, clothes were purchased largely for special occasions or were given as gifts on festivals, significant birthdays and other auspicious occasions, or when someone went for an interview or landed a job. We didn't go shopping as we do today, and it certainly wasn't the recreational activity it has become.

Amma was also an inspired and thrifty cook. She would not throw away vegetables that were a few days old, but would rather use them to make a variety of delicious dishes. Shrivelled cucumber and ridge gourd that had been in the storeroom for a few days were cooked with ground coconut and spices into a mouth-watering *kootu* (stew) to be eaten with rice or chapatti. Bits of carrot and a handful of leftover peas were transformed into delicious fried rice. These were little surprises for us. Traditional cooking used all the parts of a vegetable. The stems of amaranth greens were not discarded, my mother would make them into a delicious curry with ground spices and coconut, which would accompany the main rice meal. I've never tasted banana peel chutney anywhere else but in my mother's kitchen. The peels of the raw banana, though tough and fibrous, would be painstakingly chopped, parboiled, then sautéed with lentils, spices, coconut and tamarind and ground into a coarse one-of-a-kind *thohayal* or chutney. Mixed with rice and ghee, it is a delicious first course in a traditional vegetarian meal. Peels of ridge gourd would be similarly ground into a spicy thohayal. My mother would even make a delicious *gojju* (a sweet-sour relish) with orange peel that we would eat with *adai* or rice and curd. Her *manga kottai kootu* made with the seeds of ripe mangoes was another mouth-watering dish.

Like many households in those days, ours didn't have a refrigerator. Women had various ways of making sure leftover food was not wasted. My mother followed an ingenious and traditional recipe: leftover beans kootu, rasam, sambar and brinjal curry would be combined in a heavy stoneware pot with the addition of a little oil, homemade ghee, curry leaves and a pinch of asafoetida. A teaspoon of sambar powder would bring it together. My mother would slow-cook this concoction, stirring it frequently till it became the appetizing amalgam we called *yerichakari*, which loosely translates to 'well-cooked'. We would eat this with freshly cooked rice, accompanied by potato chips or fried appalam.

I remember Annam Athai would take the trouble of keeping the leftover rice cooked for dinner in water to prevent it from going bad. The following day, she would squeeze the water out and mix it into curd rice adding curd, milk and salt. The curd rice would be garnished with toasted mustard seeds, chana dal, curry leaves, ginger and green chillies. On special occasions, she would add dehydrated buttermilk chillies fried in oil. Day-old rice was also made into a variety of flavoured rice dishes with lemon or coconut. The peel of the jackfruit, along with skins of mangoes, bananas and other fruits and vegetables, would be given to the cows or used as compost for the garden.

My thoughts go back to Miss Esther, my fourth standard English teacher at St Helena's in Poona. She joined the school in 1938 and had come from a small town near London. She was petite and pretty with a commanding voice and had a way with ideas and words. She asked us to introduce ourselves to her, which itself was novel. She would give us unusual homework assignments and ask us to illustrate our writings with drawings. One of the words she introduced us to, which I had never heard before, was 'thrift'.

Miss Esther encouraged us to learn through activities as well as writing. There was a large biscuit tin in the classroom on her desk. She would remind us every Friday to save pencil stubs and used erasers and bring them to school. We would collect all the pencils, erasers, crayons and little pencil sharpeners in the tin. At the end of the term, all the unused paper from our exercise books would be carefully removed and re-sewn into fresh exercise books with brown paper covers. The entire class, led by Miss Esther, would visit the orphanage next to the school and whatever we had collected would be distributed to the children there.

Thinking back on those days, I realize it was during the Second World War. Miss Esther's teachings on thrift made sense in the context of the war effort and in encouraging the public, even children, to participate and feel a sense of collective responsibility. She would also ask us to bring old clothes, shoes and whatever was in reasonably good condition and could be used by others. Girls also took classes in needlework and knitting. In these classes, we were encouraged to make useful things like handkerchiefs, napkins, little booties and bonnets to give to the needy.

The next time I heard about thrift was 60 years later. When I stayed in Los Angeles with Lakshmi, then a university student, she and I visited thrift stores. We spent some delightful afternoons in the thrift store run by the university, not knowing what we would find. Now I enjoy browsing in thrift stores on

Cape Cod. I find them to be treasure troves of memorabilia: English Wedgewood china, cuckoo clocks, baking dishes that were used in the 1950s (taking me back to that time when I was in Berkeley), trinkets and toys and jewellery that reminds me of Victorian era pieces. In fact, I much prefer the thrift stores with their treasures of bygone days, to what the malls have to offer.

It has been a long journey from Miss Esther's class in 1938 to the thrift stores in America in 2019. Back in those days, the motto was to 'save for a rainy day' and while at home, my uncle would repeatedly say, 'Waste not, want not.'

Today, as I move around my neighbourhood near Boston, I see furniture, clothing and household goods piled on the street waiting for the trash truck. Thrift is a bygone idea. It is easier to throw something out and replace it, rather than get it mended, in this 'make, take and trash era'. In buying the latest fashions or latest model of gadgets, we tend to accumulate goods. In some European countries, there are a growing number of people who buy at second-hand stores because they want to conserve resources by reusing goods. I have heard of an entire mall in Sweden devoted to selling second-hand goods to encourage people to shop sustainably.

Old habits die hard. These days, I automatically switch off lights and turn off taps. My daughters express their concern when I walk in the dark, from one room to the other in our home. But it is difficult for me to change the habits I developed at a very young age.

The International Epidemic

In the summer of 1941, my father was transferred from Madras to Jabalpur, in the Central Provinces. The entire family was not able to move with him as my mother had just had a baby. She stayed behind in Madras with the infant and my two-year-old sister. My father had just about six weeks to join duty on a promotion. He was also keen to move because he needed to find places in school for my two younger sisters and me. My eldest sister, Kamala, had no plans of going to college immediately, so she took care of us until our mother was able to join us a few months later.

The journey from Madras to Jabalpur was a long one and I remember the train winding its way through the forests of central India. Sarasa and I enjoyed the journey immensely, especially because we got to spend three nights in our cozy compartment. Buying and eating food sold on the platform was another thrill.

My father's friends in the Military Accounts Department had helped in finding us a house in Gol Bazar, in Jabalpur. The house was a spacious four-bedroom bungalow built in the traditional North Indian style with a central courtyard. My father had requested his friends to furnish the home minimally. So, when we arrived, we found cots and mattresses, a dining table, bookshelves and comfortable living room furniture.

Within a week of our arrival, my father accompanied us to the Christ Church Girls High School for an entrance test. At Christ Church, the principal, Miss Levi, interviewed all new students. After an anxious wait of about 10 days, it was a relief both for my father and for us when we learnt that we had secured admission to the school. Miss Levi was a small woman, stern in appearance but, as I realized later, very kind-hearted. Over the years, she became a good friend of my father's.

It was 1942, before the summer vacation, and one afternoon I received a note from the principal's office during lunch hour asking me to meet her that day. I was a bit unnerved and wondered what I had done wrong. When I went to the school's administrative office, I found Miss Levi seated in a lounge chair on the wide semi-circular verandah. That was her favourite spot, as she could keep a watch on students playing in the school compound. Miss Levi pointed to a chair signalling me to sit, and went straight to the point, 'Did you know your sister Leela has scabies? I'm sending her home right away.' Leelu was all of nine years old and I didn't quite understand what this was all about. I was worried about her going home alone. Fortunately, Narayana, our cook who had brought our lunch to school, was on his bike, heading towards the school gate. Shouting 'Narayana! Narayana!', I ran after him and asked him to take Leelu home.

When I went home that evening, I asked Leelu what had happened and she showed me a big blister between her toes. When she was not able to do the 'drill' exercises in the gym, the teacher had asked her to remove her shoes and found she had a big sore. Leelu was in obvious discomfort. The blister was itchy and painful when she scratched it. It had broken open and her socks were stuck to her feet. Kamala gently eased them off with lukewarm water. I was upset with Leelu, who seemed to have been suffering in silence. I asked her why on earth had she not let us know all these days. She had to stay home till the blisters went away.

Dr Chitappa was visiting us from Tanjore that summer. He would come once a year to see us, first in Bangalore, then in Poona and now in Jabalpur. That year when Dr Chitappa visited us, my father had been temporarily posted to the Italian prisoners' camp in Bairagarh for a few weeks' official duty. Not wanting to return to Tanjore without meeting his elder brother, Dr Chitappa decided to go to Bairagarh. He asked if I would like to accompany him. I jumped at the chance. The train ride was unusual and one of a kind for me as we travelled in a sepoy train and each compartment was occupied by Indian soldiers. There were a few white soldiers as well. All were on their way to the Bairagarh camp. Years later, I learnt that the conditions in this military camp were so unhygienic that the prisoners contracted all kinds of diseases, scabies being one of them.

Back in Jabalpur, Dr Chitappa examined Leelu's foot and gave his diagnosis, 'This is a classic case of scabies.' He cautioned us that it was very contagious and advised us to separate her clothing and bedclothes from ours, all of which were to be boiled frequently. The itchy blisters had to be treated with copper sulphate crystals, and Leelu would scream and cry in pain when they were rubbed on her sores. But that seemed to be the only remedy. She also had to use coal-tar soap, which was used for skin conditions like eczema. As I remember, no one else in the family contracted scabies and Dr Chitappa explained that Leelu's constitution was such that it was prone to skin infections. Even a small mosquito bite or a scratch would develop into a medical problem for her.

Leelu missed school for a year. At home, it was a kind of a quarantine, as she had to sleep in the annex next to the main bedroom. Coincidentally, when Dr Chitappa was staying with us, there was a warning in the newspaper that handwritten letters should not be posted from anywhere in the Central

Provinces to other parts of India. Scabies was spreading in the country and it was feared that letters would carry the highly contagious disease. The postal department was a bit too late in its warnings, I thought, because my uncle in Bombay called my father to say that my aunt had been diagnosed with scabies and most likely it had spread through post. The doctors reported that it was more rampant in the Central Provinces. But over time, it became a nationwide epidemic.

In 1941–42, there were multiple scabies outbreaks. Many prisoners in the Second World War contracted scabies in the camps. In Auschwitz, scabies was one of the many infectious diseases. This I learnt recently. In England, scabies was referred to as 'shelter rash', as people in the confined and crowded spaces of air-raid shelters contracted the disease. More recently, in 2019, I was telling Lakshmi about our Jabalpur experience with scabies and how I had visited the Italian prisoners' camp at Bairagarh around the same time. She remarked, 'What a memory you have!'

Bullying

Lettie Fernandes and I were good friends from the second to the fourth standard in St Helena's School. Lettie's parents' home was close to Fergusson College, where her father was an administrator. On weekends, we would spend the day in each other's houses and ride our bicycles together. One evening, when I was leaving Lettie's house to come home, I heard her father raise his voice in the back room and say, 'Don't you bully him!' Her brother, five years younger to her, was punching the youngest of the three siblings. I turned around and saw the father lifting his crying toddler. I found the incident upsetting.

I came home and told my parents about the incident and my father said, 'This happens all the time.' He went on to explain that in our home, as we were all daughters, we didn't encounter this kind of behaviour, which, he implied, happened more with boys.

I lost touch with Lettie when we left Poona for Madras. In Madras, I was enrolled in Good Shepherd Convent. The nuns who ran the school were very strict and would not tolerate any bad behaviour. When we moved from Madras to Jabalpur in 1941, my sisters and I were enrolled in Christ Church Girls' School. The students at the school were mostly British and Anglo-Indian girls. In my class, for the three years that I spent there, I came across only two Indian-Hindu girls: Asha Srivastava and me. The school authorities found our names too cumbersome to pronounce. Asha Srivastava became Asha Sri and my surname, Naganathan, was shortened to 'Nathan'. As a result, the staff thought my sisters and I were Cochin Jews. Our teachers were mostly English, Scottish or Anglo-Indian. Only two of our teachers were Indian—the maths master and the arts master who taught us drawing.

Three months after my sisters and I joined the school, there was a new admission to my class: a short, stocky, light-skinned girl with a freckled face and short curly hair walked in and was given a vacant bench in the front row. With attendance being taken every morning, we eventually learnt her name was Patsy Sargon.

By the third day, Patsy had moved from her allotted seat to the back row and in a few days, she showed her true nature. When the teachers were present, Patsy was very quiet and well behaved. But at other times, she would be rude, domineering and defiant. She was also a bully. Unfortunately, Asha became her target. Patsy would address her as 'You Asher', and deride her with 'Your Gandy drinks goat's milk' and then laugh. After one of these incidents, Asha didn't show up in class for two or three days. Her mother met the principal and reported the matter. No action was taken for a while and Patsy became even more belligerent.

In gym class, Patsy appointed herself as a supervisor of sorts. We were required to wear navy blue bloomers under our skirts for gym. Before the gym mistress arrived, we had to lie down on the floor in rows in preparation for the class to begin. Patsy would appear with a ruler and check that everyone was in uniform by walking down the rows of girls and lifting certain girls' skirts with her ruler.

Patsy enjoyed humiliating whomsoever she could. As with all bullies, she would pick on those who were quiet, meek and lacked the ability to retaliate. When I went home and reported Patsy's behaviour to my father, he was outraged, 'This is not to be tolerated in a school. I will come and speak to Miss Levi [the principal].' This was characteristic of him—he was very involved in our education and was a frequent and welcome visitor to every school we were in.

Patsy did not stop at bullying just her classmates. I remember her targeting one of the teachers who, again, was Indian. We would address him as 'Sir'. He would sit in an armchair placed in front of the desk. One day, as he was outlining the lesson, he shot up from the chair, looked around and underneath it. Before we knew what was going on, he started scratching his arms and legs violently. It was a bit comical, and some students started giggling. Others looked nervous and frightened. After a few minutes, Sir picked up his notebook and left the classroom hurriedly. As it turned out, Patsy had struck again. She bragged a few days later to her cronies that she had scattered some itching powder on the chair. But no one came forward to accuse her and she suffered no consequences.

Patsy knew she couldn't intimidate me, and she left me severely alone. But there was an incident when I had to threaten her with dire consequences. My younger sister Leelu, all of eight years old, was also a student at Christ Church. She was a very timid and gentle girl, just the sort to be abused by someone like Patsy. One afternoon during the lunch break, I was summoned by Miss Levi to her office. I found Leelu there, looking frightened. I asked myself, 'What now?' I learnt that a staff member from the school had found Leelu crossing the road to the boys' school and handing over something to one of the boys. The question on the principal's lips was: 'Why was your sister at the boys' school?' I asked my sister in front of Miss Levi and the answer was that one of my classmates, who turned out to be Patsy, had given her a note to be given to the boy who was waiting at the gates of the boys' school.

Miss Levi dismissed both of us, and I later learnt that Patsy was in the habit of using the junior schoolchildren to carry notes to her dates in the boys' school. I also learnt that Miss Levi was aware of this.

Patsy's father was an engine driver in the Central Indian Railways. He was never available to meet the principal. Patsy was the first generation in her family to receive a school education. Her lack of interest in her studies resulted in her failing her exams. When I moved into the Junior Cambridge class, which streamed students taking the centrally administered Cambridge examinations, she was thankfully not my classmate. She disappeared from the school because she was not allowed to sit for the Junior Cambridge examinations.

I had always thought only boys could become bullies. My memories go back to St Helena's in Poona, when I was in the third standard. The school was co-ed and we had both boys and girls in the classroom. Seating was organized such that the girls and boys occupied alternate seats in the classroom. To my left was Monish, short and with a round head and very little hair. He was a relatively quiet student and not outstanding in any way. I remember him because of this unfortunate incident: one day, when the teacher was at the blackboard, he reached out with his sharpened pencil and jabbed me on my left palm. I might have let out a scream. The teacher came over and took me to the school dispensary and bandaged my bloody hand. That was my very first experience of bullying. To this day, the scar is visible and to this day, I can't recall a reason for Monish's sudden aggression.

When I joined Queen Mary's College for my Intermediate degree, I once again encountered bullying among the women students and here it was restricted to those who lived in the hostel dormitory. During the first week of our stay in the hostel, each one of us received a personalized invitation for an 'initiation' held in the evening. None of the freshmen students had an inkling of what this initiation was about and the seniors were tight-lipped about it. We were told we would meet other hostellites and have dinner with them. We had not yet adjusted to college, to hostel life, the food, etc., so many looked forward to the event. But there were some cruel jokes played on the newcomers.

On the evening of the event, we were instructed to meet at the Garden Block—a building located a few hundred yards from the main college building. The residential dorm rooms were on the first floor of the main building, up a flight of stairs. Our invitation said we would be met at the bottom of the first-floor staircase and taken to the Garden Block. It was evening and the light was fading. We were not familiar with the college grounds and had to find our way. As we descended the stairs, the lights went off. Ghostly laughter reverberated from all sides. Some of the hostellites rushed down the stairs to find the boys who had picked up balls on the tennis courts waiting there; 'chokra-boys', as they were called in British India. There was one 'boy', John, who was a midget of a man in his 40s. He grabbed the girls by the arm as they stepped down. Those of us standing at the top of the stairs heard loud screams from below. It was frightening.

It was clear that the Garden Block was a newer building. As we freshmen climbed up the few steps into the rectangular hall, each one of us was introduced to the gathering. As I walked in, I heard 'Come in, *Lambutan* (tall one)!'—a nickname given in reference to my height. I was immediately ordered to do a somersault across the room. When I stood there not knowing what to do, one of the senior students walked up to me and said, 'I'll help you.' She made me sit on my haunches, lifted me and pushed me over. While it left me embarrassed, terrified and bruised, my performance was appreciated and everyone applauded. I was told I was a 'good sport'. Many of those seniors became my good friends after the initiation.

The young women who had just left home were unprepared for this hazing and some were treated in the college sick room for shock, where they remained for a whole week. A few of them decided to leave the college and return home. In those days, bullying of this kind was quite common and was not talked about in the way it is now.

Purity Rituals in the Village of Flowers

When I was living in the hostel at Queen Mary's College, I would visit my aunt, Kamalam Athai, my father's younger sister, in the mofussil town of Poonamallee on the outskirts of what was then Madras.

Poonamallee was an idyllic village and market garden. The name, an Anglicized version of the Tamil *Poov-irunda-mallee*, translates to the 'village of flowers'. Market gardening and growing flowers for the city was the main occupation of its residents. The pre-dawn buses from Poonamallee to Madras were laden with hundreds of baskets of fragrant jasmine, chrysanthemum, *tulsi* (holy basil), *maru* (marjoram) and tuberose for the flower markets of Madras. The entire bus station would be suffused with a glorious fragrance when the buses arrived. I experienced this first-hand on one of my visits to Poonamallee. When waiting at the central bus stand, I saw baskets and baskets of flowers being unloaded. The passengers were flower growers and middlemen. Women and men carried the baskets to nearby sheds and the flowers were auctioned then and there.

I looked forward to these short trips to Athai's home, as it gave me a welcome break from hostel food that I found inedible. I was also glad to get away to the relaxing, semi-rural surroundings of Poonamallee.

One weekend, when I was on my way to see my aunt, the diesel bus broke down a few miles from the village and we had to wait. By the roadside, where we had stopped, there was a beautiful field of orange *kanakambaram* flowers. I watched, fascinated, as the plot was irrigated using *piccotah*, an indigenous method of drawing water from a well using a counterpoise lift. The bullocks walked up and down an incline and the buckets attached to a wooden shaft dipped into the well and drew the water up as the animals moved.

When I got home, I told my uncle and aunt about the delay by the roadside and my uncle, an advocate, mentioned that the owner of that garden was his client and the land was for sale. At once, I wrote to my father about the possibility of buying this land. In those days, it would have cost a few thousand rupees. My father promptly sent me a postcard, advising me to concentrate on my studies and not be distracted by land acquisition.

When I met her in 1946, Athai bore a striking resemblance to my father. She had the same angular features and the slightly stern cast of her face. But she was kind at heart and was a very caring and loving aunt. Slightly built and frail in appearance, she dressed traditionally in a nine-yard sari and wore blouses with elbow length sleeves. Her greying, curly hair was pulled back into a tight knot at the nape of her neck. I've never seen her without a large *kumkumom pottu* (vermillion), signifying the auspicious status of being married, adorning her forehead.

Athai's life revolved around her husband, an advocate or pleader at the Mofussil Court, her grown children, and the cows and calves that were part of the family. Her house was a traditional village house—spacious and with a central courtyard open to the sky. There were two small rooms, a kitchen and a verandah. One of the rooms was my uncle's office and the other was a kind of storeroom with a variety of furniture, metal trunks, large pots and pans (which were used occasionally during events), and a mixed lot of household goods that could easily have been given away. So actually there was very little privacy, as there was no space for private bedrooms and everyone slept in the open corridor. For me, this was a new experience. There was a rosewood swing in the middle of the hallway but no real furniture. We sat on the floor on reed mats.

Athai was very affectionate and welcoming. I remember how she cared for me when I sprained my foot and spent a weekend with her. But she was also very rigid and uncompromising in her habits. Her life was governed by rules of purity and pollution. She strictly observed the customs followed by married Brahmin women. A preoccupation with purity and ritual governed her life. The ritually pure state was to be maintained throughout the day and shaped everyday activities, such as cooking, eating, cleaning house, bathing and so on. Maintaining a physical distance from visitors, household help and vendors who came to the door was also part of this ritual behaviour. Whenever a family member went outside the house, when my uncle returned home from the courts for instance, he would have to go to the well to wash his feet, hands and face. Only after a change of clothes would he come and sit down for his coffee in a silver tumbler, silver being non-polluting.

Athai's day began at 4.00 a.m., when the rest of the household was asleep. I would find her walking around the side of the courtyard with a wicker basket and a long bamboo pole. She would use the bamboo pole to grab her dry sari, blouse and a towel from the clothesline and expertly manoeuvre the clothes into the basket, taking care not to touch them. She would then take the basket to the well in the backyard and have a cold-water bath drawing the water herself. She explained to me once that before her bath she was in an impure state and so could not touch her basket of clothes. Bathing meant applying fresh turmeric paste on the face, the heels of the feet and the ankles, and pouring buckets of cold well water over one's head.

Athai's life was new and strange to me, as my mother did not observe all these rituals. One morning, I woke up with a jolt to find Athai bending over me and sprinkling cold water over my body. She then moved to my cousins who were sleeping close by on the same verandah and gave them the same treatment. When I quizzed her about her actions, she smiled and said, 'Not only is it time to get up, but the body in sleep is like a corpse.' The sprinkling of water was to counter the evil spirits. The sleeping body was in a liminal or in-between state, a state of danger. To purify the spot where the sleeping, corpse-like body was lying, water mixed with cow dung, a purifying substance, was sprinkled once the bedding was rolled up.

After we had woken up, Athai dragged the reed mats that served as our bedding to the courtyard, doused them with the cow dung water and left them to dry. Cow dung water would then be sprinkled around the entire courtyard to cleanse and purify it after the night.

The reed mats, as I understood later, were pollution-free while cotton bedding, mattresses, etc., were not. There were cotton pillows that my aunt would not touch. Thus, there were no cotton sheets spread on the mats. We cousins had to take the pillows and mats when dry and stack them up in the next room to be used the following night. Athai slept on an easy chair because she suffered from pleurisy and her headrest was a Rexine-covered pillow. Rexine, as I understood, could not be contaminated the way cotton could.

The furniture in the front room where my uncle saw his clients was made of wood, mostly benches. This was to ensure that clients of different castes did not pollute the furniture. Wood was the best option. Only my uncle's chair was upholstered and had a Rexine cushion.

I found Athai's eating habits to be peculiar. She had her meals sitting in the kitchen by herself, with a big bowl of water placed near her. Every time she served herself cooked food, she would dip her fingers in the cold water. I also noticed that the bowls of yoghurt, buttermilk and ghee were placed at a distance from the cooked food. Athai explained that cooked food is polluting whereas the other food is not, and therefore she washed her hands every time she served herself. Ghee was an exception. It was cooked, but since it was a product of the cow it was considered pure. As we were vegetarians, the question of meat did not enter the discussion.

As long as I have known, Athai has always kept cows. In the daytime, they were tethered to a tree in the backyard. At night, they would be brought into the cowshed that was part of the main house, off the central courtyard. The house would smell of cow dung and cow urine—a strong odour for me but which didn't seem to bother Athai and her family. Soon after she bathed, Athai would lead the cows to the well and give them a bath. This would be followed by Gopuja, a ritualistic worship of cows. Turmeric and red vermillion would be smeared on each cow's forehead. Athai would then milk each cow after using castor oil as udder cream. The cows would then be fed.

With the fresh milk, which she boiled, she would make herself a steaming hot cup of coffee and drink it while sitting in the kitchen on a wooden plank. Athai's coffee tumbler was also made of silver, and she would pour the hot coffee down her gullet and swallow it with a gurgling sound. The tumbler never touched her lips. It seemed like torture to an onlooker. When I questioned Athai, she said, 'You will not understand all this. You've been to a Christian convent school.'

These were some of my earliest encounters with 'purity and pollution' as anthropologists say, which I learnt from my aunt, as my parents did not observe any such practices.

There was no elaborate grocery shopping in Athai's house. My uncle, the advocate, would return from the courts with one or two vegetables like bitter gourd or snake gourd, or rarely, lady's finger. My aunt grew red pumpkin in the backyard and also drumstick (moringa), banana plants, curry leaves and chillies. She had planted mint and coriander around the well. There were also two coconut palms and a *narthanga* (bitter lemon) tree. If she did not have any vegetables in the kitchen, she would pick some drumstick or raw banana for lunch. The food would be simple but delicious—drumstick sambar and raw banana dry curry, a thin rasam and rice. I never had chapattis at her house.

There was always a supply of fresh buttermilk and freshly made ghee from home-churned butter. My first course for lunch would be steaming hot rice topped with a dollop of boiled lentils over which Athai would pour a generous helping of ghee. This was a delicious starter to an equally delicious meal.

There was no breakfast at Athai's house. The day would start with coffee and move on to a meal at around 9.00 a.m. Tiffin would be served at around 2.00 p.m. For tiffin, Athai would make steamed idlis with fresh coconut chutney made with homegrown coconut, chillies and coriander leaves. My uncle liked dosai served with sambar and spicy molahapudi. He was also fond of onion chutney as an accompaniment to dosai. It was made with raw onion, coconut and red chillies. Uncle was the only one who ate onion in the house, and the chutney would be made especially for him. Athai would not eat onion or garlic.

It seemed strange to me that Athai preferred to eat alone sitting in the kitchen with the door ajar. I made bold to ask her why, and her response was a matter-of-fact, '*Anda mattu karan varuvaane* (The boy who took the cows for grazing in the village common would come into the courtyard).' Athai felt she didn't need to say more, that it was understood that she did not want his shadow to fall on her while she was eating. Though a short bus ride from my college in Madras, my aunt's home was a world away from the life I had known hitherto and continued to live in Madras.

Athai's orthodox and rule-bound life prevented her from travelling even to her dear siblings' homes. She never visited us in Poona and went to Tanjore only once, as I remember. She didn't leave her home much. She didn't seem to think she was missing out by adhering to her orthodox ways.

An Auspicious Morning

In the summer of 1950, I was again spending a weekend in Kamalam Athai's house. In fact, in the first two years (1946–48) when I was a student in the intermediate course, I spent many a weekend and short holiday with Athai and her family. They were very fond of me and welcomed me even when I appeared on their doorstep without notice.

One morning, before dawn, there was a lot of commotion and excitement in the house. Athai, with her daughters Kanthi and Sharada, was bustling in and out of the backyard and cowshed. I could dimly sense their movements but couldn't figure out what it was all about. I heard shouts of 'come here' and 'lift that thing' (all in Tamil) amid the groans and bellowing of the cow. All of a sudden it was quiet. Under the light of a kerosene lantern and with the help of the cowherd, a young female calf was born. It was a joyous moment for Athai and the entire family. This was the third female calf born to the cow and the first time I witnessed the birth of a calf at home.

Soon after, pails and pails of water were drawn from the well and the mother cow and calf were given a good bath. The calf, struggling to stand on its forelegs, would just flop to the ground and then try again. Athai smeared freshly ground turmeric on both the mother and the newborn, and put a big pat of red vermillion powder on their foreheads. She gave them thin rice gruel and a banana each. Her next move was to her domestic altar to the kitchen from where she brought a lit camphor lamp and moved it in a clockwise motion three times around the cow and calf. In the meantime, the cowherd came back with a flower garland and threw it round the horns and neck of the cow. She was a beautiful animal, not the hybrid kind. She had white greyish-brown horns, and a gentle and obedient demeanour.

I was both intrigued and impressed by the way Athai looked after her cow. Later, the cow and calf were led to the cowshed but tethered a few feet apart. My Athai was visibly exhausted but very happy. She slumped into her easy chair in the courtyard and said, 'Normally, when girls are born in succession in families, we feel it's a headache and are not altogether happy, for we are more concerned about how we would get the girl married. But in the case of a cow, it means prosperity. Lakshmi (the calf) very soon will start giving us milk, and I hope she will also have girls like her mother.'

An Outdated Ritual

In the summer of 1947, at the age of 55, my father retired from the Military Accounts Department in Poona and moved to Tanjore where he built his retirement home. I was a second-year intermediate student in Queen Mary's College in Madras at the time. I met him at Egmore Station where he boarded the Boat Mail. He was happy and was looking forward to retired life, long walks and reading. In fact, Appa, like many of his colleagues, was offered a post-retirement position at the Staff College in Wellington in the Nilgiris. But, as he told me, he wanted a complete break from his working life of 35 years and looked forward to enjoying life with his family and making new friends. He also suffered from asthma and the cold Nilgiris climate would likely not have suited him.

Sometime after the Tamil New Year in April 1952, I received a detailed letter from Dr Chitappa reminding me that Appa's *Shashtiapthapoorti* (sixtieth birthday) was to be celebrated that summer and it was good that I would be home during that time. Considered a milestone, the sixtieth birthday is thought to represent a turning point in one's life and so this was not unexpected. Chitappa said the ritual part of the function would be held in the morning at the *muhurtam* (auspicious time) followed by an evening reception. He had started compiling the list of relatives and friends to be invited and asked me to let him know if I had any special friends to add to the list.

Dr Chitappa also entrusted me with the job of buying a nine-yard silk sari for my mother for the occasion and a pair of silk dhotis and *angavastram* (cloth covering the torso) for my father. He advised me to go to Mettur where his paternal uncle, the chief irrigation engineer, was posted. His uncle, my grand-uncle, would drive me to the town of Arni—known for weaving and for silk—where I could pick and choose the items of clothing right where the weavers lived and worked. Chitappa also wanted me to buy silk saris for my father's sisters, my sisters and myself; silk skirts for all the younger girls; and traditional dhotis for all the male relatives who would be attending.

The following weekend, I took a train to Mettur where my grand-uncle's son met me and drove me to their official residence, a beautiful, spacious British bungalow not far from the Mettur canal. The sound of flowing water was a constant backdrop to all the conversations in the house. The following morning, my grand-uncle, his son and I drove to Arni in Tiruvannamalai district, west of Madras. Arni is known as one of the most important silk centres of Tamil Nadu. In those days, the quaint township reminded me of my visits to Poonamallee and Kamalam Athai.

In Arni I saw handloom silk looms for the first time, with men and women busy weaving yards and yards of silk cloth of different textures, designs and colours. It was fascinating and a one-of-a-kind experience for me. We must have gone to about three or four homes of weavers where I had to select the gifts. My aunt had not accompanied us and as the only woman, I was left to make the choice. It was difficult and mind-boggling for me.

That day, in the short space of a few hours, I was given a tutorial on the sari colours that were considered appropriate for such an occasion. My uncle said no black, no navy blue, no white, no biscuit or cream colours, and no maroon because that is a combination of red and black (although the latter was my father's favourite colour). They nudged me towards greens, yellows, orange and bright red (also known as *kumkum* colour). I must have looked at and set aside dozens and dozens of saris because of the colour, the design, the type of sari border and other considerations. Finally, for my mother, I chose a very appealing yellow with a red border and with no gold lace. I must add here that my mother loved that sari and we all thought she looked gorgeous that day.

The birthday event was very well attended. There must have been close to 35 to 40 relatives on both my mother's and father's side, and about 25 to 30 of my father's friends from Tanjore and Trichy showed up. Everyone who attended the morning's ritual feasted off banana-leaf plates. One of the sweets served was jalebi, my father's favourite, freshly made in our kitchen. The entire meal was prepared by three professional cooks with Annam Athai supervising them. It was what they would traditionally call *kalyana shapad* (wedding feast).

The ritual was performed in the garden where my parents sat on chairs. Water from the well was drawn and relayed in brass pots by the women relatives, and finally the priest poured the water, mixed with a few drops of Ganges water, over my father's and mother's heads. There were several such relays with the sonorous chanting of Vedic prayers. I noticed that two or three pots contained turmeric water and two others contained neem leaves. When the ritual was concluded, the priest gave my parents permission to go and wear their new clothes. A pity that there was no photographer in attendance—I don't have a single picture of that day.

Later that evening, Dr Chitappa, tired but happy that the function went off well and without a hitch, came and sat next to me and said, 'Thank you for going to Arni, what do you think of the function?' To that I replied, 'It's a beautiful function. I don't think I will ever see one like this again being performed. You've taken a lot of trouble.' Then I asked him why in the mid-twentieth century, when medicine has improved and people live much longer, people continued to celebrate their sixtieth birthdays so elaborately? He smiled and said, 'There are no answers for such questions.'

The celebration of my father's sixtieth birthday also seemed out of character given what I knew of him. To explain, I will need to meander on to another story. My elder sister Kamala's marriage was arranged when she was just 16 and still in high school. Although I was just 10 years old at the time, I remember my father's lack of enthusiasm about her being married so young. His ambition was for all his daughters to be well-educated and independent. After her wedding, Kamala returned to Poona to complete high school and so she never got to know the young man whom she had married. And it was destined that she never would, as a few months after the wedding he contracted typhoid and succumbed to it. My parents were devastated; Kamala became withdrawn and depressed and refused to return to school. She instead opted to learn music in the village where Dr Chitappa lived with his family. Dr Chitappa cared for Kamala like his own daughter, but the extended family of my father's relatives were very orthodox and treated her as many widows were treated in those days. My father was incensed at the cruel treatment meted out to a young and innocent young girl and vowed never to participate in what he saw were meaningless rituals. He removed his sacred thread—which Brahmin boys wear from the age of eight or nine—signifying their status as a member of the twice-born caste. Kamala married again and was happy, but my father, from then on, refused to participate in arranging his other daughters' weddings or even to perform his role as father of the bride on the wedding day.

Knowing this about my father, I was all the more puzzled by the ritual celebration of his sixtieth birthday. I never asked him about it, but I suspect that once again family and custom prevailed.

A Promise to Keep

I would like to delve into some family folklore and share a story told in my extended family. Different versions exist and I am not sure how much fact and fiction developed in multiple retellings of the story, but this is the version I remember well.

On one of my mother's visits to Bangalore, I told her about the snake that we found swimming in the fishpond in our Benson Cross home. She listened to me calmly and then asked, 'What did you do? I hope you didn't kill it.' I replied that it was saved and went on its way. She added, 'This brings to mind my father's relationship to animals and in particular, the serpent.' Now, I remember my mother saying it was her father, but I heard from my sister that it was our great-grandfather who had a special relationship with snakes. Whether it was Chinnasamy, my mother's grandfather, or her father, Panchapakesa Iyer, is not clear. But it seems that either one or both of them had a remarkable sensitivity to animals, and in particular to snakes.

Panchapakesa Iyer worked in the land records office in Madurai. He lost his wife when my mother was barely four years old and lived as a widower for decades. He seems to have been a loner. My mother remembered him as being very quiet, not socializing much and preferring his own company. In fact, he seems to have been a recluse. I know him only from an old black and white photograph. He had a flowing white beard and we children used to refer to him as *Dadi Thatha* (grandfather with a beard).

Dadi Thatha's close friend in his early years was Venkatraman Iyer, who later became the sage Sri Ramana Maharishi. My mother reminisced that her father and Ramana used to play together as children in the small town of Tiruchuli, about 45 km from Madurai, where they grew up. My grandfather was religiously inclined and used to sing devotional songs. He named his son and daughter—my mother—after the deities Bhuminatheswara and Sahayavalli of the Siva temple in Tiruchuli.

Even as a child, my grandfather appears to have demonstrated an unusual compassion and sensitivity towards animals. He would not want to harm even mice or insects. When young boys tried to catch squirrels or stoned birds, he would admonish them to leave them alone. In those days, the floors of houses were plastered with mud and cowdung that would attract ants. My grandfather felt that the ants wandering around in the house should not be harmed. Interestingly, his friend Ramana also cared deeply for animals. In the Ramana Maharishi Ashram, in the temple town of Tiruvannamalai, we would find many animals and birds freely moving around.

I've heard that as a young man, my grandfather went to Tiruvannamalai and met his friend Ramana with the idea of joining him and giving up his worldly life. But after hearing him out, Ramana told him that he was not yet ready for *sanyasa*, as he was a householder and had the responsibility of looking after his young children. And so he should return to his family, which my grandfather did.

One of the most bizarre and interesting stories that my mother told me about her father was something she had heard from relatives. As an employee of the land records office, my grandfather travelled to far-flung villages around Madurai. He would spend the night alone sometimes in old, dilapidated houses and pass the time by singing devotional songs at night.

His sonorous voice would attract both humans and animals. Villagers would bring him food and stay to listen to his singing. The story goes that snakes would come into the house, slither up the wooden pillars and drape themselves on the wooden rafters and beams. Apparently, the vibrations of the music would calm them.

Grandfather would also talk to the snakes with compassion, telling them not to be afraid and to come and lie down. He would have bowls of milk ready for them. As grandfather sang with half-closed eyes, the snakes, which were cobras, would twirl their hoods in a circular motion and strike the ground in front of him seven times. The interpretation was that they made a promise not to hurt him or his family for seven generations. At dawn, the snakes would disappear.

Another story my mother narrated to me was one about her elder sister who was in her parents' home for the birth of her first child. A snake crawled in at night when she was lying down on a mattress on the floor. She was naturally alarmed and screamed in fear. My grandfather reassured her saying, 'You will not be harmed. They have promised me that they will not hurt any of my family.'

What follows may seem like a digression, but these are rambling tales and the anecdote that follows seems to somehow bring together different moments in my family's history. As honours students in Geography at Queen Mary's College in Madras, my classmate Nallama and I used to revise for exams sitting outside the library. One April evening, when we were outside the library late at night, we saw a magnificent spectacle that I remember vividly. A ball of fire streaked across the sky and fell into the ocean. We were excited upon seeing what we thought was a meteor or a falling star. The next morning, the newspapers reported the passing away of Sri Ramana Maharishi in his ashram in Tiruvannamalai. It was 14 April,

Tamil New Year's Day. Nallama came excitedly to my room and asked if I had seen the papers. I had not. We both rushed to the library and read about Ramana Maharishi's passing. What we had seen as a falling star was strangely coincidental to the passing of this great soul. Nallama said she felt as if the two of us had been blessed.

Fateful Encounters

Readers of my first book *Tiffin* might recognize some elements of this story. I have included it here, as what was an accidental encounter became a turning point in my life.

Dr Paramasivam was a close family friend and he would stop by our home in Tanjore now and then to chat with my father over coffee. Sometimes, he would stay and have tiffin with us.

As the chief archaeological chemist at the Brihadeeswara Temple in Tanjore, he was working with a team on a project to expose the eleventh-century frescoes of the Chola period* at the temple's sanctum sanctorum. The work involved laboriously peeling off the superimposed layer of thirteenth century paintings.

In the summer of 1953, when I was home for the vacation, Dr Paramasivam made a hurried visit home to ask my father if I could play host to his two friends—Sankho and Ira Chaudhury—who would be visiting Tanjore. He himself would be away in Madras and so would miss seeing them. Sankho was an acclaimed sculptor at the Fine Arts Department of M.S. University of Baroda and his wife Ira was known for her pottery skills. Both had trained at Shantiniketan, the

*The Cholas were one of the longest ruling dynasties in South India. The Chola empire stretched from the ninth to the thirteenth centuries, but the Chola kingdom existed around the second century. Literature, art and culture flourished during the Chola period.

educational centre based on Rabindranath Tagore's vision and located about 95 miles from Calcutta (now Kolkata). They were on a holiday in Ootacamund (now Ooty) and were planning to visit temples, as they were interested in temple art and aesthetics. They were visiting the seventh-century Ucchi Pillaiyar temple built atop Rockfort, in the town of Trichy. The temple complex built on a rocky outcrop is a landmark attraction for visitors to Trichy. But when they were climbing up to the temple, some urchins conned Ira and stole her handbag, leaving them stranded as the handbag had all their money and train tickets! The station master, a sympathetic man, allowed them to phone Dr Paramasivam, paid for their tickets and loaned them a few rupees. A few hours later, Sankho and Ira arrived in Tanjore.

Sankho and Ira instantly connected with my parents. They were a joyous and fun-loving couple. Sankho had a hearty guffaw and Ira had an easy grace that we felt instantly comfortable with. My mother felt she was back in Bombay and chatted with them in Hindi, which surprised and pleased them. They were keen to go to Chittanavasal, the beautiful ninth-century Jain cave temple in Puddukottai district. I accepted their invitation to go with them, and the three of us left by bus the following day. We got to know one another a bit during that trip. Once at the temple, I was amused to see both of them lying on their backs for a good part of the day, admiring the frescoes on the temple ceiling. My parents invited them to high tea the next day and prepared a special tiffin as they were leaving for Madras by the night train. Amma made *rava* idlis and *paal poli* (a dessert with milk), which they greatly enjoyed. After the meal there was music and dance, and we all sang with Ira and Sankho joining in. I lost touch with them after they left for Madras that night.

In early August 1955, I was teaching in Queen Mary's

College, having completed my master's in Human Geography. I was also the secretary of the dramatic association at the college and was up to my neck in supervising rehearsals for a programme of music, dance and plays in Tamil, English and Hindi. We had just a few weeks of rehearsals left. Chief Minister K. Kamaraj was to be the guest of honour. Needless to say, there was much excitement on campus.

Rukka at Queen Mary's College

A few days before the event, around six o'clock in the evening, the college office sent word that there was a phone call for me. In those days, there were no phones in the staff quarters where I lived, and all incoming calls were through the college administrative office. I requested the office to pass on the phone number of the caller to me, but with everything going on, I completely forgot to return the call. Ten days later, the office paged me again and I took the call this time. The voice on the phone was deep and I liked the sound of it: 'Hello? Am I speaking with Rukmini? I am Chamu Srinivas, a friend of Sankho, my friend at M.S. University of Baroda, and I'm in town for a few days.' He drew me into a pleasant and interesting conversation, and we decided to meet the next day. The office also handed me a letter from Sankho received two days earlier! Sankho's introduction was very Sankho. It read: 'Although a pipe-smoking brown Englishman from Oxford, he is an interesting person. Get him talking about Mysore, his hometown, and you'll make him emotional.' I understood this when I met Chamu.

The next day, when I responded to a knock at my door, I found a figure crouching down. I saw a head of grey hair. Chamu had bent down to tie his shoelace. 'Sorry about that,' he smiled apologetically. 'Come in, Mr Srinivas,' I responded. I offered him tea in an attempt to ease the situation. 'I'll take a rain check on that. Call me Chamu, please.'

My accommodation at the staff quarters was fairly spacious, though sparingly furnished. There were enclosed verandahs on two sides, one of which served as my study. Chamu observed, 'A nice, airy, well-lit study.' He was interested in the courses I taught and smiled as he picked up a volume, 'So you use my colleague and friend Darryl Ford's book…is it for the undergraduate level?'

We talked about my department, a little about my schooling, nothing in particular. Nearing lunchtime, when I was wondering what I could offer Chamu for lunch, he said, 'My friend Ramachar has generously loaned me his car and driver for the next two days. May I take you out for lunch today? I am not familiar with the city, so you get to choose the place.' I did not know much about eating out in Madras, so I suggested the Ramakrishna Lunch Home, a vegetarian eatery in Parry's Corner. I had been there a couple of times with college friends.

I realized on that first day that Chamu did not talk much about himself. In fact, I did most of the talking over masala dosai, gulab jamun and coffee. I talked mostly about my work and my family. As we drove back to Queen Mary's College, Chamu told me a little bit about himself, his mother and his family in Mysore. I learnt that he had resigned from a lecturership at Oxford University to start the Sociology Department at M.S. University in Baroda, and was still getting used to the change. We browsed in a bookstore on Mount Road and stopped at P. Orr & Sons, the famous 'time' outlet where Chamu got a chain fixed on his pocket watch. Back in the car he said, 'How thoughtless of me, I should have bought you a wristwatch.' He must have noticed I was not wearing one. 'Would you like to have mine?' The Smith man's wristwatch was his first gift to me. Dropping me back to college, he said he was free the following day and if I was inclined to go out he would very much like to spend time in Mahabalipuram. And we did. This was my first experience at the shore temples and the day went by ever so fast.

Chamu was relaxed the second day, telling me more about his brothers and sisters. I got the feeling that he wanted me to know about his background and did not want me to have any surprises. I was attracted to his deep voice, his simplicity and his sense of the absurd.

Chamu was to leave for Baroda the following morning and when I remarked on how quickly the past two days had gone, he surprised me with, 'I will be back in Madras in a few weeks to finalize the arrangements for the International Anthropological Conference being held later this year between the fifth and seventh of November.' I received an invitation to the conference and enjoyed meeting scholars from around the world. I also got to spend more time with Chamu when he was back in Madras that November. The day after the conference ended, he expressed a wish to meet my parents and the rest of my family. When I told him that I too had wanted to invite him to Tanjore, he simply said, 'I read your mind and it should not surprise you to know that I feel the same way you do.' And we left for Tanjore.

My parents were very welcoming. The day went by without any questions asked or any answers expected. It was just one of those pleasant family gatherings. By the time we left for Madras that night, my parents knew that I had come with Chamu to introduce him as someone special in my life. And they were happy for me. That he was a member of the *Shrivaishnavaite* sect, an Iyengar, and that we were *Shaivaite*, Iyers, made no difference. And as Chamu told me later, he liked the interaction between me and my parents, particularly with my father and among us sisters.

Chamu wanted me to meet his family too, and so we left for Mysore. I felt comfortable with him and was not nervous about meeting his family, who were very welcoming. There was a painted portrait of his parents in the main hall. Chamu had told me that his father had passed away when he was in his teens. Pachu, the eldest son, stepped in as the head of the household to discuss his younger brother's forthcoming marriage.

Chamu in 1955

Chamu's mother was excited that her son had brought home his future bride. The evening we arrived from Madras, she took me to her Srinivasa *gudi* (temple). The following day, we shopped for wedding saris and a few essential gold ornaments. I did not grow up in a family that placed much importance on jewellery and she was pleasantly surprised at my refusal to buy heavy gold jewellery. But it was fun shopping with her.

On that first visit to Mysore, I met the celebrated author R.K. Narayan, Chamu's friend from his teenage years, and he insisted Chamu and I visit his mother and have tiffin with them. The previous evening, Chamu had presented me with a copy of *Swami and Friends*—Narayan's first novel. I must confess I had not heard of R.K. Narayan till I went to Mysore, for I had grown up reading Thomas Hardy and Somerset Maugham.

We had delicious rava uppuma and coffee with Narayan's mother and his two sisters-in-law. Narayan, or Kunjappa as he was known to family and friends, was delighted that Chamu was marrying someone from the same sect as him (an Iyer). From the moment we met, I felt connected to Kunjappa. I felt I knew him from before.

Chamu claimed that Kunjappa saw in me the likeness of his dear wife, Rajam, whom he had lost. Indeed, Kunjappa frequently said, 'Rajam was also tall and slim, like you, Rukka. My meeting with her was under very unusual and unorthodox circumstances. I was visiting relatives in Coimbatore, and at the public water tap in the street, my eyes fell upon this tall, young, slim girl who came every day with a *kodam* [water pot]. She would fill the pot from the tap under my window and go her way. One morning, I dared to ask her what her name was. I went home to Mysore and announced to my mother that I had found Rajam, whom I wished to marry.'

'That was indeed quick and unconventional,' I remarked.

'Well, very like Chamu,' Kunjappa responded and laughed that inimitable laugh, throwing back his head a little.

On my return to Madras and to college, my father sent me a news cutting from *The Hindu* that read, 'This year's recipient of the coveted Rivers Memorial Medal awarded by the RAI [Royal Anthropological Institute of Great Britain and Ireland] is Dr M.N. Srinivas, Professor and Head of the Department of Sociology in M.S. University, Baroda.' My father excitedly asked whether I knew about it, to which I replied that I did not have the faintest clue.

BARODA, DELHI AND BEYOND

The Artful Dodger

Chamu and I were married in my parents' home in Tanjore on 21 November 1955, and we left for Baroda the same night. Chamu was on a week's leave from his university in Baroda and the journey by train was three days long.

The night train from Bombay arrived before dawn at the Baroda station. As the train steamed into the station on that chilly morning, Chamu briskly moved our luggage to the 'off side' instead of onto the platform. We were the only passengers in our first-class compartment, so there was no dearth of space in the corridor. Two of the four porters clambered in and, doing a sort of a relay, transferred each piece of luggage from one to the other in a well-coordinated and swift move. When all our luggage was offloaded, Chamu jumped down with the help of a porter and two of them helped me clamber down. 'Why was Chamu doing this?' I wondered. Why not just disembark onto the platform? It was certainly not to dodge and avoid the ticket collector, for our tickets had been checked more than once during that night journey. We waited, standing precariously on the siding, till the train steamed away from the platform. Crossing the sleepers, clambering up and on to the other platform, we made our way and mingled with the passengers. Then followed a short cab drive to Alkapuri—the beautiful suburb of tree-lined avenues and little lanes—which was to be my first house with Chamu. I was greeted by Chamu's major-domo, Ramchander, with a tray of thin and savoury *khakhra* and hot coffee. For a Maharashtrian, Ramchander's coffee made with the South Indian percolator was excellent, I thought. A short, young man in his 20s, with a smart, close crop of jet-black hair and clean-shaven pleasant face, he folded his hands and greeted us with a namaste. Ramachander was a man of few words but he would sing to himself most of the day. It seemed a great way of driving away boredom. His favourite was Maharashtrian *abhang* music, a kind of devotional poetry sung in praise of the Hindu god Vithal or Vithoba, which I had first been introduced to as a schoolgirl in Poona when my mother learnt music from a Mrs Sule.

As Chamu and I were enjoying our first cup of coffee of the day, I heard sounds of traditional band music with pipes and drums, and even before I could gather my thoughts I heard Chamu say under his breath, 'Here is that rascal Sankho.' And sure enough Sankho was there, entering the front gate, singing loudly to the accompaniment of instruments. He made a show of garlanding both of us for an 'auspicious welcome'. Sankho preferred tea and had a cup with us before he left. Chamu knew his friend only too well and had successfully averted this embarrassment earlier that morning at the Baroda railway station by getting down on the wrong side of the tracks.

Sankho returned a couple of hours later with Ira, his wife, and Savita and Nanubhai Amin—all dear friends of Chamu. Ramchander gave us a hearty breakfast of *thali peeth*, made with rice flour and chopped scallions, and accompanied by mint chutney and strong masala chai. He surprised us with *kobbari mithai,* a sweet made with coconut and jaggery. I was touched by his thoughtful and friendly gesture.

A Misunderstanding in Deobandh

Soon after we arrived in Baroda in November, Chamu announced that I should be ready to pack and travel in a few weeks' time. 'Don't think you're settled in Baroda,' he laughed. I asked him later where we were going. He said, 'To Deobandh, near Saharanpur in Uttar Pradesh. A group of American scholars, sociologists and anthropologists are conducting field studies in Deobandh and have asked me to go visit them at their research site, and I've agreed.'

And so it turned out that in the last week of, I think, December of 1955—the year we got married—we left Baroda for Delhi. In Delhi, we stopped at my aunt's house for a couple of days and then drove to Deobandh. I knew nothing about social anthropology, or the kind of research that anthropologists conducted, so I didn't know what to expect.

We drove over flat land with wheat fields as far as the eye could see. Women and men could be seen working in the fields, the women with their faces veiled. The long drive ended with our arrival at the site late in the evening. A cluster of well-lit white tents stood out in the darkness. To my eyes, it looked eerie and I felt uncomfortable. One of the researchers came out to greet us. I later learnt that he was the director of the project. The team appeared to comprise a senior American anthropologist and the men and women who worked with him—all of whom were white Americans. There were a few Indian interpreters, all of whom were men.

That evening, a meeting was held for Chamu to get acquainted with the research and the researchers. It was cold in December, but it was warm and cosy inside the tents. Every tent had a generator and mobile heating. An unexpected luxury at a rural field site! I seem to remember hearing that the research was funded by the Ford Foundation. That evening, I heard Chamu and the research team talking late into the night.

While I was not an anthropologist, I had done field work when I was a student and was curious to learn about the research that was being conducted. I was also eager to have a look around the field site.

The next morning, I accompanied a group of three young American women with one Indian male interpreter to the village. The women researchers were dressed in Western clothes, one wore a pantsuit, another was in a long dress paired with a coat as it was chilly. I was, as usual, dressed in a sari and had covered my head with my sari's pallu, following Chamu's advice to keep my head covered while in the village. I remember being a bit surprised at the dress and demeanour of the women researchers.

They had short hair and no head covering. They were slim and flat-chested. I have gone into details of their appearance because it had a bearing on what followed. In strong American accents, they asked me if I could speak the local language and I responded that I could speak, read and write in Hindi.

The village was about a mile away from the tents and, after a bit of a walk, we reached some dwellings. Children ran around and goats were tethered to wooden stakes around the house. The children came up to us, curious about our presence.

Some elderly women, bent over with age, leaned on wooden canes as they sat on their haunches outside the houses. They gave us a keen look. All the women were fully covered in *salwar kameez*, with their dupattas covering their heads and faces. Outside one of the huts, an elderly man was seated on a charpoy. The interpreter greeted him and the old man signalled to him to come sit on the charpoy.

The women welcomed us. As we bent down to enter the low doorway of one of the huts, we could smell food being cooked and there was smoke in the air. I could smell hot rotis being baked. We walked into a large, dimly-lit room with a low ceiling. The floor was surfaced with cowdung. There was no furniture other than a charpoy. I sat down on the floor. The researchers stood around awkwardly. Maybe they found it difficult to sit on the floor. Noticing their discomfort, one of the village women shouted to a boy, '*Kursi ley aao* (Get a chair).' He brought one heavy wooden chair and placed it there. Then the charpoy was pulled closer and an elderly woman indicated to the researchers to take a seat. About three or four other women stood around, closely watching and sizing up the arrivals.

The village women were very hospitable. One of the elderly women ordered chai and *nashtaa* (snacks), and soon after some of the younger women brought brass plates laden with *barfi*, along with some coloured sweets—orange, green and white. Pointing to the sweets, a little boy standing nearby said, 'Indian flag!'

It seemed to me that this was the first time the researchers were meeting this particular family. They didn't seem to know the women and there were no friendly greetings. They took out their notebooks and asked me to relay their questions to the women as none of them spoke Hindi, leave alone the local dialect. It was an awkward interaction to say the least because we had not spent any time introducing ourselves or getting to know the women.

There seemed to be a number of questions which the

researchers wanted quick answers to. I don't remember all the questions, but some were very personal and seemed insensitive to me. I tried to convey to the researchers that we needed to get a sense of the family and the relationships the women had with one another, but they wanted to get done with their survey questions. I was a bit taken aback when questions moved into the area of sexual behaviour. One of the American women asked a pointed question and directed me to relay it, something along the lines of 'What kind of relationship do you have with your husband? Do you sleep in the same room? How many times a week do you have intercourse?' I felt embarrassed and the villagers looked at one another and giggled when I translated the questions. There was a ripple of laughter all around and the Americans didn't know why the women were laughing. To them, this was a serious question. They were busy scribbling in their notebooks and seemed oblivious to the atmosphere in the room. After a while, I conveyed to the village women that we would return the next day and we walked back to the tents.

The next day, I returned to the village with the team and the interpreter. The moment the researchers entered the haveli with a male interpreter, the village women drew their *ghunghat* even lower to cover their faces. The interpreter tried to ease the situation by telling the women that he was from a neighbouring village and that he belonged to the same community as they did. But he was not able to get them to talk. He felt it was best that he left. And he did soon after.

At the end of each day, there would be a discussion with the research team in the director's tent where the researchers would report the happenings of the day. Chamu was present and took notes on such occasions. Following these disastrous visits, it was decided that male interpreters should not accompany women field researchers as the village women were not forthcoming with information in the presence of a man. So, there was no man accompanying us when we went to the next house. I was an observer, so I did not say anything. But I was a bit surprised at how the research was being conducted and it seemed to me that it would not go well or yield the desired results.

Chamu was supposed to stay there only for a few days. He held a brief meeting with the group the final morning of our stay, and we said our goodbyes and left at midday. It was not until some days later that I heard of the unfortunate incident at the field site.

It appeared that the researchers' prying questions had not only embarrassed but also angered the women in the haveli. When one of the young female researchers went to the village to continue with her questioning, she least expected what would follow. The women closed the door behind her and tore her clothes to see if she indeed was a woman. She had been asking excessively intrusive questions and the village women were suspicious of her.

Chamu and I discussed the incident back in Delhi and he was disturbed at how unprepared the research team was and was shocked at what had transpired.

Many years later, I remember one of Chamu's young Indian colleagues at Delhi University went south to Tanjore district to do fieldwork. As he did not know Tamil, I put him in touch with my parents who had moved to Tanjore. My father, as ever interested in young students and intellectually curious about their work, took him under his wing. He gifted him a couple of *veshti*s that men wore in South India, along with a kurta. This was to be his garb in the field to help him blend in with the locals as much as possible. My father's home, about 15 km from the village, was a getaway for this young researcher when he left the village and came into town. My father helped transcribe some of the Tamil documents from the research and facilitated his stay in other ways. He even gifted this young scholar a sacred thread. Chamu had told him how important it was for him to have the caste mark (the mark or symbol that orthodox members wear to designate their caste, usually of sacred ash or vermillion) on his forehead when he went to the village.

I'm sure this preparation and advice eased his entry into the village community and facilitated his research.

Rukka outside a mosque in Deobandh

Makhijani's Dilemma

The Housing Allotment Office at Delhi University was efficient. Within a few weeks of joining the Sociology Department in early 1959, Chamu was allotted Staff Bungalow Number 14 on Cavalry Lane—the first of six red-brick bungalows on a quiet dead-end street on the campus. This became our home, where we lived for 13 years till we left Delhi in 1972.

14 Cavalry Lane was a gracious two-storey, red-brick bungalow with a front verandah overlooking the lawn and garden. I was told these bungalows were built during Sir Maurice Gwyer's tenure as vice chancellor of Delhi University. There was a towering neem tree on the street opposite the house and a number of birds—owls, vultures, parrots, crows and peacocks—used to nest in it. Once we even found a large anteater foraging under the tree. We spent most of our waking hours on the front verandah, from where we could see the garden and all the happenings on and around the tree. We would also have our morning coffee, breakfast and evening tea there.

The main entrance door of the house led to a corridor off which were a bath and a toilet; a bedroom on the left; and living and dining rooms on the right. The staircase between the kitchen and bathroom opened onto the first floor with two additional bedrooms, a bathroom, a study and an open terrace. Treetops and birdcalls lent the illusion of living amid nature and far away from the bustle of urban life.

Chamu was keen to settle in without delay. The immediate reason was that his good friend and colleague from Manchester, Max Gluckman, the anthropologist, was stopping in Delhi for three days on his way to Canberra. Chamu had invited him to stay with us and Max was due to arrive in four weeks. Needless to say, we were both keen to make his stay comfortable. This was Max's first visit to India.

Chamu felt that the bedroom on the ground floor with an attached bathroom would be suitable for our guest. There was just one snag—both the toilets in the bungalow were Indian-style, where one had to squat on one's haunches. Max, we were sure, would not be comfortable, even though his visit was a short one. So, we requested the university civil engineer to replace the Indian-style commode on the ground floor with a Western one. Several letters were sent to the university estate office following which, late one evening, a stocky man with greying hair, dressed in a black suit and tie appeared on our doorstep. 'Mr Shiriniwas!' he hollered. Just as Chamu opened the door, he started off. 'I do not understand why you want a Western-style commode. You are Indian and Hindu, are you not?' he asked in an accusatory growl. I rushed from the kitchen. 'Please come in,' I heard Chamu's calm, unruffled voice.

'I am Makhijani, university civil engineer. I have seen your letters. Only Christians have Western-style commode. Cavalry Lane bungalows were built many years ago and many families have lived here without any complaints.' Even as Chamu tried to explain, 'I have no complaints,' Mr Makhijani waved his short arm in a dismissive gesture and turned to leave. He felt he had said his piece and the interaction was over. He went past Chamu and me into the corridor and sat on his haunches with his hands resting on his knees. 'This is the easiest way to relieve yourself!' A good part of the evening was spent in explanations and counter-explanations. But Mr Makhijani was adamant. Finally came a concession: 'I will install an Anglo-Indian commode which your guest from England can use.' That was the first time I heard of an 'in-between'—neither Indian nor Western, but both. Chamu was not annoyed. He was highly amused that he, a social anthropologist, was being tutored by a civil engineer on how Hindus relieve themselves and should relieve themselves. How many civil engineers with such a passion for 'Indian culture' does one encounter?

The Ice Box and 'Meat Safe'

Timmy, our mongrel dog, went bounding down the corridor, came to a sudden halt on the porch and barked threateningly. I followed him and saw a tall, lean, cadaverous-looking middle-aged man at the gate. On spotting me, he alighted from his bicycle and said, '*Salaam Memsaab*', and introduced himself as Ibrahim, the university carpenter. How on earth did he know that I was desperately in search of a carpenter, I wondered?

I went up to the gate, led Timmy back into the house and Ibrahim followed me, taking care to lock the gate behind him. The fragrance of sweet *paan* and the acrid smell of beedi wafted from him. From that day on, I never failed to sense Ibrahim's arrival—his arrival would become obvious from the smell of paan and beedi. He would always greet me respectfully with his usual 'Salaam Memsaab'. As I got to know him, it became more of a friendly greeting.

Ibrahim seemed to know the layout of 14 Cavalry Lane. He left his bike leaning against the short, red-brick parapet wall on the side, walked to the back of the house and emerged at the side door. He shook his pathan slippers off and washed his feet under the garden tap. As he entered, I saw him at close quarters. His face was heavily lined and he had a small, hennaed goatee. He wore loose white pyjamas and a full-sleeved striped shirt with a black waistcoat that had seen better days. He removed the embroidered cotton cap from his head, tucked it under his arm and walked in. He then told me in

Hindi, 'I can make just about anything, Memsaab: bookshelf, pantry shelf, bench, stool, table, anything!'

We discussed the pantry shelves and he stepped into the kitchen and, fumbling in his waistcoat pocket, produced his metal-rimmed spectacles. With our cook's help, he took measurements. Then suddenly, he turned around and asked me pointedly, 'Don't you have a fridge, Memsaab?' He seemed surprised that a professor's house did not have a refrigerator. I said, 'No.' Then he added, 'I can make you one.' I wondered what he meant. He explained that he could make an ice box and sounded very confident. Taking out a piece of crushed paper and a pencil from his waistcoat pocket, he proceeded to sketch a long box with compartments. It seemed interesting and I thought would serve our needs. He said he had made a few like it before. So, I asked him to go ahead. Before he left, he asked for an advance of 200 rupees, to which I agreed.

A few weeks later, a lorry stopped at our gate with Ibrahim following closely on his bicycle. Four men brought in the pieces of furniture I had ordered: kitchen stools, a wooden bench and pantry shelves. Lastly, they staggered in with a huge, five-foot-long rectangular metal case. Ibrahim directed the men to place this box in the corridor, as, he explained, it was too big to be placed inside the kitchen. I had never seen anything like it before. 'This is the ice box, Memsaab.' Ibrahim cheerfully and proudly lifted the heavy lid. He explained to me that there were zinc sheets hammered in on a wooden frame with a felt lining between the double metal layers. A perforated tray on the bottom was designed to hold ice blocks, above which were two other trays and side brackets made of metal. Both the trays and brackets were divided into compartments for fruits, vegetables, milk, butter and cheese. The ice box stood on four sturdy legs. I asked Ibrahim how it would keep things cool and he lifted the bottom-most tray and showed me a deep compartment and said, 'Ice from the *barafkhana* [ice factory] should be filled here.' He showed me another opening under which there was a sliding tray to collect all the melted water. This was indeed an ingenious design, which needed no electricity to function.

Ibrahim had arranged for the ice to be delivered every few days from the ice factory across the Jamuna. A tempo soon arrived and stopped in front of the house. Two men got out, carrying blocks of ice on their heads and filled the ice compartment. Our cook was thrilled and busied himself with arranging the fruits and vegetables in the trays.

Ibrahim was ready to leave when I asked him how much I had to pay him. He wanted the amount in cash because he had no bank account. On receiving the notes, he counted them very quickly and returned 200 rupees to me with a smile, 'Remember?'

That evening, when Chamu returned home after a day of meetings at his department, I heard him say as he walked in, 'And what is this coffin doing here?'

Ibrahim would stop by every now and then. He became a handyman of sorts and did repairs around the house. Returning from the department, I would find him playing with Timmy on the lawn of 14 Cavalry Lane. They had become friends.

The ice box served us till we left Delhi in 1972. It was so cool that Timmy, and then Kittu who followed Timmy as the family dog, used it as air-conditioning and would lie down next to it on hot summer days, and the cook used to sit on it.

The last time I saw Ibrahim was when he came to say goodbye the day we were to leave for Bangalore and helped us with the final packing.

I mustn't forget to mention the meat safe, too, that Ibrahim made for us. I still have it in our home in Benson Town in Bangalore. While all the other furniture Ibrahim made was of *sheesham* wood (Indian rosewood), the meat safe was made of teak. I remember the meat safe in my mother's home when I was growing up, and the safe Ibrahim made was similar to it. When I married Chamu and travelled to England, his former landlady, Mrs Jones, with whom we stayed in Oxford, told me her meat safe was a hand-me-down from her sister-in-law. It had an intricately carved panel of flowers and vines. Mrs Jones used this airy cupboard for storing eggs, milk, butter and, of course, meat. In Mysore, in Chamu's mother's home, there was a 'milk safe', which was used to keep tasty homemade sweets and delicacies.

The meat safe made by Ibrahim was raised eight inches off the ground. It was a smallish cupboard with three removable shelves. He had designed the top of the meat safe artistically with a series of whorls. The front and sides were covered with wire mesh for a free play of air and to keep insects out. We would place a bowl of water under each of its four legs to prevent ants from getting in.

The meat safe stood side by side with the 'coffin' in the corridor. It was a place to keep loaves of bread, biscuits for us and dog biscuits for Timmy (and later, Kittu), as well as bottles of jam and pickles. It also became a treasure house of tasty treats: homemade sweets like gulab jamun, Mysore pak and homemade eggless cake—our cook Krishnan Nair would make a delicious upside-down pineapple cake and that, too, found a place (for a very short time) in the meat safe.

Mary Nana

The scene that I barely forget, even after all these decades, is of my little daughter Lakshmi playing with the water from the garden hose on the lawn of 14 Cavalry Lane. It was a hot summer's weekend and she was dressed in a muslin *jabla* (tunic) and shorts. A flock of sparrows covered the lawn and she was running after them. I sat on the porch, keeping an eye on her.

An Ambassador taxi stopped in front of our gate and a short, fairly plump woman stepped out, holding a pink parasol above her head. She wore a pink *chikan*-work (embroidery) cotton sari and carried a thick cotton handbag. As she walked up the driveway, I saw she was middle-aged and had curly hair that was turning grey. When she came closer, I could see her red stone earrings that were decidedly South Indian. And I could not miss the cross hanging from a chain around her neck.

I went down the steps halfway to greet her. She smiled at me, a cheerful, gap-toothed smile that transformed her face. After settling her taxi fare, she pointed to Lakshmi and asked, 'Is that the baby?' When I nodded, she remarked, 'Very thin.' Lakshmi, of course, was deeply absorbed in playing with the water and chasing the sparrows.

I was grateful to Dharma Kumar, our family friend, for finding me what turned out to be a gem of a nanny for our daughter. Dharma and Chamu were good old friends—Dharma had studied Economics at Cambridge while Chamu studied Social Anthropology at Oxford. And now, years later, Dharma was a faculty member of the Economics Department at Delhi University. She was a frequent visitor to our house on Cavalry Lane.

I had casually mentioned to Dharma at one of our dinner meetings that I needed somebody to stay home and look after Lakshmi when I went to work. I was a lecturer at the Geography Department in Delhi University. It did not take her long to come up with a solution. 'I have just the person, Rukka. She speaks Tamil and American English!' Dharma threw back her head and laughed. She went on to explain that the person she was thinking of would be out of work soon. 'She works for the current American ambassador who is leaving and, I am told, the incoming one does not have young children.'

Mary was quite managerial, if not bossy. And she was clearly accustomed to taking charge. At that first meeting of ours, she wanted to see the inside of our home and asked detailed questions about where her 'quarters' would be and where the baby slept. She asked, 'Do you have a nursery?' I offered her tea and as we chatted, I asked her what salary she expected. Surprisingly, her reply was, 'Anything you give, Madam.' Her one condition was that Sunday mornings and every Christian religious holiday she should be given the day off, which I thought was reasonable. I later conferred with Dharma, who suggested that Mary be given 500 rupees a month as salary. So, I opened a bank account for her and deposited the money every month.

Mary told me a little bit about herself: her deceased husband had been a writer (clerk) at a tea estate in the Nilgiri Hills, from where they had moved to Delhi, and for the last 20-odd years, she had been working as nanny for American diplomat families in Delhi. Her husband was buried in Delhi and on All Souls Day, she would make it a point to visit his grave.

A few weeks after our conversation, Mary arrived with a hold-all and two black trunks. Her luggage was deposited in the little cottage at the back of the property that adjoined the garage. This was a self-contained one-bedroom unit with a verandah, bathroom and kitchen. I had assumed that she would like the privacy. But within a week of her arrival, she surprised me by saying she wanted to move into the main house because her quarters were 'haunted'. There seemed to be no way to reassure her that the cottage was safe, so I gave in and she moved into the bedroom on the ground floor, which was also Lakshmi's nursery, and that became Mary's room.

Mary Nana took charge not only of Lakshmi but also the entire household staff, which included the cook, the gardener and later, the young Nepali boy who joined us, Ratan Lal. Ratan was an orphan and Chamu had decided we should give him a home and train him for a job. But over the years, Ratan turned out to be an excellent cook. He learnt to make both South Indian and North Indian foods—the best idli and dosai, along with chapatti and dal.

Mary had her own ideas about how Lakshmi should be raised. She would plan the day, starting with breakfast, after which she would take Lakshmi for a stroll in the pram, sometimes following the university band. Then lunch, afternoon naps, another stroll in the evening and so on. In short, in planning the days for Lakshmi and herself, she also planned our days. For example, on a weekend, she would come up with 'Let us go for a drive with *magaa* (the child).' And she would have her own shopping list of biscuits, chocolates, toys and clothing. She loved outings and would accompany us to shops, parks, the zoo—in short, wherever we went. Chamu quipped that we should raise our living standards to suit Mary

Nana. He said we lowly Indian academics would not compare with the white American diplomats she was used to living with. We were a step down for her.

Mary Nana with Timmy and Lakshmi

Mary made friends easily, no matter whether it was a university professor or his wife, or the university gardeners. She soon got to know almost everyone in our neighbourhood and on the campus. She always had information about events and activities, such as the annual flower shows, Indira Gandhi's visit to the campus, and social events like campus marriages. In fact, it was she who encouraged me to admit Lakshmi to the newly instituted experimental pre-school on the campus. She had stopped by on one of her strolls with Lakshmi and picked up the application form.

Mary identified with our family completely. We never thought of her as a paid domestic and she did not regard herself as one. It was not unusual for her to walk into our living room whenever we had company and expect to be introduced. She was always invited to join us during our mealtimes and sometimes she would oblige. She felt so comfortable with us that she would make decisions about reorganizing the nursery as well as the living room. She took charge of the vegetable patch in the back garden. With Lakshmi pottering in the soil with her, Mary planted radishes, tomatoes, beans, carrots and spinach and suggested that I have one row of curry leaf plants. Her walks around the campus pushing Lakshmi in her pram were also opportunities for foraging and gathering bits of wire, string, nails, buttons—all of which she felt 'would come in handy'. She would also collect seedlings and plants—tomato seedlings growing in the storm water drains were replanted in the back garden and grew lushly, and her gardener friends would also give her seedlings. One day, Mary came home with a young mulberry plant and said it would attract birds that Lakshmi was fond of. She planted it in full sun in the middle of the vegetable patch. She would keep a watch on her garden and harvest the produce, ordering our cook, Veluswamy, to use them.

Mary's gardening, at times, took an unusual turn. There were young fruit trees: peach, mango and a *sitaphal* on the north side of the house next to the cricket field. Though they were mature, none of them bore any fruit. I asked Mary if she had any suggestions to make them yield. She simply assured me that they would. And one day, I found the sign of the cross scratched into the bark of each tree. Surprisingly, the trees did yield after that.

Her faith was unshakable. She would leave for church early every Sunday and return late in the afternoon after a shopping spree in Chandni Chowk: beers for Chamu; a set of handkerchiefs for me; gifts for Lakshmi; and for the new baby, Tulasi, flowers and fruit. One Sunday, she returned with the parish padre and invited him to stay on for tea. She had bought pastries for the occasion.

Mary had a little altar in the nursery with a picture of Christ and every night, without fail, she would say her prayers before turning in. I would find the nursery light on past midnight and Mary sitting on a *moda* (wicker stool) with her rosary in her hand, nodding, fast asleep. When I went to wake her so she could sleep comfortably on her bed, she would insist that she was praying and wide awake. Chamu feared that she would burn down the house one day as she would light candles on the altar in her room for her prayers before falling asleep.

Mary protected her faith determinedly. Anything to do with Hinduism was shunned. In our household, our cook, Veluswamy, was from a village in Tinneveli district in Tamil Nadu and was a very religious Hindu. He would offer a coconut and flowers to the family deity, housed in a small shelf in the pantry. Knowing this, Mary did not want him to add coconut to any food he cooked. She would tell him firmly, 'I will not eat anything that has coconut in it.' She would sulk if he added coconut as a garnish and I would have to intervene and remind him to take out Mary's share separately before he added coconut to anything.

When Chamu and I, with our two daughters, visited the Vatican, we brought Mary a gift of two rosaries blessed by the Pope. Mary spread the news all over the campus. It was the thrill of a lifetime for her.

It is rare to find someone like Mary. On our annual summer holidays to Mysore and Tanjore, we would leave her in charge of the house and Lakshmi's canine friend, Kittu.

And when we went abroad and stayed away for a year at a time, Mary wrote us long letters in Tamil to keep us informed about herself, the house, Kittu and the visitors to the house, as well as what was generally happening on the campus. She remembered all our birthdays and would send us cards and letters. I can't imagine even a relative ever identifying so closely with our family.

When we left Delhi for Bangalore in 1972, I assumed Mary would come with us. She had become a family member and was from South India. But Mary was adamant that she would not leave Delhi. She wanted to be buried near her husband and saw leaving Delhi as abandoning him. Sadly, we had to say goodbye to Mary Nana and all of us missed her dreadfully.

The Garden at 14 Cavalry Lane

The bungalow we were allotted in Delhi had a 40 ft lawn in the front and an equal spread of yard space at the back. I was excited at the prospect of having my own flower and vegetable garden. The university *maali* (gardener) appeared at my door, offering his services and explaining to me that he had been working as a gardener in the same bungalow for over five years but that the previous professor's family had no interest whatsoever in gardening.

Within weeks of moving into our new home, I started gardening feverishly. I went to the Sundar Nagar nursery, where I over-indulged my passion and bought several dozen rose plants. I remember my mother telling me that roses grew well in North India. My neighbour sent her maali, Vishnu, over and we spent the weekend digging beds on all four sides of the lawn and planting roses. He introduced me to the Okhla sludge, which people in the university bought in lorry-loads to use as manure for their gardens. Once a year, he and I would drive to Okhla (on the outskirts of the city) and order a lorry-load of the sludge. I was told that Okhla sludge was the well decomposed cake-like mix of sewerage and organic compost that was dried and sold as fertilizers. I don't know if the sewerage was treated because there was a noxious smell to the fertilizer. The first time the sludge truck came to our door, one of our neighbours, Mrs Dasgupta, walked in and offered to 'share' half the sludge, saying it would be too much for one garden. I didn't realize then that she wanted to save a trip to Okhla. The drive to Okhla on the outskirts of the city had to be planned, for the entire trip took three to four hours.

The garden at 14 Cavalry Lane took an interesting shape. Since it was the first of the six houses from the main road, it was a corner plot. I planted a Lady Palmer, a popular variety of bougainvillea at the time, which had pink and white blooms—a gift from the novelist Ruth Prawer Jhabvala. With proper sunlight, it flowered throughout the year. Along the driveway, on one side was a hedge of the long dark-green Dhaka lemon. The hedge bordered the lawn. On the other side of the driveway, alongside the neighbour's wall, were several plants of *Raath ki rani* (night-blooming jasmine). We enjoyed the fragrance of the Raath ki rani flowers; though the plant was on the other side of the wall, in Professor Nagendra's garden, it flowered on our side. Chamu's gift was variegated bamboo from Shillong. He was also keen on having *Amaltas*, a variety of laburnum. I found it in a nursery on Mall Road and planted it near the gate. In the summer, when it bloomed against the backdrop of the red brick wall, it was a stunning sight. The roses I planted bordered the lawn. We had some bulbs—dahlias and tuberoses—another of Chamu's favourite fragrances. Near the water tap, we planted sugarcane and a few banana plants gifted by a South Indian friend in Karol Bagh. On the ground floor, outside Mary Nana's bedroom window, was a mango tree and a sitaphal tree, both given by our dear friend Nanubhai Amin and sent with detailed planting instructions. Nanubhai had a keen interest in plants and it equalled his boundless interest in global cuisine. He was an innovator, an entrepreneur, an agriculturist, who never tired of experimenting.

Rukka with baby Tulasi in the garden

Leading from the driveway to the garage at the back of the house was a pergola where I had planted a grapevine. Though it did not bear much fruit, the squirrels enjoyed whatever little it did. Bordering the house, at the back and opening out onto the main road, was a conservancy lane that led to the servant's quarters for the six bungalows on Cavalry Lane. The patch of land between the back of the house and the conservancy lane housed the kitchen garden. I planted a row of four to five curry leaf bushes and another of three or four moringa trees sourced from a nearby nursery in Model Town. The moringa plants fared well in afternoon and evening sun and we harvested the drumsticks. An annual gift to Chamu's childhood friend, S.L.N. Simha, working at the time at the Reserve Bank of India in Bombay, was home-grown drumsticks. Every time Chamu passed through Bombay, he would take some in a cloth bag for his friend.

The mulberry sapling Mary Nana dug out from the side of the road during one of her strolls with Lakshmi in the pram, and that she planted became the centrepiece of the back garden. It was the red purplish variety of mulberry and attracted many birds. I also grew cabbages, *knol khol*, potatoes, onions and sometimes lettuce, though unsuccessfully. But it was a lot of fun.

My university colleagues would ask whether I was entering my garden in the annual university flower show—a competitive sport on the campus—where university wives (yes, it was mostly the wives as I remember) would show off their gardening prowess. I hadn't planned to, but my friends and colleagues encouraged me. I did not receive any prize, and that was okay by me. There were many keen home gardeners who would prepare for the competition for months. And as I learnt later, they also had the expertise and advice from the Sundar Nagar Nursery. The second time I entered the flower show, I won a silver cup. This was largely due to the efforts and care of my gardener, Vishnu. He continued tending my garden till we left Delhi and 14 Cavalry Lane for Bangalore in 1972.

I gave Vishnu a farewell gift of the silver cup, which we had won together in 1963. He was touched and said, '*Didi*, this garden is yours, you should keep the prize.' I was very sorry to leave our home and garden after 14 years, not knowing whether the next occupant would be interested in tending to the garden. I mentioned my concern to friends and colleagues at the university who were only too willing to come and take away the plants to give them a good home!

The 'Horse Doctor'

When I was growing up, a family doctor who lived in the neighbourhood was seen as an indispensable member of the community. In most cities where I've lived in India, we've had neighbourhood doctors who either made house visits or had their clinics nearby where patients could drop in without appointments.

Dr Mitra was highly recommended by Chamu's colleagues at Delhi University. His clinic in Kamala Nagar adjoined the university campus and this was an added advantage to all the university families living on the campus.

I remember Dr Mitra as middle-aged, short and balding, with small hands. He wore ill-fitting full-sleeved shirts. Buttoning it over his generous tummy must have been a daily challenge. Even during Delhi winters, he wore heavy, leather sandals that had seen happier days. Thick, dark-rimmed spectacles completed his uniform. Of course, in the 1960s, most spectacles were heavy-rimmed.

Dr Mitra was a man of few words. Chamu would make unsuccessful attempts at engaging him in small talk and often a nod would be the only response. I don't remember him smiling much either but he had a pleasant, if remote, expression on his face.

We would often see Dr Mitra in the evenings, walking briskly on the main street in Kamala Nagar to his clinic and then up the stairs, swinging his black bag containing his stethoscope and a flashlight. Sundays and holidays were no exception. Patients sitting on the steps would make way for him when they spotted him a few steps away. They would greet him with a 'Namaste, Doctor Saab' as they stood up. A brisk nod was his response.

The west-facing clinic would be draped in the evening sunlight, and in summer the heat and the glare within made one quite uncomfortable, to say the least. There was no fan and the seating for patients was organized with a few chairs and benches on either side of the narrow waiting area and against the wall, which was painted a bilious green.

Dr Mitra was not only a general physician but also did his own compounding. An anteroom with half a dozen shelves of labelled bottles of different sizes containing powders, pills and syrups lined the back and sidewalls. After a diagnostic meeting lasting a few minutes with each patient, Dr Mitra would retire to the back room, which had a glass partition, and would pound away with a pestle and mortar, stir the liquid, concocting a few ounces of a mixture, often pink or white and sometimes light brown. He would noisily type out the label with the dosage, date and duration on an ancient typewriter and laboriously spread the glue to stick it onto the bottle. The bottle would be handed to the patient through a porthole in the glass partition. This would be accompanied by a paper slip with his charges specified, which were exceedingly nominal.

We would visit Dr Mitra for seasonal coughs and colds, cuts and grazes, indigestion and insomnia. He had a liver tonic that he would give to nutritionally-deprived children with distended stomachs, and a cough and cold medicine that he would dispense every Delhi winter.

A few years after we became his regular patients, a story circulated among Delhi University staff that Dr Mitra had successfully treated a wounded horse on the streets of Kamala Nagar. He was called to the site of the accident—an

Ambassador car had collided with a tonga head-on and sped away. The poor horse had fallen to the ground, frothing at the mouth and writhing in pain. A crowd of bystanders who were witness to this tragic incident hailed Dr Mitra as a saint when they found him bent over the wounded animal to treat it. He examined the horse's heart and injuries and called the veterinary hospital to send their animal ambulance without delay.

Dr Mitra's compassion might have been his undoing. The next time I overheard a mention of Dr Mitra was by the librarian at the Ratan Tata Library in the 'D' School (the way Delhi University was sometimes referred to). She was recommending 'the horse doctor' in Kamala Nagar for all minor ailments to a young student. I did not find this funny. Later when his practice suffered a downturn, people attributed it to his dedication to treating our equine friends.

The Animal's Friend

One of the first words my daughter Lakshmi uttered excitedly was *chidiya* (bird), as a swarm of sparrows pecked at the grass on a sunny afternoon on our lawn at 14 Cavalry Lane. Mary Nana was sitting nearby on a moda, throwing seeds for the birds. I can never forget that sight. Another memorable visual was Mary pushing the pram on Probyn Road on the campus, and four or five dogs following the trail of breadcrumbs that she was throwing for them.

Love for animals and birds is common in my family as well as Chamu's. Lakshmi, from a young age, was very fond of and sensitive to animals. She was also curious about the natural world and would spend a lot of time outdoors watching the birds, ants and squirrels in the garden—a lifelong interest.

My friend, the librarian at Delhi School of Economics, was a dog lover and told me stories of how she had adopted four dogs. She also mentioned that near her home in Model Town (a neighbourhood in Delhi), an English lady had started a farm for stray and rescued animals. I mentioned this to Chamu. A few years later, for Lakshmi's birthday, Chamu's plan was to go to this farm to get her a puppy.

We drove to Model Town in my black Fiat one winter morning, but had trouble finding the shelter. After asking many people, we were finally directed to a large compound that was overgrown with shrubs and trees. The structures were dilapidated, and we wondered whether we were at the right place. Then we saw a sign: 'The Animal's Friend'. Near the gate, there were a few horses and donkeys, a peacock and lots of chickens running around.

We had heard of the Englishwoman, Crystal Rogers, who was running the shelter. We walked in hesitantly to find her seated on a charpoy with a tin of kerosene by her side. Two men were holding up the hind leg of a horse and she was concentrating on taking out the maggots from the horse's hooves and dropping them in the kerosene tin. This was an unforgettable scene.

After she had bandaged the horse's foot, she turned around and Chamu told her that we were there to pick up a puppy for our little daughter. She told us to come back in a week or so. When we returned, she narrated the sad story of a dog that had been run over by a car, leaving behind four or five puppies that were only a week old. We could have our pick.

Chamu wanted a small dog that would be easy to take care of. Lakshmi wanted a white dog. She had been reading fairytales and stories of unicorns and other magical animals. The puppies were all cream-coloured and Crystal Rogers assured us they were Pomeranian pups and would suit our young daughter very well. We selected one of the puppies and wrapped him up in Chamu's Exeter College scarf and beret as it was a cold day. Lakshmi named the puppy Krishnaswamy, 'Kittu' for short. She wanted the puppy to have an Indian name.

Kittu was adorable and became Lakshmi's constant companion and friend. He grew up alongside her in the nursery, where Mary pampered him too. When we went to the United States a few months after adopting Kittu, we left him in the care of Mary Nana and Veluswamy, who spoilt him thoroughly. Lakshmi did not want to leave Kittu and wanted to stay back with him and we had to persuade her that he would be looked after and that we would only be away for a year. Although Chamu had a chance to extend his visiting appointment, we missed Kittu and wondered whether he would be missing Lakshmi, so we went back home to Delhi.

While we were away, Mary wrote me long and detailed letters, giving news of the house and garden, but it was mainly about Kittu. Once we returned, Kittu remembered us and even greeted us enthusiastically, slobbering all over us and running around in delight. But he was no Pomeranian! He had grown to be a tall handsome dog that looked like a mix between an Alsatian and a Labrador.

Kittu

When we left for Bangalore in 1972, Kittu travelled with us by train. We packed special biscuits for him from Kamala Nagar, which we hoped would tempt him to eat even when he felt anxious on the train. There were no air-conditioned compartments, so we had to find ways to keep our compartment cool for him. Big trays of blocks of ice had to be bought along the route.

Kittu lived with us to a ripe old age in Bangalore.

Coincidentally, we learnt that Crystal Rogers had also moved to Bangalore where she set up CUPA—the Compassion Unlimited Plus Action animal shelter.

The Upside of Losing One's Way

When Chamu accepted the invitation from Dr V.K.R.V. Rao, vice chancellor of Delhi University, to start the Department of Sociology at the Delhi School of Economics, it had meant closing shop in Baroda. We moved in the winter and stayed with Kamala Achchaiah, a long-time friend of Chamu's from Oxford and, within a fortnight, moved yet again to the Delhi University campus.

Our allotted university bungalow was on a corner lot and to one side of the road was the university cricket field. The open space, rimmed with trees, attracted lots of birdlife. At night, we would also hear the howling of jackals, which was unnerving at first. They would come down from the Ridge, a forested area adjacent to the campus, to forage in the garbage bins.

Within a week of moving into our new home, I heard Chamu calling out one day, 'Rukka! Are you ready, let's go for a walk.' He was very particular about his morning and evening constitutional. We had no idea of the layout of the campus, so we just walked down the main university road with a troop of monkeys following us and dashing across the street, paying no mind to the traffic, which, thankfully, was sparse early in the morning in those days. We passed Gwyer Hall, the men's hostel block, and turned left onto a rough path which led to a gently rising scrubland. Thorny bushes and tall trees with large rocks and anthills formed a distinctive ecology and the area was home to a wealth of wildlife. Peacocks were seen strutting about. I once saw an anteater, and there were plenty of wild hares. We didn't see any snakes, but there were many tall anthills that could have been the homes of snakes, and our friends and colleagues reported coming across the slithering reptiles. Chamu and I would walk right up to the top of the Ridge and make a roundabout at the monument at its summit where many locals exercised in their pyjamas and cleaned their teeth with neem sticks. We would return home in time to get ready to go to the university. On one occasion, we lost our way and found that one of the paths led to Sabzi Mandi, the wholesale vegetable market. That was quite a long trek for me back home. But from then on, I visited Sabzi Mandi quite frequently.

When I felt more confident about walking in the area, I began to venture out on my own. One day, I decided to walk up the Ridge. It was later in the forenoon and Chamu had left for the university. I lost my way, but instead of turning back, I continued and found myself walking downhill.

I had heard stories about the Ridge. Not only were there stories of snakes, but of people who had gone missing, and there were reports of children being kidnapped. I warned Mary not to go anywhere near the Ridge with Lakshmi in her stroller. That day, to find myself lost on the Ridge was unnerving. As I kept walking, the path opened onto a tarred road and I was relieved to stumble upon a row of well-kept cottages with gardens. I told myself I couldn't be far from the university and luckily, I came upon a young woman outside one of the cottages, watering the plants. As I approached her, I saw she was in Western clothes and wore her hair short. I made bold to start a conversation and said, 'Your garden looks beautiful!' She responded warmly and said, 'Thank you.

Are you from here?' I said, 'Actually, I am coming from the university and I've lost my way. I have to get back to my family.' She asked me if I would like to come in and have a cup of tea, and I gladly accepted. Over tea, I learnt her name was Ruth and told her mine was Rukmini.

I asked her for directions back home while I explained where I lived. She said, 'You can either go back the way you came or [gesturing with her hand] go down the other way, and you'll come to the West End Hotel. We are in Civil Lines. Take a left and you will find the university area.' It was quite a long walk for me. Eventually, I came across familiar roads. I passed by the School of Social Work and found my way home. That was quite an adventure.

Within a week of meeting Ruth, there was a loud and determined knock on our gate. I went out and was pleasantly surprised to see her. I invited her in, and we sat on the lawn as was the custom in Delhi, where, for part of the year, the lawn would become the place for meeting and entertaining. I learnt that Ruth was married to an architect and that she was a writer. She was also curious to know more about Chamu and me. Before she left, she said, 'You must come again and this time with your husband.' So, one evening, on our way to dinner at H.Y. Sharada Prasad's house on Mall Road, we stopped briefly to say hello to Ruth. After meeting her, Chamu said, 'She's an interesting person. She's certainly not English. She must be from the Continent.'

A few months later, Ruth came by again. It may have been during one of the protests on campus, perhaps a student gherao. Chamu would be away for long hours at the university, staying there late into the night as protesting students would surround the university buildings, till their demands were met. Faculty and administrators in the building would not be able to leave for hours; sometimes they were trapped till the early hours of the morning. So, I would send him dinner from home and other faculty would similarly get food from their homes. And so we were not able to spend time with Ruth and get to know one another.

Some years after we moved to Bangalore, Chamu's boyhood friend from Mysore, the well-known and acclaimed first national librarian of independent India, also known as the 'Father of Indian National Bibliography', B.S. Kesavan, came by one evening. Chamu and I looked forward to his visits. He was a great conversationalist and raconteur. His hearty voice and laughter still echoes in my ears. Whenever Chamu and Kesavan met, they would chat about books and authors and this time, the conversation turned to the novel *Heat and Dust*, which had garnered a lot of attention. I can't remember what Kesavan said about the book, but Chamu turned to me and said, 'You remember Ruth whom you befriended on your walk to the Ridge? She's won a prize for her book *Heat and Dust*.' It was only then that I realized that I had chanced upon Ruth Prawer Jhabvala on that day when I was lost. I am now curious to see the movie *Heat and Dust* based on her novel.

On Keeping a Diary

I was influenced by my father in many ways. Keeping a diary was one of them. It was my habit to sit and chat with my father at the end of the day. Sitting in his bed, propped up by many pillows, he would either be reading a book or writing in his diary. Every day, he would painstakingly record everything he did, whom he met and what else happened in the lives of family members. He would note the days his brother or sister visited, when peasants would bring the produce from his family's land, and the days when he visited his friends. A separate section of the diary was for daily household expenses, and for budgeting and recording bills due and paid.

I admired my father for being so organized. In spite of all distractions and his illnesses, he never failed to write in his diary. I adopted this habit of his. I think I started writing in my diary when I started going to college, and my father's annual gift of a diary encouraged me to keep going.

In fact, some years ago, when I was cleaning out a bookshelf in our Bangalore home, I chanced upon one of his diaries and it brought tears to my eyes. The ink was faded, but I could still read his writing and I felt transported to those days in Tanjore when we would sit together and read late into the night.

It was a coincidence that Chamu also kept a diary, but his diary reflected department meetings, appointments with colleagues and students, work-related deadlines, progress with the development of the Sociology Department, letters to publishers, his correspondence to colleagues and friends, and so on. It was completely different from my father's diary. The importance of keeping a diary was brought home to me starkly when I moved to Delhi with Chamu.

Delhi University had advertised for a Lecturership in Geography and I applied for the position. For some reason, candidates were interviewed for the Lecturership before Readers were appointed. After I was selected, I realized I had to start the Geography Department as there was hardly any staff other than myself. I was soon swamped in all the groundwork needed to set up a department, from ordering books for the library and maps for the cartography section to publicizing the programme among the affiliated colleges. This was a lot of work and it was time-bound, as the university was planning to start the MA programme the very next year. I was kept very busy. The following year, the university recruited three more staff members for the department, one of whom was a Reader and later became the department head.

The department attracted many students in the first year and that was very encouraging. One of the feeder colleges was the women's college Miranda House, and another was one of the men's colleges, both on the campus. I was excited and looked forward to teaching.

I, along with two other staff members, drew up the programme of study together with course syllabi. I was fully absorbed in this work and in arranging the cartography section when the other members joined. As was my habit, I entered all the details of the growth of the department from day one in my diary.

Sadly, things soured within a year. Among the faculty, there seemed to be a rift for reasons I could not fathom. Over time, I could sense a distancing between other staff members and myself. I was not invited to faculty meetings, and I felt excluded. There was an undercurrent of tension that was palpable. I continued, hard as it was, with my classes and advising students.

Things went from bad to worse. As I remember, one chilly winter morning, the doorbell rang, and I went to see who it was. Chamu had already left for his department. Two university officials were standing on the front porch and they told me they were from the vice chancellor's office. They handed me an envelope, took my signature and left. What could it be—the question raced through my mind. I had already received my letter of appointment. On opening the envelope, it appeared to be a legal document, a 'show-cause notice' addressed to me and the charge appeared to be 'dereliction of duty'. This was a bolt from the blue and I couldn't for the life of me fathom what it all meant. Fortunately, Chamu came home a couple of hours later and I handed over the letter to him. He calmed me down and said, 'We'll sort this out, don't worry.'

Chamu had not eaten that morning before rushing off to the department, so I gave him his breakfast. He said, 'Come, sit here,' and read the letter out loud again and said, 'Charges have been brought against you by the university authorities for not doing the job you have been selected for. But you have been going every day to the university. What do you do when you go there?' So, in my confused state of mind, I tried to explain to him that over the past year, I had been setting up the library and the cartography unit, going to different stores to buy the surveying instruments and, in addition, had been busy drawing up the syllabus for my courses. I had also visited campus colleges to publicize the new programme. All this even took up a lot of my time and energy.

A couple of days later I would have to face the one-man commission appointed to investigate the matter. I felt angry and humiliated. I connected the behaviour of my colleagues in the department to the accusation brought against me. But I was still flabbergasted as to why and how such a thing could happen.

I appeared before the Dean of the Faculty of Law at the university who indeed was the one-man commission. As I walked into his chambers, an elderly balding man stood up from a hard, wooden chair. He was lean and wiry and had a stern face with deep-set eyes. He gestured to a chair and asked me to sit down. 'Have you read the notice?' he asked. 'Yes,' I responded. His next question was: 'Now what do you have to say about it?' He also explained to me what the show-cause notice letter meant. I said I was stunned to receive the notice and could not think why it had been sent to me. The charge that I had not been teaching classes regularly seemed a complete fabrication.

He said, 'Don't use the word "fabrication". That is what *you* think it is. Now you tell me your side of the story.' At this point, I took out my little blue pocket diary. I handed it to him and said, 'This speaks for itself right from the day I went for my selection interview. I will leave it with you.' Seeing I was overwrought, he calmed me down, 'Let me go through this and we will meet later.' He then walked with me to the gate of the building.

I walked back home in a daze, wondering why on earth this charge had been brought against me when I had done my all for the Geography Department and the students.

A couple of days later, I met the Dean while walking on campus and he recognized me and said, 'Don't worry, it's all settled.' I have no idea what he meant by that. But I do remember that my first-year master's student came home a few days later and said, 'I'm sorry, Mrs Srinivas,' and handed me a red diary. This turned out to be her own personal diary. 'I heard about the charges brought by the university against you, and I thought this might be helpful. This has all the details of your classes.' She had kept detailed notes on the classes she had attended, including the lesson plan, readings, discussion and so on. From her diary, it was clear that I had not missed a single class. She told a colleague who happened to be visiting us at home that my classes were very lively and engaging.

Talk among students was that there were two clear factions in the department, the North and the South, and since the North Indians dominated numerically they thought they could do everything in their power to oust the South Indians. As it happened, a few months later, a full professor was appointed head of the department and the atmosphere changed for the better.

I never heard back from the vice chancellor's office and Chamu thought I shouldn't expect to, given the way university bureaucracy works.

R.K. Narayan wrote *The Dateless Diary*, the year we all spent in Berkeley. It is a delightful and fascinating read. Well, mine was a diary of dates for which I am thankful.

The Japanese Inn Outside Tokyo

Chamu had been invited several times to the Department of Anthropology at the University of California, Berkeley. He refused many of these invitations, as he felt he was needed at Delhi University where he had built the Sociology Department. He had worked long and hard to place the Sociology Department on a firm footing. In the early 1960s, he finally felt he could leave to spend a few months in Berkeley. I was also looking forward to visit my friends in the San Francisco Bay Area.

We decided that the long journey across the Pacific would be more manageable with a couple of stops, especially as we had a young child travelling with us. Lakshmi was in kindergarten and I had to work hard to persuade the Mother Superior to give her leave, so that she could accompany us.

Chamu had a long-standing invitation from Professor Chie Nakane, the head of the Anthropology Department at Tokyo University, so we decided that a stop in Japan would be a good way to break up our journey. Then, from there, we would stop at the East-West Center in Honolulu, before flying to our final destination, San Francisco.

Professor Nakane had arranged for us to stay at a Japanese inn outside of Tokyo. We arrived at the inn at dusk after a long flight and a fairly long drive from the Tokyo airport. It was past dinner time and the twinkling of lights as we drove into the grounds of the inn made it look like a fairyland.

The inn was set on a hillside with well-laid-out gardens, though we couldn't see them that night. The building was a single-storey bamboo structure. I had never seen anything like it before. At night, it was dimly lit and very welcoming with strains of soft instrumental music coming from within.

I didn't know what to expect and as we—Chamu, I and Lakshmi—entered, the staff at the inn, men and women dressed in beautiful traditional garments, bowed to greet us.

I found the inn very comfortable. It was a wooden structure with a low roof. The lighting was concealed except for a few paper lanterns that were aesthetically placed. The seating was floor-level, with tatami reed mats placed all around the room. There were no chairs or sofas. I remember being struck by its elegant design. We were offered some refreshment, juice and a snack before we were taken to our rooms.

Our room overlooked a small water body, which was beautifully lit. We were tired after a long flight and ready for bed. The next morning, even before I was wide awake, I smelt incense—what a wonderful way to be woken up! I heard Chamu saying, 'Come, see, it is simply beautiful outside!' and it surely was.

The front of the inn did not give an idea of the landscape around it. But the side entrance opened out onto a garden with a little bamboo bridge over a rivulet. It was all a masterpiece of landscaping.

Lakshmi, Chamu and I went for a stroll in the grounds before breakfast. It was a brisk day, sunny but not warm. There was a traditional garden with lots of ferns and bamboo and temperate trees including fragrant magnolia. And unlike gardens in Delhi, there weren't many flowers at all. The garden was not very large but was peaceful to walk around in. It was dotted with little statues of monks, children and so on. I found it magical.

An artificial stream with goldfish and koi separated the front of the inn from the grove of conifers beyond. We took a relaxing walk by the stream. Lakshmi had fun running back and forth over the wooden bridge. There were low tables and benches placed strategically all along for people to stop and rest. We lost ourselves wandering in the gardens, and suddenly realized that we had to get ready. Professor Chie Nakane would be there shortly to fetch us.

Two days were really not enough to enjoy this beautiful idyllic sanctuary. One could not imagine the hustle and bustle of the city just an hour away.

Breakfast was another one-of-a-kind experience. We were ushered into a long, rectangular sun-filled room, where the guests were already seated on mats on the floor. We joined them at the low tables. I did not find the smell coming from this room appetizing and Chamu was a little embarrassed to see the expression on my face. We took our places at one of the low tables that was laid out with exquisite crockery, breakfast plates, teacups and chopsticks.

There was a uniform breakfast for everyone. We were served a bowl of steaming hot glutinous rice with a raw egg broken into it, seaweed and two small pieces of fish on the side. Being vegetarian, I couldn't eat any of it. I found the smell and the sight of the food nauseating. Chamu stopped me from walking out. I thought I could have some tea. There was fragrant hot jasmine tea but without milk, which I was not used to. I asked for milk and was told they didn't have any. I don't know what Chamu ate or how he managed. Lakshmi ate a little bit of the rice. I starved.

Mid-morning, I asked for some fruit and one of the women brought us some apples, which we devoured. One of the staff came to our room and told us the baths were at the end of the hallway. I took Lakshmi along with me and when I opened the door to the bath it was no bathroom that I recognized. There was a huge rectangular swimming pool-sized tank of hot water. I could see the steam rising above it. A number of completely nude men and women were jumping in and out of what they called the bath. I was unprepared and even slightly shocked by what I saw. That was my first experience with communal bathing. I had never even entered a swimming pool before and everyone was nude!

I walked out with Lakshmi and asked if there was a place where I could have a bath by myself. The inn staff could not comprehend my request for a separate bathing room. It took me very long to make myself understood but, at last, the staff was able to accommodate me. I was taken to another large room where again there was another tank of very hot water. There was no one else there. I felt exposed in that large space, and Lakshmi and I had our baths in fear that anytime someone would enter. Both breakfast and bath were a disaster, I felt.

The second day I went for a bath much earlier in the morning and found I could bathe in privacy. I lived on apples the two days we were at the inn and was hungry all the time. Professor Nakane did try and help and brought me some crackers.

We did a little sight-seeing in Tokyo, travelling everywhere by public transport. What a different experience from back home in India! Here, boarding the bus was very orderly; the staff on the buses, the drivers and conductors who ushered us to our seats were all uniformed women. Every time the bus doors opened and people got down, the staff would thank the riders with '*Arigato gozaimasu* (Thank you very much).' We also travelled by the bullet train from Tokyo to its environs. This was another wonderful experience. Needless to say, the trains travelled at lightning speed. They were spotlessly clean and everyone was very orderly. At every stop, travellers could buy hot, steaming tea in disposable clay tea pots—one of which we brought back to India as a souvenir. Children snacked on crunchy dried cuttlefish and hard-boiled eggs, which were also sold on the station platforms.

What impressed me was the meticulous care with which the Japanese kept their surroundings clean. Each person was responsible for his or her own trash. The lady sitting next to me with a young child gathered all the eggshells and carefully put them in a bag which she took away with her. From another bag, she took out a wet cloth with which she cleaned her young child's fingers and face. I noticed another child, sitting nearby, had little boots on, which were covered with plastic overshoes. I assumed they were protection against the rain. But I was told that the child had one pair of shoes that should be protected. Children were taught to conserve resources from a very young age.

Looking back, I'm grateful to Professor Chie Nakane for the experiences both inside and outside the Japanese inn.

Encounters in America

Growing up in colonial India, I went to schools managed by the British. My teachers were from either England or Scotland, the exams that we studied for were the Junior and Senior Cambridge examinations, and the books that we read were written by English authors. As a child, my only encounter with American culture was through the very few Hollywood movies I saw and my elder sister's collection of chocolate wrappers featuring Hollywood stars such as Norma Shearer, Greta Garbo, Clark Gable, Errol Flynn and others—glamorous and oh-so distant.

After I married Chamu and we travelled to America, I didn't know what to expect. We left Southampton in mid-November 1956 on *RMS Queen Elizabeth*, the luxury liner. On the ship I was very seasick. I didn't get to know many of the passengers because I stayed in my cabin. I missed out on many of the film screenings, musical performances and dancing. But some days, Chamu would encourage me to move around and lead me onto the deck. I was the only woman in a sari on that ship. And the other passengers kept a friendly distance from me till they realized I could speak English. One of the women, more outgoing than the others, invited me to dance and I ventured out one evening, much to Chamu's amusement. I did enjoy the evening, although it was not easy dancing in a sari.

We arrived in New York on 21 November and it turned out to be Thanksgiving Eve. We were met by a representative from the Rockefeller Foundation who announced to us that a dockers' strike was in progress and so we would have to unload all of Chamu's 20-odd trunks of his books and papers ourselves. After some heavy lifting, we managed to get a cab to the Abbey Hotel that stood between the Avenue of the Americas and 7th Avenue.

It happened to be our wedding anniversary and, to celebrate, Chamu took me to see *The Pajama Game* on Broadway, the first-ever Western musical I had seen. It was great fun, and a whole new world opened up before me. I was enthralled by the sights of New York. I had never experienced a city on this scale. It seemed like many large cities put together. Everything seemed big in America—big buildings, wide roads and vast distances.

At our hotel, someone recommended an Indian restaurant. I think it was the Woodlands, and so Chamu and I had a delicious South Indian vegetarian meal, with a few traditional dishes on the menu. This was a delightful surprise, as I hadn't expected to enjoy a sumptuous South Indian meal in New York.

We left New York to go all the way across the country to Berkeley, California, where Chamu was on a Rockefeller Fellowship. On our way west, we stopped for a couple of days in Chicago where Chamu was to attend a conference. Milton Singer—an anthropologist at the University of Chicago and a good friend of Chamu's, who I had met in Madras in 1955 before Chamu and I were married—met us at the airport and drove us to the university faculty club. Chamu stepped forward with me in tow to register for a room for two nights at the faculty club. The middle-aged woman at the desk asked Chamu mechanically, 'I hope you won't have blacks visiting you?' to which Chamu responded, 'I am black myself.' Milton was deeply embarrassed and upset and ushered us out saying,

'Chamu, come let's go.' He then took us to the Windemere Hotel, not far away. As we checked in, he advised us not to explore the neighbourhood on our own as it was unsafe. 'I will come and fetch you.' I was surprised to learn that in America, just a couple of blocks this way or that, the city could be a very different place.

In Chicago, I met Chamu's academic friends—anthropologists Sol Tax, Robert Redfield, Fred Eggan and others. Who should we bump into in Chicago but Chamu's childhood friend from Mysore, the novelist R.K. Narayan, who was also passing through on his way to San Diego. Coincidentally, he, too, was a Rockefeller Fellow that year. He joined us on the train trip out west, as he was bound for San Diego, but he was so homesick and felt so comfortable with Chamu and I that he decided to disembark in Berkeley instead of proceeding on to Southern California. Narayan's book *My Dateless Diary*, published in 1960, is based on a journal he kept during the time he spent in Berkeley.

Travelling by train across the country was such an adventure. The Vistadome offered panoramic views of the countryside we passed through, and the geography I had studied came alive. In Berkeley, we settled into a cozy little house on Peralta Avenue, which had an apricot tree and a lemon tree in the backyard. Chamu's colleagues showed us around Berkeley, where the stores were, where we could get groceries, the post office and so on. Chamu went to see an eye doctor, and his optometrist Ed Mogerman and his wife Frieda became our good friends and introduced us to their circle. So, our circle of Jewish friends in the Berkeley–Oakland area grew.

Rukka with Frieda Mogerman in Berkeley

My women friends were intrigued by Chamu and I, our 'Indian culture', the food I cooked and the fact that I was a vegetarian. They thought my 'outfit', the sari, was 'exotic' and elegant and wanted to know more about how I wore it. My friend Miriam, an accomplished seamstress and weaver, lived in Oakland with her doctor husband. She was very interested to see all my saris, the different textures and patterns. She asked if they were pre-sewn and whether she could sew them at home. She enthusiastically organized an afternoon with three of our women friends to have a viewing of my saris and have me 'wrap' them in saris. I had kept several saris out for the ladies to choose, and they excitedly picked out their favourite colours and fabrics, marvelling at the gold lace and intricate weaves. They were intrigued by the six to nine yards of material and the way it was folded and wrapped around. Miriam grilled me with questions: 'Were the saris part of my "trousseau"?', 'Which ones had I worn at my wedding?', 'How expensive were they?' We took photographs and they stayed on for an Indian vegetarian dinner I had prepared.

I don't think I realized how different I must have looked to Americans who might not have encountered an Indian woman in traditional Indian clothes. Even in the mid-1960s, when Chamu and I lived in Palo Alto, Indian women in saris were an uncommon sight. Sometimes people would stop me on the street and compliment me. At other times, my sari was seen as a problem. The driving school instructor in Stanford decided that I couldn't learn to drive in a sari and with chappals on my feet. He was concerned that I would cause an accident and told me I would never pass the driving test if I showed up in a sari and chappals. He asked me several probing questions: 'Had I driven in India? Do many women drive in these clothes in India? Were there many cars on the streets in India?' Maybe I was the first Indian woman in Indian clothes that he had come across. After a few unsatisfactory lessons at the driving school, Paul Hockings, then a postdoctoral fellow in anthropology at Berkeley, who had visited South India for his fieldwork, took over and taught me how to navigate the boulevards and freeways of California. I was so grateful to have someone who accepted my culture and helped me get the confidence to drive. Decades later, I find that my sari excites both admiration and curiosity. Post 9/11, when Lakshmi and I were walking around the neighbourhood where we live near Boston, a neighbour who was in her garden called out to us in a friendly way to say 'Hello'. We stopped to exchange greetings, and she said gesturing to my sari, 'That's beautiful', and then asked conversationally, 'Are you from Pakistan?'

Growing up in an environment where we spoke and heard different languages and went to English-medium convent schools, I still feel a bit taken aback when people assume I can't speak or understand English because I wear a sari. These days when I go for my medical check-up, the nurse often assumes I will not understand her and addresses my daughters instead. On a couple of occasions, I have been asked whether I need an interpreter. At the Cambridge Center for Adult Education, where I taught Indian vegetarian cooking, I demonstrated recipes from various regions in India and took along a map to show where the food came from. The students were surprised that I spoke fluent English and asked me where I had learnt such good English. I've been asked if I had lived in England, or whether I had taken English lessons before coming to America.

Rukka and Lakshmi

I hadn't realized what a challenge a purely vegetarian diet would be until I travelled to England and America. In America, by the mid-1960s, there was a beginning of acceptance of vegetarian food habits with the counterculture movement, but little understanding of vegetarianism. I still found it difficult to get a vegetarian meal when we went out. Our friends would take the trouble to make a multi-course dinner for Chamu and me and, interested in food as I was, I would go into the kitchen to watch. On one occasion, I found my host had thoughtfully made lentil soup for us. But in the kitchen, while she ladled the soup, I found her picking out bits of what I later learnt was sausage from Chamu's and my bowls. She thought this was a perfectly acceptable dish for a vegetarian. I was faced with the dilemma of what to do with the soup. She had also baked fresh bread, but had topped it with an egg wash. I don't eat eggs and find the smell of eggs off-putting. So now I had soup and bread, neither of which I could eat. After a while my host saw my discomfort and said, 'I'm sorry, Rukka,' and took away the bowl.

There were other friends who understood what it meant to be a vegetarian and they were more enterprising in putting together a vegetarian meal. I remember the first Passover* dinner Chamu and I were invited to at Miriam and Frank's home. Miriam was an enthusiastic cook. She would often come over to spend afternoons with me, watch me cook a vegetarian meal and grill me with questions. She surprised us at the Passover dinner with a new appetizer she had concocted and named 'Mysore Mandu', a kind of vegetarian samosa, in honour of Chamu, who came from Mysore. As I remember, the Mysore Mandu was crunchy and delicious, with herbs, chickpeas, water chestnut and spices, and Miriam had even made a dipping sauce for it.

That reminds me of the way some people addressed Chamu, whose name was Mysore Narasimhachar Srinivas. Not used to the convention of South Indian names starting with a place, they would assume 'Mysore' was his first or 'Christian' name and call him 'Mysore'. This amused Chamu, who later told the story with a quiet smile but was too good-natured to correct his hosts.

I found Americans very direct and informal compared to the British. They would very quickly be on first-name terms. When we moved into our house on Perry Lane in Menlo Park,

*Passover is a major Jewish holiday that commemorates the emancipation of Israelites from slavery in ancient Egypt.

our neighbour across the street, Virginia, came over the next day with a cake she had baked to welcome us. How charming, I thought, and invited her in. Such pleasantries are exchanged in some neighbourhoods even today. When Lakshmi moved into a house recently, her next-door neighbour brought a plate of cookies and left it on the porch. Her neighbour from the opposite house invited her for a meal till she had her kitchen up and running.

Rukka and Chamu, Berkeley 1956

Our neighbours on Peralta Avenue, May and Bob Muir, were from Scotland. The day after we moved into our home, Bob came over and introduced himself. He said he was something of a handyman: 'If there's anything around the house you need help with, I'd be happy to help.' How generous and friendly, we thought. When Bob's wife May heard we were driving down with friends to Los Angeles, she said, 'You must stop at Solvang! The food is fabulous. Try the smorgasbord.' We did stop at Solvang and found a picturesque Danish village where we could sample some Danish delicacies. That was the first time I had seen a smorgasbord meal. It was a big disappointment as I couldn't eat a thing. There was a lot of meat. Even the *aebleskiver* (apple fritters), which looked oh-so appetizing, smelt strongly of eggs. I was famished and, later that evening, it was a relief to go to Millie's Pizzeria.

Pizza was a reliable standby for vegetarians. In those days, distinctions between vegetarians and vegans were not made as they are now. This brings to mind our good friend and the well-known writer R.K. Narayan's first experience of eating out in Berkeley in 1956. He, too, was a staunch vegetarian and this was his first trip outside India. Narayan, or Kunjappa as we knew him, lived close to the International House on the Berkeley campus and befriended some students who took him out for a meal at a local pizzeria. The pizza was served steaming hot, like a thick pancake, and Kunjappa liked the look of the little red discs of tomato on top. But the tomatoes tasted different. One of the young students explained what 'pepperoni' was and, when he realized Kunjappa was a vegetarian, he removed the pepperoni discs from half the pizza and offered it to him. Kunjappa called me the next day and told me of his disastrous evening out, then asked for simple rice mixed with yoghurt ('curds rice')—he referred to it as 'cleansing food'. He was a frequent visitor to our home and would stop by on his evening walk and stay for dinner. He liked my South Indian vegetarian cooking and would often opt for simple rasam and rice or curds rice and a vegetable curry or sambar.

I was amazed at the large grocery stores in America, but I remember explaining to Kunjappa the difficulty of getting vegetables suitable for Indian meals there. The local grocery store had vegetables I was unfamiliar with. Celery, lettuce, broccoli, asparagus and artichoke would not lend themselves to Indian cooking. Ruth Mandlebaum, whose husband David had done fieldwork in the Nilgiri Hills in South India, took me to the Co-op in Berkeley, where I was thrilled to find rice flour, garbanzo (chickpea) flour, basmati rice, various types of legumes and lentils, and even fresh coconut!

I discovered that Draeger's, a speciality food store in Menlo Park, also carried more food options for vegetarians. One of my Jewish friends suggested I go to Chinatown in San Francisco. So Chamu and I took the F train to San Francisco and found our way to Chinatown. The first time it was quite an ordeal—we walked for miles and thought we were lost. But we finally found grocery stores. In those stores, there was a display of the vegetables I was familiar with, like white pumpkin, yellow pumpkin, bitter gourd, Colocasia leaves, small purple brinjals as well as green chillies and fresh coriander—so essential to Indian cooking. Once to my delight and surprise, I even found banana flowers and raw plantains. But I had to learn the American–English terms for these vegetables. What I knew as lady's finger in India was okra, fresh coriander was cilantro, white pumpkin was winter melon and bitter gourd was bitter melon. An elderly Chinese gentleman sitting on a large stool waved to me and said, 'I speak Indian.' Chamu responded by raising his hands in a namaste, which brought a wide smile to the gentleman's face.

Rukka and Chamu at Half Moon Bay

I went crazy in the store, wanting to buy all these vegetables which I hadn't seen for months. But Chamu gently dissuaded me, reminding me that we had to carry everything we bought and walk back. When I mentioned spices, he said, 'Not this time. We can explore the spice stores next time.' We trudged back to the train carrying our heavy bags, and when we reached Berkeley, we walked home. But I was thrilled! The day had been worthwhile. When I found I was getting low on the spices I needed, I thought we could explore San Francisco's Market Street. The Armenian and Greek stores carried slabs of tamarind pulp and also coriander and cumin seeds, along with saffron, bay leaves, cardamom and cloves. Chamu was fond of the baklava and Turkish halwa, which he said resembled the sweets from the well-known sweet shop Indra Bhavan in Mysore. We found a couple of Middle Eastern stores, which did carry some of the spices I needed, like cumin, dried red chillies, turmeric, sesame seeds, cinnamon sticks and bay leaves. I also found 'fava beans', which is similar to what we called 'double beans' in India, a favourite of ours. I was pleased and relieved that I could find many of the spices I needed for the vegetarian dishes I make, though it required a trek.

America offered other surprises. When we lived in Menlo Park, I learnt that our new neighbours had moved their house, literally, and brought it with them. The house had been transported from their previous address, on what seemed like a plank on a truck and placed on the site. It was a marvel! I had never heard of anything like this!

Certain American social customs were also alien to me. Though I was used to my classmates in the senior classes in Christ Church School in Jabalpur going out for dances with boys on the weekends, I never knew the term 'dating' till I came to the United States. The importance of dating was brought home to me starkly when we lived in Palo Alto.

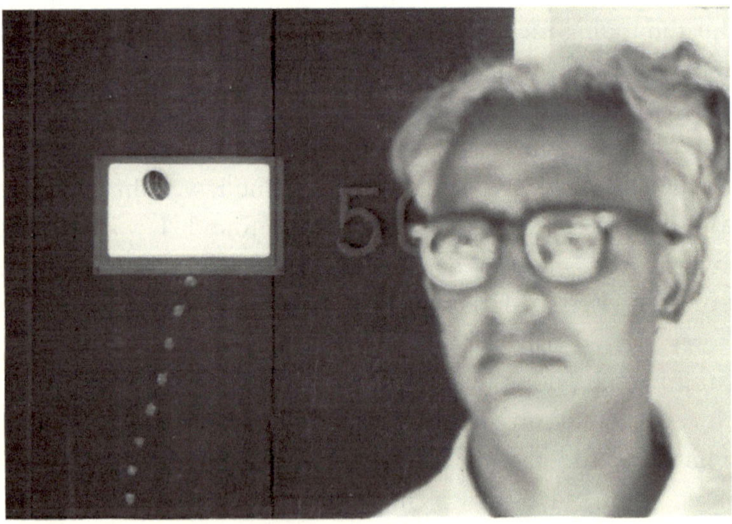

Chamu outside his study at Stanford

I enrolled for an evening course in childhood education at Stanford. One entire evening we spent discussing dating among adolescents. Everyone there was curious about me—the only Indian woman in the class. They quizzed me about dating, marriage, caste and so on, and wanted to know if I had had an arranged marriage. They were surprised to learn that Chamu and I had met through friends in a very non-traditional way. Their curiosity extended to questions about Chamu's and my caste and community, and whether I allow my children to date. It was a lively discussion.

Most of my Jewish friends in Berkeley and Palo Alto had teenage children. I found that the mothers were preoccupied with their children's social lives. And there was a lot of anxiety over who they were going out with, and in some cases, there was anxiety regarding their children not dating at all. One of my very close academic friends, whose son was at university on the East Coast, was panicking that he might date girls who were not Jewish. She would relay her worries to me when we met for lunch. From across the country, she would try to set him up with 'good, Jewish girls' and he was too good-natured to tell her off. To me, this was, in some ways, like the matchmaking arrangements in India. In those days in America, inter-racial marriages were less common and I remember one of our Jewish friends being in shock when she discovered her daughter was living with a young African-American man—a professional in finance whom she later married. Of course, dating was not the custom among most South Asian families living in America, and even in the late 1990s, I've known of families moving to India suddenly to prevent their children from getting into the dating scene.

Out of Fire, Rebirth*

I find my memory growing sharper with the passage of time and now decades later, certain images and conversations keep returning.

I came home one Friday evening in 1969 from the Geography Department at the Delhi School of Economics, where I was a lecturer. It had been a particularly long and tiring week and I was looking forward to a quiet weekend. As was my habit, I made myself a cup of tea and desultorily opened the day's mail. I remember being excited, reading a letter from the director of the Center for Advanced Study in the Behavioral Sciences (CASBS) in Palo Alto, inviting Chamu to join the group of Fellows at the Center for the year 1970–71. My earlier experience of Chamu's Fellowship year at the CASBS in 1964–65 was memorable—meeting old friends and making new ones, exploring, and introducing my young daughters, Lakshmi and Tulasi, to the beautiful sights of California.

Chamu had received many such invitations to spend a year or two away at various research institutes, but he accepted only a few of them due to the pressure of work involved in building the Sociology Department at Delhi University and making it a Center for Advanced Study. This time, he was pleased with the invitation, as it would give him the much-needed time away from his teaching responsibilities

---

*From *Remembering Chamu: A Study in Resilience*, prepared for the MN Srinivas Centenary Panel at the American Anthropological Association Minnesota, November, 2016.

and the stress of administrative chores, and allow him to work on his manuscript from his fieldnotes on Kodagehalli in Mysore.

The next few weeks were spent sorting out, filing and packing all of the village study research papers and edited fieldnotes that had 'languished for decades in steel trunks and had to be worked on', as Chamu would often tell me. This had been on his mind for a while. All his research data, mostly handwritten sheets, scores of tablets with hand-drawn maps, many photographs, letters to him from his friends and small address books wrapped in plastic sheets were packed in four plywood 'tea chests' that had an inner silver-foil lining. They were addressed to the Center in Palo Alto. I delivered the precious tea chests and trunks to the American Express office in Connaught Place in New Delhi. The booking office clerk asked me, 'How much do you want to insure this consignment for?' I heard myself say, 'This is uninsurable; it is the work of a lifetime and cannot be evaluated moneywise.' The clerk smiled in response.

I came home and told Chamu that the trunks and chests would be sent soon and would take three months to arrive.

In late August, Chamu, Lakshmi, Tulasi and I flew to San Francisco, each of us looking forward to a different year. We settled comfortably in our new home in Palo Alto. Lakshmi and Tulasi joined the neighbourhood school and enjoyed a new way of learning. I enrolled to audit a couple of courses on secondary school education at Stanford. Preston Cutler, the assistant director of the Center, suggested places to buy a second-hand car and we bought a blue Chevy convertible. Chamu was working hard on earlier commitments and dissertation manuscripts of students to 'clear my table before I turn to my Kodagehalli notes', as he would say. He waited eagerly for the arrival of the tea chests.

In late fall, American Express sent us the notification that the goods had arrived and were in the warehouse in San Francisco. I drove with a friend to pick up the trunks and arrangements were made to transfer the trunks and chests to the Center. We both heaved a sigh of relief. Chamu could now plan his writing schedule.

He had moved into Study Number 19 at the Center and was looking forward to starting serious writing. His study was not large enough to take all the four trunks and two chests, so while some were stacked in his study, a couple had been placed in the alcove next to a phone booth that was adjacent to his study.

Soon after the trunks arrived, Chamu received the news that his mother's health was failing and that she had been hospitalized. He contemplated returning to Mysore, which would mean being away for at least a few weeks. He would be on the phone with his brother and sister, late at night and in the early hours of the morning.

Needless to say, Chamu was very distracted and distraught. Here he was with the gift of precious time to write his long-delayed book, but the importance and significance of that paled in comparison to the thought and fear that he might not see his mother, his dear Amma, or hear her voice again. He decided to leave for Mysore to spend a week with his mother. But when she was informed of his decision, she would not hear of it. She told Chamu's elder brother, Pachu, 'Chamu has gone to America to write an important book and I do not want him to be disturbed.' The following morning, we got the sad news that Amma's health was deteriorating rapidly and her end was only a matter of hours. She was peacefully listening to the chanting praise of Lord Narayana.

The next day, in the wee hours of the morning, we both reached out for the telephone on hearing the ominous ringtone, dreading the news from Mysore. 'Chamu, this is Preston Cutler. There has been some vandalism at the Center. Can you come up?'

I left Lakshmi and Tulasi, still sleeping, and drove Chamu to the Center. We drove in utter silence. All cars were stopped at the entrance at the bottom of the hill by police vans, firefighters and a couple of ambulances. Chamu had to explain in some detail that he had been called by the director and asked to come immediately. I left Chamu with a group of Fellows walking up the hill in the dark and rushed home to my daughters.

Around midday, Professor Sol Tax brought Chamu home. Sol, a senior professor of Anthropology at the University of Chicago, was also a Fellow at the Center that year. A friend of many years, he was visibly upset at the senseless damage caused by the ROTC (Reserve Officers Training Course) protesters who had found no other avenue but arson and violence to express their condemnation for the Vietnam War. They had randomly planted Molotov cocktails in several places at the Center, with one in the phone booth next to Chamu's study. The elegant redwood timber study went up in flames, devouring all his notes and books. Chamu commented that the notes he had unpacked were 'sitting ducks' in the study. He seemed very calm and collected.

Sol stayed late into the evening. He played the role of an elder brother and counsellor to Chamu. It had been a tough week for Chamu and many of his colleagues were concerned for his physical and emotional well-being. A couple of my friends, who were wives of the Fellows, suggested I get psychiatric help for him. I knew Chamu wanted to be left alone. He was a person of immense inner strength, not to be defeated by such things.

He mentioned to me several days later that Sol had reminded him of the fear that anthropologists lived with—the fear of losing their field notes. 'This is a challenge for you, Chamu. Don't lose heart.'

The Center was in mourning. The fire affected all the Fellows. Many of them came over to our home. I remember the day vividly—burly American men in tears hugging Chamu. They were curious about Chamu's stoicism and asked him if it was his Hindu upbringing that made him so calm.

Two days after the fire, Chamu received the news that his mother had passed away. His brothers and sisters urged him not to come home. Chamu kept the grief of his loss to himself. Those days, Fellows were assigned a secretary to help with correspondence, typing of manuscripts and other such work. Chamu's secretary was a very pleasant woman in her 40s called Joan Wambrun. I called Joan and told her of Chamu's mother's passing, and then the news spread to all the Fellows. Some of them came over to offer their support and condolences and broke down and wept.

This was a very difficult time for Chamu and for all of us in the family. That same week, as I was driving with Lakshmi and Tulasi on Junipero Serra Boulevard to fetch Chamu, not far from the Center, I smelt smoke in the car. I jumped out with the children. The car caught fire right before my eyes. Helpful passersby took charge of the situation and called the emergency services. One of them very kindly drove us to the Center. It was evening, about 5.00 p.m. I told Chamu and Preston what had happened. Preston arranged for the car to be taken to the mechanic and was thinking of ways to get us another car. In the meantime, that evening, Jackie Mann, a good friend, visited us and very generously told us she had two cars and could loan us her car till we got a replacement.

Help for Chamu's work came from various sources. A grant from the Ford Foundation helped to bring over V.S. Parthasarathy. Partha had been Chamu's research assistant in

Kodagehalli decades earlier and was now technical assistant in the Department of Sociology at the Delhi School of Economics, where he was pursuing his PhD. Partha arrived at the Center within a few weeks. A couple of days after the fire, there was an offer of help from a total stranger, Karen Brown, whose special skills and experience were invaluable in salvaging partially burnt and charred sheets of paper. I joined many of the Fellows' wives to help with the salvaging. It was a very delicate process of separating the charred pages, placing each one between thin plastic sheets; clipping them on a wire in a hot shower to steam them and make them supple was the next step. Many of the sheets were charred at the edges and margins and there was hope of saving them, but there were an equal number of sheets that crumbled to black ashen dust when they were lifted. This was a one-of-a-kind experience for all of us, a very sad one indeed.

Chamu had lost his dear mother and his precious fieldwork material within a span of 48 hours. Knowing Chamu never wore his grief on his sleeve, I simply hung around, a silent companion. He went back to Study Number 19 soon after the restoration and started writing in earnest. His secretary, Joan, became so involved with the fieldwork data that she and Chamu worked even over weekends and holidays. On a few occasions, when Joan drove Chamu home, she would stay on to have dinner with us. I saw how, in fact, she was now 'living' in Kodagehalli. She spoke of Kulle Gowda, Nadu Gowda, Nachcha and other villagers with affection and said she felt she had visited the village. When we bade goodbye to her at the end of our stay in Palo Alto, she hugged Chamu and thanked him for her Mysore village experience of Kodagehalli through Chamu's *Remembered Village* Rampura. I would say Joan was the first reader of the book even before it was published.

The week before we left the Center in mid-1971, the Fellows organized a farewell party for Chamu. There were several touching speeches by colleagues, especially his volleyball team members, and the office staff, including the janitor and the gardener, each one with a story highlighting Chamu's empathy for the other and his self-deprecating humour—which only reinforced what I knew and loved about him.

What hangs in Chamu's library and study in our home in Bangalore is a memento, a framed drawing of a magnificent Phoenix rising from the fire, signed by all the Fellows and the staff at the Center. Below the framed drawing is an inscription: *Ex Igni Renascimur* (Out of fire, Rebirth)—a constant reminder to me of the Chamu I knew.

Ex Igni Renascimur

The Orchard Garden, Palo Alto, 1970

Our home in Palo Alto in 1970-71, when Chamu spent a year at the Center for Advanced Study in the Behavioral Sciences in Stanford, was 1046 Amaranta Avenue. The house belonged to Dr Dreisbach, professor in Environmental Studies at Stanford University, and he was away that year. True to his interests, there were lots of plants in his garden, which was unlike other gardens in the neighbourhood. The front yard was a wilderness of overgrown holly bushes and other shrubs that attracted many birds. Every summer, the blue jays would get drunk on the overripe and fermented berries and Lakshmi would anxiously look out for neighbourhood cats that preyed on them.

The backyard was beautifully designed with a spacious patio, surrounded by an orchard: cherry, plum, fig, persimmon and several almond trees could be found there. There were apricot and black walnut trees on the street and the ripened fruit would fall on the sidewalk and just lie there. The first time I saw an artichoke plant was in the Palo Alto house. I had eaten artichoke earlier, but had never seen it grow.

I was puzzled as to how to use all the fruit that ripened. I hated to see it go to waste. My neighbours helped me out. Dee Dee Hornum lived next door and said she would help. Joan Warmbrun suggested we invite our friends over to enjoy the garden. So, in summer, we would invite our friends for the day and they would enjoy lounging in the sun, an al fresco lunch and picking the fruit to take home. Sol Tax, who was also a Fellow that year, came over one afternoon and was delighted to see the fig tree laden with fruit. He told us he could eat only a few, as they were high in cholesterol. John Gumperz, a well-known linguist, came with his young son, who climbed every tree and harvested all the fruit, which our friends shared among themselves.

From these friends, I learnt how to make jams and jellies from ripe fruit. In return for the fruit, I received several gifts of tarts and pies. Lois Paul brought me a rich, dark persimmon cake that she said would last for months in the fridge, and it did.

Partha, who had been Chamu's field assistant during his research in a Mysore village and had come to Palo Alto to help Chamu with retrieval of his fieldnotes, visited our house in Palo Alto almost every evening and over the weekends. He, too, was taken with the orchard. When the almond trees bore fruit, he offered to harvest the ripe almonds and to shell them. We spent two weekends shelling the almonds until our fingers were sore. Two big sacks were filled and stored in the garage. Partha fondly hoped that all these almonds would be shipped to Mysore and got a rude shock when Chamu laughed off his idea and said we could distribute what we had shelled to our friends and the Fellows at the Center.

The Baba in the Garden

One hot summer afternoon, in the New England suburb where I now live, Lakshmi came home and excitedly showed me a bunch of greens she had in a bag. 'Do you recognize this?' I said, 'Of course, it's ponnaganni keerai. Where did you find it!' She told me it was growing like a weed on a nearby farm where she had volunteered to help for a couple of weeks in the summer. The farmworkers were throwing all the ponnaganni, which was growing like a weed in onion beds, onto the compost heap. The last time I had cooked this type of greens was when we were in Bangalore. I had made it with lentils and tomatoes, and it was a favourite dish to eat with chapattis. I grew both the green and pink varieties in my garden as a border for my flowerbeds and the plants would multiply rapidly during monsoon. It was only when I visited the farmers' markets in the United States that I heard it being called purslane.

The stems of the purslane that Lakshmi had brought were already wilting and I was in a hurry to plant them. I requested Popsi, my son-in-law, to dig just outside the deck, near the back porch, where the soil was friable. The porch was part of an extension added to the house and cut into the back garden and lawn. I spent quite some time on the sunny porch on summer afternoons.

Popsi came with a shovel and asked me where he should dig. I pointed out a strip on the side where a butterfly bush (Buddleia) used to be. I marked out a rectangular piece where there was plenty of sunlight and where the soil was good. Popsi started digging. I had gone back indoors when he suddenly called out. We all rushed out. I was concerned that he might be hurt. Popsi showed us a small white object covered with soil in the palm of his hand. He thought he had dug up the root of a healthy plant. But it was hard, like a stone. He didn't know what it was.

When we washed the dirt off, we discovered it was a figurine, four inches high, of a saint I recognized as Shirdi Sai Baba. When I turned it over, I found the sculptor's name etched at the back—S. Patnaik. I was simply stunned!

We washed off the mud and examined our precious find. The detailing was incredible: Baba's thoughtful face; his wise eyes; his fingers and toes; his clothing; the cloth covering his head and his posture, with one leg crossed over the other; and his hand resting lightly on his knee in a relaxed yet pensive pose, was beautifully chiselled. I don't know the material the figurine is made of, but it is an ivory colour.

We thought and thought but couldn't explain how the figurine had come into the garden. Could someone have dropped it there? But who? And when? The house was constructed by an Italian builder, Mr Camarano, in the 1950s or 1960s. He had also built other houses in the neighbourhood, we were told. There was a medium-sized statue of the Virgin Mary in the back garden when my daughter Tulasi and her husband bought the house. The seller was the very same Mr Camarano. There were no other owners of the property.

When we told our friends and relatives about discovering Baba's figurine in the garden, they were astonished and each gave their own interpretation of this mystery. Many told us we were blessed, as Baba had chosen to come to our house.

Given the way I was brought up, we were all the more surprised that Baba had chosen to make an appearance in our garden in Boston. I grew up in a household where neither parent was ritually inclined. Religion sat very lightly on them. Our rented home in Poona was a modest two-bedroom bungalow and our landlord lived above us. My mother's kitchen had one cupboard for her spices, pickles and powders, and another for her pots and pans. A third smaller cabinet with a projecting table, carefully placed in one corner, held the figures of the deities that my mother worshipped. There was no separate 'pooja room'. My mother did not have time for elaborate poojas though she did light the oil lamp every morning and evening to the strains of soft, mellow bhajans that she kept humming.

The news of 'Baba coming home' travelled far and wide to our friends and family in India, some of whom are devotees of Shirdi Baba, and told us we were fortunate to be the recipients of his love, mercy and protection. My relatives in the United States made a trip to our home to see Baba and get his blessings.

He now occupies a place in the company of other deities in our modest pooja room. One never knows what treasures a garden holds.

BANGALORE

The Move

We returned to Delhi in the autumn of 1971 after an eventful and somewhat challenging 18 months in California. What else happened in those 18 months is another series of stories.

Back home, Chamu's department and staff were waiting for his return to inaugurate the Advanced Centre in Sociology, for which Chamu had worked tirelessly with the University Grants Commission and the Ministry of Education. At the same time, Chamu, the artful dodger, was dodging an invitation to become the next education minister.

The chief guest at the inaugural event was Dr V.K.R.V. Rao, the former vice chancellor of Delhi University, who was a member of the Planning Commission at the time. Dr Swaroop Singh, the then vice chancellor, was happy that during his tenure the Sociology Department had gained the status of an advanced centre. I was also invited to the function that evening. Dr Rao came up to me and announced that he was coming home after the event as he wanted to talk to Chamu and me. Over a cup of hot South Indian rasam, he said that his efforts at starting an institute for social sciences in Bangalore had now become a reality, and that Shri Dharamveera, the then governor of Karnataka, was keen that it should begin functioning soon. He added, 'Chamu, you will be my joint director. You'll have to leave soon to set it up, I will join soon after.' His manner was such that he gave Chamu no option to say 'no'. I dare say that Chamu felt inclined to be of help in starting the institute, partly because it was going to be in Bangalore, in his home state. But he was also reluctant to think of moving at this stage of the Delhi University Sociology Department's growth.

That December, we went to visit our friends Nanubhai and Savitha Amin in Baroda for a family holiday. A couple of days after we arrived, Nanubhai mysteriously announced that we were all going to Ahmedabad the next day, and would meet someone of interest to Chamu. Chamu's curiosity was aroused. While in the car, he asked Nanubhai about the reason behind the sudden trip to Ahmedabad. Then Nanubhai told us in detail about Chhaya Shastri, an astrologer who did his predictions by measuring one's shadow. Nanubhai had consulted this astrologer and thought he and his rather unusual practices would intrigue Chamu.

In the heart of Ahmedabad, we stopped outside a modest home and were led up a rickety staircase to a room overlooking an open terrace. There, a middle-aged man sat at a desk. After exchanging greetings with Nanubhai and chatting with him, he asked Chamu to step out onto the terrace and measured Chamu's shadow with a wooden stick. He made some calculations and then took out some palm leaf scrolls from which he read. He told Chamu that he was a great scholar and a sceptic when it came to astrology, and that he, Chamu, had come reluctantly to test Chhaya Shastri. Among other things that we found eerily accurate, he said that fire had and would continue to follow us, but would not harm us personally. Chhaya Shastri then said that he saw a sudden movement and change of place for Chamu and our family. He also said Chamu had been seriously ill a few times in his life and that my horoscope (which he also cast) was protective of Chamu's and had pulled him through and would continue to do so.

When we went to see Chhaya Shastri, we had not decided to leave Delhi at the time. Many of our friends at the university advised us against it. But over the course of the next couple of months, Chamu made up his mind to take on the challenge of starting an institute in Bangalore and was excited about the move. He had long felt that there needed to be an institute of excellence for the social sciences in South India, or 'South of the Vindhyas' as he put it. And he was also looking forward to moving to Karnataka, where he was from, and closer to his hometown, Mysore.

We made preparations for the move. All our personal belongings, furniture and other household goods, including our car, were sent by a EVK (freight) wagon ahead of us. The wagon had to be insured and Chamu made arrangements to do so through a third party.

We arrived in Bangalore in May and settled into a rental home in Jayanagar, one of the new residential localities. Our dog Kittu had made the journey with us by train. Chamu's books, which had been sent by lorry, arrived on time and were unpacked and arranged in the basement of our home. But we had not received any news of the freight wagon in which all our belongings—furniture, household goods and Fiat car had been sent.

After several anxious weeks, Chamu received a cryptic telegram from the railway minister's office: 'EVK wagon number...involved in fire. Contents transferred to EVK wagon number...' Chamu wrote to the railway minister to get further information. We then received a telegram from the chief engineer of the Bangalore railway division, saying that the EVK wagon containing our belongings had reached Bangalore Cantonment station. So, Chamu and I went the next morning and were taken to the siding where the wagon was parked. To our utmost horror, we saw a burnt-out shell that was our Fiat, along with a couple of sticks of furniture.

We learnt from the chief engineer that the original wagon

had been declared 'sick' and put on the siding in Gooty Junction, where it most probably had been burglarized and then set on fire. The chief engineer seemed to suggest that it was a known practice of railway dacoits. He then recommended that the shell of the car be towed to the TVS workshop on Kasturba Road to see if it could be salvaged.

Chamu and I were in a state of shock, but a further shock awaited us. On contacting the insurance people, we were told that no insurance papers had been filed! We simply couldn't fathom how this misunderstanding could have occurred. We now had to plan and replace all our household goods. I set about renting essential pieces of furniture from Saleh Ahmed. I had to quickly get the house in order, as we were expecting houseguests. We didn't want to buy a new car. We had bought our Fiat from a friend in Mysore and had driven it all the way to Delhi. We didn't feel like junking it. We left the car at the TVS workshop on Kasturba Road and it was rebuilt. I drove it in Bangalore for the next three decades.

I drove all over the city in our rebuilt car and felt safe doing so, but I was totally unaware of the workings of the engine and so on. Once when I was driving on Nrupathunga Road, I found flames coming into the car from the bonnet. Fortunately, there were no passengers that day. I jumped out while the car was moving. It eventually came to a slow stop ahead. Passersby gathered around me and threw sand on the flames till the smoke died down. Then the car was towed to the workshop and once again made roadworthy.

When I think back on these untoward fiery adventures, they bring to mind the predictions of Chhaya Shastri, all those years ago.

The Bangalore City Survey

In 1973, I joined the Institute for Social and Economic Change (ISEC) as a research associate. In those days, the Institute was temporarily housed at Carlton House. For me, personally, the location was convenient. My daughters attended Sophia High School, which was within walking distance of the Institute.

Carlton House has an interesting history. It was built by the British auctioneer Carlton in 1880 for his residence and later became the home of Sir Mirza Ismail, the Dewan of then Mysore state. The spacious bungalow housed all the departments of the Institute, including Economics, Statistics and Sociology. The Geography Unit was in the annexe.

I was appointed the chief field investigator in the Geography Unit chaired by Dr V.L.S. Prakasa Rao, who was our colleague at Delhi University and had also moved to Bangalore. My main responsibility was to collect data in and around the city for what I believe was the first attempt in recent years to do a systematic study of the urban expansion of Bangalore and its environs. The study was undertaken under the aegis of the Indian Council of Social Science Research (ICSSR). I worked in coordination with the City Planning Department and the Land Records Office in Bangalore. Dr Vinod Tewari, a statistician and urban geographer who worked closely with Dr Prakasa Rao in Delhi, and Dr Prakasa Rao himself, were responsible for the analysis and mapping. I was happy to be associated with the project. And the work involved field study, which I enjoyed!

More importantly, as a result of the fieldwork, I got to know the city first-hand. Driving my 1950s vintage Fiat, I travelled the length and breadth of the city and its outskirts, stopping every now and then to admire the purple jacaranda in full bloom, scarlet gulmohar and pink-blossomed rain trees, with their canopies spreading across the street. I also remember many more Peepal trees in the city and streets lined with native fig trees that hosted many types of birds and bats. I felt fortunate to live in the city. Not only did I enjoy my work, I also made many friends.

From the Land Records Office and the Bangalore Development Authority, earlier known as the City Improvement Trust Board (CITB) of Bangalore, I collected information about the development and radial growth of the city. Visiting a few slums across the city was particularly interesting to me. Though I was armed with a questionnaire for my survey, I realized soon enough that participant observation would be the more effective way to learn about and appreciate the lives of the slum dwellers, many of whom were in-migrants. They were the bulwark of the workers on whom the middle class depended on a day-to-day basis. I am thinking of the Siddapura slum adjoining the Lalbagh Botanical Gardens in South Bangalore, the slum that supplies the neighbouring upper middle-class households of the localities of Jayanagar and Wilson Gardens with their domestic maids, gardeners, home watchmen, municipal street cleaners and other supporting help; of the Pottery Town slum in North Bangalore, from where the residents of the neighbouring Williams Town, Benson Town, Richards Town, as also those of Jayamahal, source not only their vegetable vendors, carpenters and household help but also the clay pots for their well-maintained gardens and mud images of Ganesha for Ganesha Chaturthi celebrated every year. When I moved to live in Benson Town and visited Pottery Town more frequently for introducing my senior class students to the basic elements of fieldwork, the Ganesha idol-making had reached gigantic proportions witnessing ever-larger mud Ganeshas ordered by institutions and temples.

Street in Pottery Town
Image Courtesy: Athreya Chidambi

The dhobi ghat slum in Ulsoor, adjoining the precincts of Indira Nagar and Mahatma Gandhi Road near the Gurudwara, was another focal point. I was introduced to this locality by one of its illustrious residents, Shri Byrappa, a building contractor for the well-known and prestigious architecture firm, Chandavarkar and Thacker. Bearded and impressive, Byrappa was an active member of the slum community. I got to know him well over a period of two years and he remained a friend. He and I spent many hours sitting on the cement platform around the temple in the slum, discussing the haphazard growth of the city. He introduced me to his friends in other squatter settlements and slums and willy-nilly facilitated my research. I ultimately conducted a detailed study of three slums: the Murphy Town slum, bordering the connecting road between Ulsoor and the newly developed extension of Indira Nagar;

the Pottery Town slum settlement along the Bore Bank Road, running parallel to the railway tracks through Benson Town; and the Siddapura slum settlement between the localities of Wilson Garden and Jayanagar 1st Block and adjoining the Lalbagh Botanical Gardens.

The Bangalore City Survey, which lasted for over two years, led to the publication of the Bangalore City Survey monograph, initiated and supported by the Indian Council for Social Science Research.

When our family moved to Benson Cross Road, my husband and I familiarized ourselves with the neighbourhood during our evening walks. That is how we stumbled upon the Pottery Town settlement. When I mentioned my discovery of Pottery Town to my new neighbour, she exclaimed, 'Oh! That dirty place with young louts from the slums!' To me, neither did it seem dirty (anyway, not more so than other neighbourhoods I have visited) nor did I encounter young men whom I would call 'louts'.

Ganeshas in Pottery Town

Image Courtesy: Athreya Chidambi

In fact, the slum study I did for the Bangalore City Survey was eye-opening for me. Contrary to my earlier impression and expectation of a higgledy-piggledy assembly of hutments and *kutcha* houses crammed together, with no space to expand, I found there was some organic structure in the development. I was able to continue with my exploration of this type of settlement which I began when working on the Bangalore City Survey.

Chamu and I walked through long, narrow but well-swept streets with semi-detached single-storey modest houses. A signboard read, 'Drive Slow'. It is true that there was no proper arrangement for surface drainage and I jumped over improvised bridges of brick and granite stepping stones, trying to navigate the streets that had pools of stagnant water. Though it was part of the city, the atmosphere was very rural. Ducks and chickens strutted about freely. There were small one-room tenements and single-storey houses along narrow streets and lanes, some unpaved. The houses fronted onto the street and there were little patches of marigold plants or a flowering jasmine creeper in a tiny space. We stopped to admire the sight.

Goats and cows tethered to moringa trees growing on the roadside also lent a 'rural' air. Very often, there would be a sheaf of moringa leaves tied low on a tree trunk for the goats to chew on. As I stopped in the middle of the road to avoid the scurrying fowl, an elderly sun-tanned woman emerged from a doorway with sheaves of leaves which she shoved before the goats. She recognized Chamu and me as strangers to the area and asked if we were lost. 'No. We are admiring this street,' I replied. She invited us into her home, took us through the long narrow dwelling to a backyard garden. You would never have thought such a beautiful and fragrant space existed behind the huts. There were several sweet-smelling jasmine plants, a couple of tulsi shrubs and a few bright-orange marigold bushes.

Three moringa trees, tall and laden with drumsticks, as the long pods were called, caught my eye. She said immediately, 'Whenever you need flowers for your pooja, or moringa leaves and drumsticks for cooking, come over and help yourself.' What generosity! And that too to complete strangers, I thought and said so to Chamu. I had not cooked drumstick leaves in years after leaving our home on Cavalry Lane in Delhi, where I had grown six trees in our back garden.

From that day on, the woman, whose name I learnt was Vanaja, would stop me with a gift of a handful of drumstick stems with luscious, fresh green leaves and half a dozen fresh drumsticks. She was thrilled when I gave her a few Easter lily bulbs from my garden. Her highly developed sense of reciprocity goaded her into gifting me with *omum* (carom seeds) plants and from then on, we were on a plant-exchange relationship. One day she visited me in my home on Benson Cross Road, and a few days later, she arrived with three of her grandchildren to show them our backyard jackfruit tree laden with fruits. She did not return home empty-handed.

As I learnt from Vanaja, moringa could be propagated by cuttings as also with seeds. I planted a moringa sapling in our garden at Benson Cross, as far away from the house as possible, for it was well known that the trees attract a particular type of hairy caterpillar.

On my repeat visits to the slums, I was invited inside the dwellings of the slum dwellers. And each time I entered, I would be simply stunned at what I saw. I had to reframe my impressions and assumptions of the interior of a house in a slum. I was welcomed into neat, clean, well-organized spaces, some with front hallway, where I was invited to sit. The seating area led to a small kitchen space that was the hub of the house. The kitchens had wooden shelves on which gleaming pots and pans of burnished brass and copper were neatly arranged. A couple of skillets hung from hooks on the wall, and all the food was cooked on a woodfire stove. Beyond the makeshift cotton curtain was the family bedroom. Bedding rolls were neatly stacked against the wall and a reed mat was spread on the floor. In one house, a baby's hammock cradle was slung from the ceiling. In a couple others, I was surprised to find a calendar with an image of Jesus Christ next to which was a framed picture of a Hindu goddess. In one Christian household, I learnt that the daughter-in-law of the house was Hindu.

I was grateful for the insights I acquired into the life of those living in Pottery Town through my connections with residents like Vanaja.

Adventures in Wine-Making

I grew up in a family of teetotallers. My father was an asthmatic and although advised by his doctors to take a glass of alcohol occasionally to get good sleep, he never made a habit out of it. He preferred to rest against a pile of pillows throughout the night.

In one of his letters to me after I visited England, he asked me whether I had tasted wine. In fact, the first time I had wine was in England. When Chamu and I travelled to New York by sea, alcohol was plentiful on the ship. Yet I was not tempted, as I was seasick. Chamu, however, would have a glass of whiskey in the evenings while writing.

When in California, our Jewish friends would invite us home for the Jewish holidays and wine would always be part of the festive meal. I got used to enjoying a glass of wine. Our friends thought Indian snacks of samosas, pappadam and pakodas went well with drinks. In California, the Center for Advanced Study would organize two trips every year to the Napa Valley wineries. It was there that I got to see the entire process of making and bottling wine for the first time.

When we moved to Bangalore in the 1970s, I discovered that the Bangalore Blue grapes were delicious and my Parsi friend told me they were also good for making wine. Paul Hockings, whom I met when he was a postdoctoral fellow in anthropology in Berkeley, used to come frequently to South India for fieldwork in the Nilgiris. He would have a base in Bangalore and would visit us in our Benson Town home. On one of Paul's trips to Bangalore, we drove to Mysore, passing vineyards on the way, some owned by movie stars. There were baskets of grapes for sale on the roadside. We would buy the Bangalore Blues and the extraordinarily sweet little green grapes for Chamu's mother and his siblings whenever we visited Mysore in the grape season.

I wanted to try my hand at making wine at home, so I set about finding out where I would get large-enough containers. My friend Savitha Amin in Baroda suggested that I try using the large pottery jars that we used for making pickles. That set me off to Avenue Road in Bangalore. Locating the street was my first challenge. I stopped and asked many people, and they sent me off to the City Market. From there, I found my way up Avenue Road, a one-way street. Avenue Road is a vibrant market area with small shops and footpath stalls. Abutting Avenue Road was Raja Market, a cavernous deep-set space of small stalls selling everything from buttons and lace to jewellery and spices. The narrow streets and side lanes off Avenue Road bustled with every kind of vehicle, as well as pedestrians and animals. The street seemed to be never-ending and I drove slowly and carefully to avoid any untoward incident.

I came to the Mysore Bank Circle and was on the point of giving up when, to my surprise and delight, I saw a roadside display of large glass jars—some clear, some blue and some green—on the right-hand side. I finally settled for the clear glass jars and bought three. By sheer accident, the store opposite had weighing scales for sale and looking at them, it occurred to me that I would need weighing scales too. I bought one with brass pans which I could place on a table, and triumphantly took it home. I felt ready to start on my wine-making adventure.

The process, I found, was laborious and there were many

challenges. Once the grapes were bought, they had to be immediately squeezed, otherwise they would spoil. I did not have a mechanical grape press. In Italy, I had heard that grapes were pressed with hands and even feet, as they were stomped on in large vats.

After dinner, I would sit down to squeeze the grapes with my hands. I would also use a wooden butter churner, as no metal could be used on the grapes. The pressing of the grapes would take hours. Once, I remember calling Chamu at midnight to help me as the grapes were in danger of spoiling. He came downstairs bleary-eyed and agreed to help. He asked me whether there was an easier way of doing this. The squeezed pulp and juice had to be strained in a muslin cloth. I reserved the skin and pulp for making jam. Maybe this was my parents' influence, they would never waste anything.

The glass jars from Avenue Road worked well except that they were not really meant for making wine and had no air-locks. This posed a problem. The first couple of batches turned out vinegary. I wondered if it was the grapes that I had bought from the orchards on Yelahanka Road. I gave my friends some of the vinegary wine and they used it for salad dressing, saying the flavour was excellent. But my objective was not to make vinegar, and I felt disappointed.

I struggled on with the advice of my Parsi friend who encouraged me to document each stage of the process, with dates and times like a 'wine diary', and so I did. The end product this time was not a complete failure. Chamu tasted it and pronounced it dry but not bad for a first try. I felt pleased.

On one of his visits, I told Paul Hockings about my experiments in wine making and my struggles with the improvised containers and so on. Paul seemed interested. I knew him to be very resourceful, but beyond asking questions about the equipment, he said nothing at the time. Several months later, I received a postcard from Paul, telling me to look out for a parcel in the mail. And a few months after this, I received a mysterious parcel. The customs label read 'enema kit' and it was from Paul in California. On opening the 'enema kit', I found that it was a wine-making kit, a compressible plastic jar with an air-lock—a gift from Paul. I was thrilled! How very thoughtful of him to have sent me the kit and to find this ingenious way of getting it past the customs.

The first batch of wine that I made with Paul's gift was a success. Chamu and I enjoyed it—it was neither sweet nor dry. One day, Chamu's young friend from Mysore, Raghu, who was now working in the United Breweries in Bangalore, stopped by and I told him about my wine-making adventures. He was very surprised and immediately interested. He stayed on to dinner and had a taste of the wine. He said, 'I can't believe how good it is!' He then offered to take it to his lab and test it for the alcohol content. Soon after, Raghu called excitedly and informed Chamu that the wine had passed the test in the lab and it was declared an excellent vin rose!

Our friend G.V.K. Rao, who was then the chief secretary of Karnataka, would visit us once in a while. We gave him a taste of the home-made wine. He was astounded by the quality and felt it was an unusual hobby for someone like me. He marvelled at how I had learnt on my own. Being the chief secretary, he immediately suggested that I start a women's cooperative for wine-making and offered to put me in touch with some people. But it would have been a full-time occupation, so I didn't take him up on it.

Go with the Flow

'So how did you decide to become a teacher?' was the question posed to me by R.K. Narayan. We were in Berkeley in 1956, when both Chamu and he were Rockefeller Fellows. Not a day would pass without Kunjappa stopping by around six in the evening and staying on to have dinner with us. He once said, 'My day is not complete without my curds rice, Rukka. If nothing else, just give me some curd and rice, and a vegetable cooked the South Indian way.' That was not too much to ask, I thought, and in any case I enjoyed cooking. As always, Kunjappa had an agenda, and what I did not know at that time was that as a freelance author, he was penning his collection of essays, *My Dateless Diary,* on his observations of his first visit to the United States. It turned out to be a bestseller.

'So, to get back to it, Rukka, how did you decide to become a teacher?' And before I could respond, he continued, 'Did you go with the flow? Because I went with the flow too, as my life was not planned. And I'm happy this way.' I smiled saying, 'I don't know what you mean, Kunjappa, but I certainly didn't plan on becoming a teacher.'

It happened this way. I was studying Human Geography at Queen Mary's College and, while writing the last paper for the Intermediate exam, the supervisor at the examination hall thrust a form into my face and said, 'Rukmini, sign this.' Not giving it serious thought, I just signed and returned the form, not realizing how consequential that signature was to be.

As I learnt later, Madras University was starting a new course in Geography for the honours and MA programmes and they had vacancies for women students from Queen Mary's College, three from the arts stream and three from the sciences, along with six students from a local men's college. Just before I left the college for my summer vacation, the head of the Geography Department, Dr Iravati, informed six of us that we had been selected to join the honours course in Geography at the university. I was a bit puzzled, though happy, that the head of the department thought well of me to include me in the very first batch of honours students. However, I also felt a little uneasy as it left me with no choice.

I had earlier wanted to study English Literature at Loyola College where I had participated in debates. That's how I got to know Father Murphy, an Englishman and scholar from Oxford. Father Murphy was a charismatic speaker and he encouraged students to take part in public speaking, debates, essay writing and so on. I liked and respected him greatly. But I learnt from him that Loyola did not admit women.

When I went home to Tanjore, I broke the news of my being selected to the honours programme to my father. He was very pleased and encouraged me to stay on in the programme. I returned to Queen Mary's College and registered for the very first honours programme in Geography at Madras University.

When I completed my masters in Human Geography in 1952, another pleasant surprise awaited me. Mrs Radha, a senior colleague of Dr Iravati, called me to her room and informed me that there would be an additional position of a tutor in the Geography Department in Queen Mary's College and that I should apply for it. It never occurred to me to turn down what seemed to be an opportunity. So, from the summer of 1952 to 1953, I was a tutor, earning a grand salary of 100 rupees a month. Subsequently, a lecturer post was created in the College and I went to the Madras Public Service Commission to interview for the post. To my surprise, a few weeks later, I learnt that I had been selected. So, Kunjappa, now you see how strange are the ways of fate; you might think of yourself as the chief player and yet not really be one in your own life.

When I married Chamu in 1955, I abruptly resigned from Queen Mary's College and moved with him to Baroda and then to Delhi in early 1959. The Vice Chancellor of Delhi University, V.K.R.V. Rao, had invited Chamu to start a Sociology Department at the Delhi School of Economics. When Dr Rao learnt that I had a masters in Geography, he said, 'Oh, I'm also finalizing the starting of a Geography Department at the DSE.' I applied to the Geography Department and, to make a long story short, I was the first to be appointed in the Department. Thereafter, I faced many challenges of starting a postgraduate department and the first year was spent in building a library collection with a cartographic section.

In my efforts I received help and advice from Dr B.N. Ganguly, who was the pro-vice chancellor at the time. He was very interested and supportive of the new Geography Department, and of me. As I had a master's in Geography but no doctorate, the University had to find a more suitable head of the department. Fortunately, and to my delight, this led to the appointment of Dr V.L.S. Prakasa Rao, who had been one of my teachers at Madras University.

He and I together were keen that the curriculum include field studies, especially of rural areas. We wanted students to visit Delhi's outlying villages and study the way of life of villagers, the prevalent cropping patterns and the lives of rural women. Under the stewardship of Dr Rao, many colleges on the campus showed an interest in the new department and soon there was no dearth of students for the MA course, which attracted a lot of women students. Dr Rao was not only keen on field work, he also established a state-of-the-art cartographic unit with a well-trained cartographer.

I left Delhi in 1972 for Bangalore. Although there was a reasonably well-developed Geography Department at Bangalore University, Chamu did not encourage me to apply for various reasons, one being that I was not proficient in reading and writing in the local language, Kannada. Many of the students coming to the University were Kannada speakers from mofussil areas.

I joined the Institute for Social and Economic Change in 1973 as a research associate in the Geography Unit for three years. But when ISEC moved from Carlton House on Palace Road to its campus in Nagarbhavi, I decided to resign. I had two school-going children and the long commute to Nagarbhavi would have meant leaving home at seven o'clock in the morning and returning late in the evening. It simply wasn't feasible. But I was eager to continue with my interest in Geography and after a while I found my way back to teaching.

I was very involved, like my father was with us, in the education of my daughters. I found that Geography, which was a compulsory subject in high school, was being treated as a 'soft subject' and the Geography teachers were either not qualified to teach or they thought that it was enough to prepare the students for the examinations. I couldn't imagine that in one of the best private schools in Bangalore, the Geography teacher did not have a degree in Geography, and, even worse, did not care to show students any maps! I was appalled to learn that students were not encouraged to refer to atlases. Even though the syllabus required the interpretation of topographic sheets produced by the Geological Survey of India, the teacher didn't think it necessary to familiarize her students with these sheets.

I decided to teach my daughters Geography and take

it beyond the textbook. To make it interesting, I told them about different landscapes and people. I went to the Geological Survey of India office and bought a few topographical sheets. That roused Lakshmi's interest in the subject. This was the first time she was looking at topographical sheets, and I could see it had become an exciting learning experience.

The experience led me to think I should teach Geography to schoolkids. I enjoyed teaching and it would be a real service. In the summer of 1980, I was wondering what to do next. I asked Lakshmi if I should apply to teach in school, and she encouraged me.

Bishop Cotton Boys' School is one of the oldest schools in Bangalore and can be traced back to the time of the British Raj. It was established in 1865 by the Reverend S.T. Pettigrew, who was at the time the chaplain of St Mark's Cathedral, with the aim of educating boys from European and Anglo-Indian families. The school was named after Bishop George Edward Lynch Cotton, Bishop of Calcutta, and has been described as 'the Eton of the East'. Following India's independence in 1947, the school came to be governed by the Church of South India. Of course, I knew nothing of this history when I drove to the school to meet the principal, Mr A.T. Balraj. I was just looking for a teaching position that was not far from our house and from my daughters' school, and Bishop Cotton Boys' School—in the heart of the Bangalore Cantonment on St Marks Road—seemed perfect in that respect.

The school's grounds extended over 14 acres. The grounds faced St Marks Road on one side and Residency Road on the other, where the main entrance gate was located. The elite Bangalore Club was a few minutes' walk from the school. A short distance away, a statue of Queen Victoria stood with a commanding view of Cubbon Park and Mahatma Gandhi Road, which used to be known as South Parade when

British military officers were stationed in the Cantonment. The coveted residential area behind the school, with large bungalows in spacious compounds and with streets named Lavelle Road, Grant Road and Walton Road, harkened back to the British Raj.

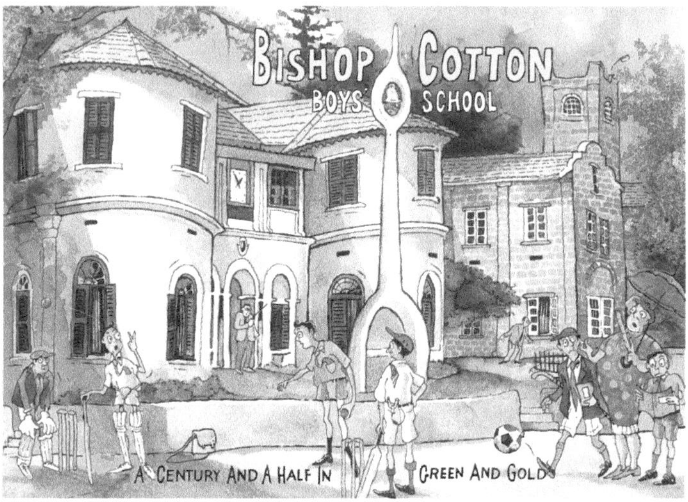

Sketch of Bishop Cotton Boys' School by Paul Fernandes

I remember being very impressed with the school and its grounds. There were four cricket fields, which gave me an idea of the importance of sports in the school. The imposing stone buildings with arches reminded me of my school, St Helena's in Poona.

When I arrived, the durwan at the principal's chamber stopped me and asked if I had an appointment. I wrote my name on a slip of paper and asked him to hand it to the principal. The half-door opened, and I heard someone say, 'Come in, Mrs Srinivas.' I was offered a chair placed opposite Mr Balraj. He asked, 'What brings you here, what can I do for you?'

My answer was, 'I can only sell Geography.'

His face broke into a smile as he said, 'Walk right in,' and then he seemed more relaxed and so was I. We talked about my credentials, where I had studied and where I had taught before. When he heard that I studied in Queen Mary's College, he beamed and said, 'My alma mater is Men's Christian College in Madras. And I have a good friend there by the name of H. Srinivasan, the same name as yours.' I corrected him and told him my name was 'Srinivas'. H. Srinivasan turned out to be my husband's brother-in-law.

Although I had never taught boys, I soon grew accustomed to teaching at 'Cottons', as it was called locally, and taught there for nearly 10 years, from 1980 to 1989.

I strongly believe that learning should neither be exam-oriented nor should it rely on textbooks alone—it should be engaging, even fun. I wanted students to be connected to their environment and learn about local culture. I organized field trips for my Geography class to the Mysugar Paper Mills in Mandya. Mr C.J. Padmanabha, my neighbour and friend from when we lived in 1st Block Jayanagar, also happened to be the managing director of the factory, and he facilitated these annual trips. I took students to Talakaadu, closer to Mysore, as I wanted them to see the shift in the course of the river Kaveri and the riverine sand dunes. This was a completely new experience for urban schoolchildren. One of the highlights of the field trip was walking into the deep cave of the Pathaleswara shrine—one of five temples of Lord Shiva that are buried in the sand dunes—and to learn that there was still a priest there who would light the lamps everyday.

The students were deeply interested in the legend of Talakaadu. In the 1600s, the Mysore Raja, a representative of the Vijayanagar family at Srirangapatna, came to Talakaadu to offer sacrifices at the temple, as he was afflicted with an incurable disease. He had left the matters of running the government to his second wife, Rani Alamelamma. But she, upon learning he was close to death, followed him to Talakaadu leaving Srirangapatna and its responsibilities to Raja Wodeyar of Mysore. The Raja coveted her jewels and deployed an army to go after her to secure them. Rani Alamelamma went to the banks of the Kaveri, threw the jewels in the water and drowned. But before she did so, she cursed both the place and Raja Wodeyar: 'Let the Thalakad become sand, let [the town of] Malangi become a whirlpool; let the Mysore Rajas fail to beget heirs.' The Wodeyar dynasty continues to retain Srirangapatna and its dependencies, and since the seventeenth century they have had to adopt male heirs. There is a warning posted at Talakaadu for all to keep clear of the whirlpool. The students were fascinated with the ecology, history and mythology of the place.

Rukka with her students at Bishop Cotton Boys' School

Another underground temple I took my students to was the Gavi Gangadhareshwara Temple on the Bull Temple Road in the Gandhi Bazaar area in South Bangalore. The difference lies in one shrine being in a subterranean sand dune and the other in a cave carved out of a granite outcrop.

Towards the end of my years at the School, students would fondly refer to me as 'Granny', as I was the oldest staff member at the time. It was very satisfying when after turning 90, I received a surprise visit from one of my former students who now lives in California. There are others who write to me every now and then. It's a pleasure to keep in touch with them.

I taught in two other schools in Bangalore, Vidyaniketan and the Mallya Aditi International School. I ended up joining both these schools by sheer chance.

At Vidyaniketan, I taught English, Geography and Mathematics. I had never taught Maths before. I had to devise ways of teaching concepts. Fractions and bill sums were taught in the fourth standard. To make fractions real, I would take apples and oranges to school, which would make it easy to explain how division worked—a whole into so many parts. The children enjoyed it because at the end of the class, they would get to eat the fruit. After fractions, bill sums would follow. I would send students on an imaginary shopping spree with a list of groceries of what they liked to eat. It only took a couple of classes for students to understand the concepts clearly.

One day, Hamsa Vithani, the founder and principal who had invited me to teach at the school, called me to her office where I found a few other teachers. She congratulated me and said, 'I like your unorthodox way of teaching mathematics.' I then learnt that her office was right next door to my classroom, and she could hear what was going on. She said, 'Students are enjoying your class greatly.' Vidyaniketan moved from Benson Town to their own campus in the Coffee Board extension near the Hebbal Lake, a commute just within half an hour from my home. But sadly I felt it was too far for me to continue to teach there as I had two schoolgoing children of my own.

In the early 1990s, I got a call from my friend Jyoti (Jo) Thyagarajan who was teaching at the Mallya Aditi International School, a private school started by a group of women, including Mrs Tara Chandavarkar of the architectural firm Chandavarkar and Thacker, well-known in Bangalore. I later learnt that the school had actually originated in her home on Palace Cross Road and was originally called 'Aditi'. Later, following an endowment from the industrial magnate Vijay Mallya, its name was changed to Mallya Aditi International School.

Jo informed me that the principal, Ann Warrior, wanted to meet me. I went to the School, which was now in Yelahanka, to meet Ann. Again, it was one of the most informal meetings I've had with the head of an institution. We talked about generalities and she told me a lot about herself. We connected and she said, 'We need someone to teach Geography in the high school.' Again, I did not want to be away from home from seven in the morning to five in the evening, so I offered to teach part-time which turned out to be acceptable to her.

Once again, I introduced students in the high school to field trips to encourage them to take the process of learning outside the classroom and get to know their environment. I took them to the Standard Brick and Tile Company in Yelahanka and interviewed the administrative staff to find out which lakes they got the clay from; what time of year was the best time to dredge the lake and get clay; and what was the process for tile-making. I helped students prepare a questionnaire—it was the first time they had heard of such a thing.

Another field trip was to the meteorological department, but this one was after school hours, so that students would get to read the various weather instruments and observe the hydrogen balloon being sent up at five o'clock in the evening. None of the students had seen a rain gauge, and it was an exciting revelation to them. They were elated when the director of the meteorological department came and spoke with them and answered their questions.

I took the students to the Geological Survey of India office, where maps were made. The cartography section, I thought, would be intriguing for them. I certainly found it fascinating. There, the data collected was tabulated and, unlike today where technology has taken over, people used to sit and plot on huge drafting tables. Students could see that the maps that they used in the classroom were being made here.

A totally different kind of fieldwork was the visit to Pottery Town, which was located off Williams Town and along the railway line. The conditions under which Pottery Town residents worked were unimaginable to my students, who came from the middle and upper classes. Again, with my help, they learnt to use surveying instruments—the chain and tape, the prismatic compass and the theodolite. Some of the boys were very impressed with what the instruments could do and they got down on their hands and knees in the mud because they were so engrossed.

I enjoyed teaching high school students. I also realized that the attention span of teenagers is short-lived and reading from textbooks is no way to make lessons come alive. By the time I started teaching in a school, I had travelled widely with my husband to different parts of the world. My observations and experiences from all these travels made the subject more interesting for me as, I think, it did for the students.

Years later, my former students would tell me that what they had learnt about the world, weather and climatic phenomena or the geological landscapes, made sense to them when they travelled. I find this very gratifying.

Although I stumbled into teaching by pure chance, I am

happy to say that I found it very satisfying. One of my students went on to study at the Massachusetts Institute of Technology (MIT) in Boston, and mentioned me as the teacher who influenced him the most. I was delighted to receive this letter of appreciation.

MASSACHUSETTS INSTITUTE OF TECHNOLOGY

Office of Admissions
77 Massachusetts Avenue
Cambridge, MA 02139

Room 3-108
Phone: 617-253-4791
Telex: 92-1473

October 3, 1986

Mrs. R. Srinivas
Bishop Cotton Boys' School
St. Mark's Road
Bangalore, India

Dear Teacher,

Each year we ask students admitted to MIT to share with us the name of a teacher who has been especially influential in that student's development.

We congratulate you on being named this year! More importantly, we thank you for the time, patience, expertise, love, discipline and all the other qualities which have had such an important impact on your students. You do the work from which we all benefit.

Congratulations again on the respect you have earned from your students.

Sd/- Michael C. Behnke
Director of Admissions

Pizza in Bangalore

Both Chamu and my daughters, Lakshmi and Tulasi, loved trying out new food at home. I would make North Indian and Gujarati dishes, Western dishes of baked vegetables, ratatouille, lasagna, eggplant parmesan and soups (for which I started growing celery). I created my own recipes for making jams, jellies, marmalade and pickles.

I wanted to bring a small Baby Belling oven from London to Bangalore but unfortunately was not able to. However, returning from one of his trips to the United States, Chamu surprised me with a Sunbeam multipurpose electric skillet. I could bake, fry, braise and steam with this marvellous gadget. It became an indispensable kitchen tool. I was excited to try some new recipes, and my family would be my guinea pigs. The verdict was always, 'Oooh, it's so tasty!' It encouraged me to use the Sunbeam even more.

My daughters liked a slice of homemade pizza every now and then. I must add that I did not know of any pizza joints in Bangalore in the late 1970s. I had no recipe for the pizza crust but with my scanty knowledge of using yeast, I managed to successfully get the dough to rise and bake a good crust. Finding the right cheese for the topping posed a challenge. Those were the pre-Internet days and none from my close circle of friends really knew or were interested in locating an outlet for different kinds of cheese. One suggestion was to try Brigade Road, one of the centres for shopping for Western groceries. And then, of course, the Patel Store on

Brigade Road came to mind. Opposite the Rex Theatre was Mr Patel's hole-in-the-wall treasure house of a store that held all sorts of imported foodstuff from far and wide: olives of various kinds in small jars that cost an arm and a leg, jams and jellies from England, crackers, peanut butter from America, tinned ham, anchovies and sardines, soy sauce, spaghetti and Tabasco sauce—a favourite of Chamu's, which he would liberally sprinkle on macaroni and cheese, soups, and use for spicing up the cheese pakodas I would make. I was also looking for cheddar and mozzarella cheese. But the small quantity of cheese available at Mr Patel's was not the solution to my quest.

I don't remember exactly how I discovered the National Dairy Research Institute (NDRI) on the road to the new suburb of Koramangala, but that discovery was a boon to me. I would drive from my home in Benson Cross all the way across the city to the NDRI. Beyond the gates, the paved driveway was flanked by tall grasses and cows grazed in the distance. The driveway led to a single-storied building that housed the research laboratory and the storehouse for the cheese.

The first time I walked in, the staff thought I was from a team of inspectors and they bowed deferentially and took me to the chief chemist's room. That was how I met Mr Rajamannar, the chief chemist at the cheese department—a tallish man with a friendly expression. Mr Rajamannar, of course, knew that I was no member of any inspection team. On the contrary, he was surprised that I had walked in without prior appointment and wanted to know the purpose of my visit. When he heard that I was in search of a constant supply of cheddar and mozzarella cheese, he sat me down and quizzed me. He was intrigued by my interest—how a 'South Indian, middle-class, Brahmin woman' was setting out on this enterprise of making pizza. We became friends instantly. In spite of his busy schedule, he found time to discuss cheese with me. He must have loved what he was doing. He had learnt cheese-making in Europe and was excited about starting it in Bangalore.

I was thrilled the first time I entered the cheese section. After putting on gloves and a covering for his hair and shoes and giving me the same to wear, Mr Rajamannar took me to a dark, temperature-controlled anteroom where wax-coated wheels of cheese were stacked on shelves. Each wheel had the production date, date of maturity and the variety of the cheese stamped on it.

When I took the cheese home and we tried it, we found that the quality was comparable to some of the best cheeses we had tasted in Europe. The texture, the sharpness and the flavour were excellent. It made good sandwiches, went well with crackers and it melted very well.

After I visited his office, I think, about six times, Mr Rajamannar asked, 'Why do you have to drive from Benson Cross all the way to the NDRI? I live in Malleshwaram. Just give me a call as to what you want and you can collect it from my house.' I went with Chamu to his house in Malleshwaram to collect cheese and as they chatted and got to know more about each other, it turned out that he knew Chamu's family in Mysore!

I lost touch with Mr Rajamannar when I stopped using the NDRI cheese and started using Jain cheese instead. It had become available and was made without animal rennet.

As I mentioned earlier, I started teaching at Bishop Cotton Boys' School after an informal meeting with the principal Mr A.T. Balraj. At the school, I would spend all my non-teaching hours in the well-stocked library and on one of my short walks to the library from the Tower Block, where I taught, I chanced upon a makeshift canteen which, in those days, operated out of a shed.

During the elevenses break, I noticed many students

rushing towards the canteen for a snack. I hadn't packed a snack for myself from home, so I walked in with a group of senior students. The smell of hot oil greeted us. There were four men busy preparing the snacks, which disappeared within no time, as scores of young boys would order two to three plates each. What was on offer was fried egg on bread, fried bread rolls with potato filling, samosas and some beverages. Being a vegetarian, I couldn't eat egg, and the other snacks were all fried and smelt of oil. I could not find anything to eat.

A few weeks later, Mr Balraj and I were walking from the library towards his office and I mooted the subject of the boys' snack and lunch arrangements in the school. After a lengthy back and forth about the need to have something other than the fried bread rolls, I must have mentioned that I make pizza, for he said, 'Why don't you offer them pizzas?' I was naturally very excited.

My working hours stretched into the middle of the night, and Chamu would come downstairs, wondering what I was doing. He would find me kneading bowls of white flour and yeast for the pizza base. Earlier in the day or the one before, I would make pizza sauce from scratch, using tomatoes, garlic, carrots, beetroot, and seasoned with oregano and a little chilli powder to suit the Indian palate. By the morning, the dough would have risen beautifully, and along with my school bag, books and papers, I would pack the Sunbeam, the grated cheese, the pizza sauce and the risen dough.

After the morning classes, I set up shop, making pizza in the corridor of the main auditorium. All I needed was a table and a power outlet. I'd be followed by dozens of boys of all ages. Racing against time, I would roll out the pizza base, work like a machine, bake enough pizzas, cut them quickly into triangles and leave them on a platter. Mr Balraj had told me, 'The boys should pay for their snacks, let them not think it's free.' So, I charged them some token amount that went into the school charity fund.

The pizzas were so popular that the school's annual fete committee asked me to have a pizza stall. The stall was a huge success. I couldn't make the pizzas fast enough with my one trusted Sunbeam.

My friend, who taught at Baldwin Girls High School, came to the fete with her relatives who were students of Bishop Cotton Boys' School. She requested me to have a pizza stall at their school annual fete, and I was happy to oblige.

Everyone who tasted the pizzas said they were delicious and it gave me a lot of pleasure to make them. I was looking for a place to make pizzas on a routine basis. I toyed with the idea of making them at home and having people pick up their pizza, but then decided I needed a place away from the house.

On the way home from school in the evenings, I used to fill up my car at a petrol bunk next to the Cubbon Park Police Station on Kasturba Road. And the owners of the petrol station, Ashok Rao, his wife Bharati and his mother, who ran the Friendly Ice Cream Stall on the same premises, became good friends of mine. They got to know about my pizza-making and encouraged me to make and sell pizzas at the petrol station. They thought it would be a good accompaniment to the ice cream. I started making pizzas at the petrol station for an hour every working day. I had a lot of fun but that did not last long, largely because, as had also happened with my mushroom venture later, the pizzas became so popular that I couldn't keep up with the demand!

Fungal Quest

As a student in the fourth standard at St Helena's Convent School in Poona, I enjoyed Nature Study classes, where I learnt more about the city and its environment than I would have from a lecture in the classroom. One nature study field trip was to Poona's well-known Bund Garden. Our teacher, young Mr Stanley, directed us to a giant old tree with gnarled roots and overhanging branches on the edge of an infrequently used walkway and simply said, 'See what treasures you can find there.' My classmates and I scrambled about, dug in the soil and found beautiful, iridescent bugs; long, pinkish earthworms; myriads of insects tunnelling their way through the moist earth; and, to complete the miniature landscape, there were soft little umbrellas, as I remember some pure white, some grey, growing out of the roots and a little distance away, there were some spotted ones. Excitedly, my friends and I gathered some bugs and the miniature umbrellas in our pockets. Mr Stanley gently transferred all our treasures into a well-aerated cardboard box. He seemed happy with our discoveries and our involvement in the field project.

On the ride back to school, we pestered him with questions and he responded with stories. 'Back when I was at school in Sussex,' he went on, 'I went on a class field trip to the countryside and there for the first time I spotted the white and sable-coloured umbrellas. And funnily, in my late teens, I worked in a "mushroom farm" near Cornwall. Packing button mushrooms for the London markets was my job.'

This was my introduction to mushrooms. I hadn't even heard the word before. When I got home, I took the mushrooms out of my pocket excitedly to show them to my father. But Annam Athai, who was visiting us, stepped in, admonishing me in Tamil, '*Chee, asingyam*! These are dirty "dog's umbrellas". Go wash your hands!' Mushrooms are called 'dog's umbrellas' in Tamil, and Tamil Brahmins stay far away from them as they grow on the ground and on heaps of manure and waste matter. But my father laid them out on a newspaper and we both examined them. They were spongy and the underside of the umbrella was beautifully segmented. My father said, 'These are called gills.' I was intrigued. I had only heard of gills on fish to help them breathe.

The next time my father took me to the Southern Command canteen for lunch, he ordered mushroom soup and requested the waiter to bring a can of mushrooms to show us. In those days, mushroom soup was only made from canned mushrooms. Unfortunately, the little umbrellas had been chopped up, but the soup was creamy and very tasty.

Mushrooms were, at one time, considered 'vegetarian protein' and were thought of as a healthy vegetarian substitute for meat. When Chamu and I were in England in 1956, we spent a few days with Mrs Jones, Chamu's former landlady in Oxford. This was the first time I was meeting her. The evening we arrived, she made a Shepherd's pie for dinner. She had forgotten Chamu was vegetarian. But at least Chamu ate eggs. When she learnt that I, too, was a vegetarian and didn't even eat eggs, she just didn't know what to cook for breakfast, lunch and dinner. The first morning, she gave me sautéed mushrooms on toast. They were delicious but I found the texture and the colour of these mushrooms to be like pieces of meat. The next day, she once again prepared mushrooms for my lunch, so I took charge of the cooking and improvized a baked rice and cheese dish which Mrs Jones enjoyed.

Fast-forward to Delhi University when Mary Nana came into our lives as our daughter Lakshmi's nanny. Mary would take Lakshmi on pram rides and explore the university campus on these long walks. She was interested in plants, in gardens and in cooking. She had lived in the Nilgiris with her husband, and she would sometimes make dishes she missed from her time there.

When mushrooms were in season, Mary would wander off to the cricket field adjoining our house. Parking Lakshmi's pram nearby, Mary would comb the field for wild mushrooms, which she called *kaalan* in Tamil. The horse dung used on the field as fertilizer was ideal for growing mushrooms. Collecting wild mushrooms is tricky, but Mary had been foraging mushrooms since her days in the Nilgiris and knew which ones were edible and which were poisonous. Her spicy mushroom curry was a gourmet dish to eat with rice.

In Bangalore of the 1970s, we could get mushrooms in specialty stores in the Cantonment. The store on Brigade Road, run by Mr Patel, was one of them. We would buy fresh mushrooms from there, as both Chamu and the girls loved mushroom soup.

One winter, I saw an announcement for a crash course on growing mushrooms at the Indian Council of Agricultural Research Center (ICAR) in Hesaraghatta. Seeing how interested I was, Chamu encouraged me to take the month-long course, six hours each day, including weekends. I didn't mind the commute—it was a pleasure those days to drive in Bangalore.

The instructor at the ICAR, Mr Rao, was a specialist in growing mushrooms and was meticulous in conducting the classes. On the first day, he distributed a few typed sheets of paper which gave us an introduction to mushrooms and mushroom cultivation. Then he took us for a field visit to the damp and dark sheds nearby and we saw—and what a delightful sight that was—little white mushrooms, which looked like miniature white parasols, embedded in friable soil in neatly stacked wooden trays.

I was completely sold on the idea of experimenting with growing mushrooms. Little did I know of the work it involved. At the end of the four-week course, when some of us showed an interest in cultivating mushrooms, Mr Rao arranged for a carpenter to come home and do the shelving. The trays were stacked one above the other in the garage and filled with the horse dung that my gardener had sourced from the Maharaja's stables at the Bangalore Palace—rich, pure, unadulterated dung that stank to heaven! The space needed to be dark, so the windows and doors were covered with several layers of hessian. To get the best results, we were instructed to wash our feet before entering the shed and keep the growing area damp, dark and sterile by spraying malathion on all the exposed surfaces four to five times a day. The spores that I bought from the department at the ICAR had to be refrigerated, so to avoid other food items from getting contaminated I bought a small Kelvinator refrigerator for the sole purpose of storing the bottles of spores.

I meticulously followed the instructions and eagerly looked for the results every morning when I went into the garage. In a few days, I was delighted to find little specks of white on the surface of the bed of the dung. And the little specks seemed to grow by the hour. By the afternoon they took on the definite shape of a parasol, and by the evening they were even bigger. It was a wonder!

I cooked the first lot I harvested—it was half a kilogram at the most. I made a hearty mushroom onion soup. A few days later, I started collecting more and more mushrooms from the 16 trays I had. That left me with the problem of what to do with them. It occurred to me that hotels might be a market for my mushrooms. So, I contacted the Berry's Hotel on Church Street. The proprietor was at first suspicious, but when I met him with samples of the mushrooms I had grown, he was very impressed and wanted a regular supply—several kilos at a time—so he could include a mushroom curry sautéed with *methi* (fenugreek leaf) on his menu. I wasn't sure at the time whether I would be able to meet his demand. But I also approached the Ashoka Hotel, where I met the young, dynamic and handsome Mr Chakravarty, who was in charge and who again was very impressed with the sample I had taken to show to him. He said, 'These are the best quality I have seen—firm and with good colour.' I supplied him with a few kilos every other day.

For the next few weeks, my harvest of mushrooms was considerable, and Mr Chakravarty was not only pleased but also said I could become his regular supplier. But he needed several kilos a day. I was pleased that he thought the mushrooms were of superior quality, but felt depressed that I could not supply him with the quantity he required and on a regular basis. He suggested that I buy a farm, which I did some time later on Hennur Road. But sadly, I could not pursue my dream of becoming a successful mushroom grower on a commercial scale because around the same time, I accepted a teaching position at Bishop Cotton Boys' School. It would have been next to impossible for me to grow mushrooms and teach. My love of teaching won the day.

Land Fantasies and Adventures

Chamu's elder brother Pachu was an English professor at Maharaja's College in Mysore. He was a very popular teacher, and a well-known cricketer and tennis player. Many of his students admired him and kept in touch with him over the years. When Pachu visited Bangalore—which he did a few times a year to attend cricket matches, visit friends and relatives and watch English movies—his former students would want to meet him. Among these students was one of the earliest chairmen of Bangalore's City Improvement Trust Board (CITB), which came into being following the City of Bangalore Improvement Act, 1945. The CITB started functioning to meet the residential and commercial needs of the city. Pachu's student and friend encouraged him to apply for a site (a plot of land) and told him that his family members should do so as well. Pachu was allotted a site on the main road in Vyalikaval, a locality near Sankey Tank and the grounds of the Bangalore Palace.

As luck would have it, one of Chamu's former classmates in Mysore was a building contractor in Bangalore. Chamu entrusted the building of the house on the Vyalikaval main road to him. Built of granite blocks, ground plus first floor, it was an imposing structure. It had a large pooja room as Chamu's mother had requested. Thangu, Chamu's sister, and I went to the Lalbagh Botanical Garden to get all the plants for the garden, including a *parijatham* tree. Chamu's mother liked the fragrant white flowers which she used for worship. Although the house was built with love and care, no one in the family was destined to live in it, and it was sold in the 1960s, well before we moved to Bangalore.

Pachu had encouraged his siblings to apply for sites in Bangalore. In the 1950s, sites in Bangalore were going for a nominal sum, a few thousand rupees in a prime locality. Pachu told Chamu that a site in Bangalore would be useful once Chamu retired. Chamu applied and was allotted a site. But we did not know where the site was.

When we moved to Bangalore in 1972 and needed a place to stay, we rented a house in the new suburb of Jayanagar in South Bangalore. The house was not the most convenient for us and there was no space for a study. Chamu initially housed his books in the basement, but the basement flooded with the first rains, and we were forced, in a sense, to look for another house. An additional reason for moving out was that our daughters' school was located some distance away on Palace Road. In those days, when there was no school bus, I had to drive them back and forth five days a week, all the way from South Bangalore to North. I came to know two other Jayanagar families who had to ferry their daughters to the same school, and they were happy to carpool, so that we could take turns. But it was still a long commute.

I've always had a deep fascination with property—houses and land. In fact, if I may digress here, when my father retired from Poona and moved to Tanjore, the rented house in New Town Colony was not the kind we could have lived in for a long time, and so he bought a site on the outskirts of Tanjore, in Rajappa Nagar. I was in my early 20s when construction on the house began and I would bicycle to the site every day to supervise. So, my interest in property, land and construction of houses goes back to my early 20s.

When we first moved to Bangalore, there was a period when I was not working. Once I would drop off the girls at school and Chamu would leave for the Institute, I would drive around in my black Fiat—no GPS to guide me—discovering new streets and new residential localities. There was not much traffic on the road in those days, and the tree-lined avenues and country roads were a delight to drive through. I would stop every now and then and ask people for directions. Bangaloreans were very friendly and in spite of it being a large urban area, the atmosphere was that of a small town in many ways. I didn't feel alienated. People would enthusiastically give me directions even if they were unsure. That sent me on many a wild goose chase, but that is how I got to know the city.

Once, when I was driving on St Mark's Road, I met a friend who directed me to Shroff's Estate Agency with its office opposite the State Bank of India. Shroff was very personable. In my very first meeting with him, he impressed me with his knowledge of the city and his experience. He asked me several questions: he wanted to know what area I was looking to move to, whether I preferred a new construction or an old bungalow, what was the size of my family, did I have a vehicle of my own or was the family dependent on public transport. I told him that proximity to my children's school and my husband's workplace was my priority. He said, 'Why don't we meet again, and I will take you and show you some houses.' I went home and reported the meeting to Chamu, who said, 'Not bad. Let's do it.'

Shroff had certain ideas about where we would like to live. He wanted to show us houses near the Bangalore Club, a much-sought-after neighbourhood. Early in our search, we saw a bungalow on Grant Road, near the Club. But Chamu vetoed it. He was clear he wanted to be nowhere near the

Club. He never aspired to be a member or spend time at the Club.

Shroff then showed us a house in Jayanagar, 1st Block, near the Ashoka Pillar. When it was erected in 1948, the pillar, a 20-ft-tall stone structure, marked the southernmost point of Bangalore, and was surrounded by fields. Though 1st Block was not near our daugthers' school in North Bangalore, it was a good residential area and we liked the wide streets and the bungalows. It was close to the Lalbagh Botanical Garden and Chamu could go for his walks there. The house Shroff showed us was No. 350 on 2nd Cross; it was a spacious ground-floor house. It had two bedrooms, a large living room, a spacious kitchen and a dining room. It was a traditional house with high ceilings, a pooja room and a traditional bathroom with granite flooring and a wood-fired *handa* to heat water. There was also a toilet outside the main structure of the house. Shroff took care to point out that it was 'a solid house'. I was also attracted to this house with its polished red cement flooring, which reminded me of my parents' home in Tanjore.

The property even had space for a small garden. Chamu was delighted to find a beautiful, mature, orange-flowering *champak* (magnolia) tree at the back of the house—and there was space along the long driveway to have flower beds, which pleased me. The neighbourhood seemed safe and quiet.

Soon after we settled in, we started going for walks. One day, we were hailed by a familiar voice, 'Hello, Professor Srinivas. So, you are my neighbour now!' Mr G.V.K. Rao was then the chief secretary to the government of Karnataka. He had facilitated the starting of ISEC and Chamu had been roped in to become the joint director of the Institute. Behind our house lived Dr Ram Prasad, who had started the Anand Diagnostics Medical Laboratory. On one of Chamu's early morning walks, he was pleasantly surprised to bump into

Dr Ram Prasad, who recognized him as Pachu's younger brother. Pachu had been his English professor at the Maharaja's College in Mysore. 'It's a small world,' Chamu said to me. We retain our connection with Anand Diagnostics. Even on my most recent trip to Bangalore, I had my lab tests done at Anand Diagnostics.

The Zamzama Hotel

Getting back to the story of the CITB site that had been allotted to us years ago, Chamu and I went looking for it with the possession papers in hand, soon after we settled into our first rental home in Bangalore. I had a memory of it being in a distant suburb of Bangalore, in one of the northern parts of the city with open fields everywhere and no proper roads at the time. The first time we set out, we came home without being able to locate the site. The second time, we went accompanied by one of the CITB field officials. He took us to an area where there was a huge open quarry and he pointed vaguely to a row of buildings beyond that quarry saying, 'That is your site.' The big board on the footpath skirting the quarry that led to the buildings read 'Zamzama Hotel'. Chamu and I looked at each other in utter bewilderment and asked the field official for an explanation. He had none to offer and simply shrugged his shoulders and said '*Hogona* (Shall we go)?' I was both extremely disappointed and infuriated that such a thing could happen. I made it my mission to go to the CITB office every couple of days to impress upon the officials that if indeed that was the site allotted to my husband, it had been illegally built upon.

I approached a friend of Chamu's who was a lawyer and he told me there was a lot of corruption and bribery involving land allocation and that we would not be able to persuade the CITB to give us an alternate site. It was at this time that we moved from our rented house in Jayanagar to our own bungalow on 2nd Cross in Jayanagar. I became friends with Mrs G.V.K. Rao and met Kanaka Padmanabha—both were my neighbours and lived on the next street close to the Ashoka Pillar. Sometimes, the ladies would meet for a game of badminton in one of the empty lots on the street. It was news to me that Kanaka's husband, Mr Padmanabha, was the chairman of the CITB which was soon to become the Bangalore Development Authority (BDA). I told Chamu I would take this opportunity to meet and talk with Mr Padmanabha about the site we had lost.

After a wait of many weeks, I succeeded in getting an appointment with Mr Padmanabha at his office in Kumara Park. The preliminaries took hours. After a long wait and being asked by various officials what my business there was, I was given a form to fill out and sign. Finally, I was ushered into Mr Padmanabha's chambers. His presence was not unfriendly, and he waved me to a chair in front of him. He was sipping coffee—a balding man in a suit. A few sips later, he asked if I wanted anything to drink. I politely declined. 'Now, how can I help you?' he enquired.

I launched into my story of how we had been allotted a site, how we had moved from Delhi and had then tried to locate the site, and found a hotel built on it without our knowledge. He listened patiently and asked me questions about Chamu, who he was and where he was from. He seemed to know who Pachu was because his eyes brightened and he said, 'Oh, I know Mr Parthasarathy.' Then with a smile, he said, 'This is an oft-repeated complaint. Let me tell you, Madam, once the site is allotted, it is no longer our responsibility. You have to safeguard it. Where do you live now?' I told him we lived not far from where he lived. He asked again, saying he knew the entire area. I told him we lived on 2nd Cross. 'So, you have bought the house behind my aunt Lakshmi Krishnappa's house?' I then told him that, yes, we had moved in recently. Then he turned the tables on me, 'Now that you have a house, why do you want a site? Sites are only allotted to those who do not have houses in Bangalore.' I responded by saying that we had paid for the site and we should be compensated for the site we had lost. I then said, 'The house is mine and the site that was in my husband's name is what I am here about.' He seemed amused by my response and asked me, 'What do you do, Madam?' I told him I was teaching at Delhi University, but I was not doing anything at the moment in Bangalore. He did not promise me anything, and I left saying I would see him again soon.

Chasing Down a Site

The next time I met Mr Padmanabha was by accident. I had gone to visit his wife, Kanaka, at their house a few streets away from ours. He walked in the door and was surprised to see me in their kitchen watching Kanaka demonstrate the making of *obburoti*—a delicacy of the Malnad region in western Karnataka. 'So, you know each other?' he asked. The next week, I returned to the BDA office to see him. After an hour's wait, I was ushered into his office. He said, 'I have some news for you, but I am not sure how it will work out. There is a stray site in Indiranagar. Would you be willing to take that?' I asked him where Indiranagar was. I was still discovering the city.

I wanted to go see the site and identify it. He briskly informed me that there was no time for that and that I had to tell him at once if I was interested. I answered in the affirmative. I left feeling quite pleased and told Chamu I had been successful in getting a site allotted to us. But it was not meant to be. A few days later, I got a call from the chairman's office, asking me to go over in person. Mr Padmanabha informed me that Chamu could not have the Indiranagar site because on the intervention of the chief minister, the site had been allotted to another retired official, a friend of the chief minister who, Mr Padmanabha informed me unnecessarily, 'is also an Iyengar'. He seemed interested in the coincidence that the official belonged to the same sect as Chamu. 'What do we do now is the question.' He went on, 'You have a roof over your head.' I once again told him he would have to make good the loss of the other site that was initially allotted to Chamu.

I made yet another visit to Mr Padmanabha's chambers a few weeks later and was rewarded with, 'I can allot you a stray site in Koramangala.' I didn't know where Koramangala was and was told that it was one of the new residential localities or 'extensions', as Bangaloreans called these new neighbourhoods, near St John's Hospital. Mr Padmanabha then told me we would have to pay as the site value was considerably more than what we had paid for the original site. I agreed. He asked me to return to pick up the papers in a month's time, which I did.

As time went by, I realized once again, that I was spending too much time on the roads, between our home and Palace Road, where ISEC was located at the time. My daughters' school schedule did not coincide with my work schedule. I left home at seven o'clock every morning to ferry my daughters and the other girls in the carpool to school, then dashed back home to pick up Chamu and drive once again to the Institute on Palace Road with him. It seemed such a waste of precious time, not to mention the sheer exhaustion of all that driving. So, I talked it over with Chamu and once more we were on the lookout for a house or a site, and this time we were determined to find one closer to our daughters' school.

Shroff was helpful as he had been before and showed us a house on Bore Bank Road—a beautiful old house with a gracious portico and a ground floor with four bedrooms. But I vetoed the house for the simple reason that it overlooked the railway line. All the trains from the South coming to Bangalore Cantonment Station and moving onto the City Station would thunder past the row of houses. Shroff also showed me a couple of newly built apartments that were just starting to change the landscape of Bangalore. I told him I had never lived in an apartment and wasn't thinking of moving into one now.

My temperament was such that I would take the car, fill the petrol tank and drive around—I did just that during the lunch hour at ISEC. Once, when I was driving near Mahatma Gandhi Road, I took one of the side streets and lost my way. I found myself on Brunton Road, a tree-lined, shady residential street with large bungalows. As I drove further, I stumbled on a vacant piece of land with a 'For Sale' sign. Then I tracked down the owner of the site who happened to be in the film industry and lived near the Cauvery Theatre, off Sankey Road. We clinched the deal and paid the owner quite a large advance. But when I returned to the site, I found that there was a collection of sewage water from neighbouring homes in front of the site. We decided against buying it and the owner of the site was good enough to return the advance we had paid. So once again, I was back on the search for a site.

This time, I decided to do my homework and drove around the areas close to my daughters' school. On one such exploration, I stumbled upon the area beyond the Cantonment Railway Station. This was a very attractive landscape with the Miller Tank bed and was in close proximity to the station, with the Palace Grounds on one side and the United Theological College (UTC) campus with its tall trees and lovely granite buildings on the other. Also, on Millers Road, across from the UTC campus, were the railway offices, public buildings set in large, tree-filled compounds. These were old English brick buildings with spacious verandahs. Further down was the Archbishop's House and opposite it was the *Eidgah* set in a mango orchard.

Rukka, Tuchi and Kittu outside the Jayanagar house

I followed the road and took a sharp turn to the left, not knowing where I was headed, stopping to ask a pedestrian what the name of the street was. He replied, 'This is Nandidurg Road.' I liked the look of the bungalows on that street. In those days, it was a quiet street. Many of the bungalows were set in large compounds with mature trees.

Once on Nandidurg Road, I turned into a newly carved-out street. The sign read, 'Ramayya Reddy Layout'. Brand new two-storey houses towered above the narrow lane. It looked like a new development and the streets were partially paved. When I later described the lanes and houses to Shroff, he remarked that I should consider investing in one of the houses, for they had just become available on the market and he happened to be the sales agent for many of them. He added, 'It will be within your budget, Mrs Srinivas, and you can indulge in your gardening hobby.' He was referring to the narrow strip of land around each bungalow. He continued, pointing out the advantages of these houses, 'There would even be a garage for your Fiat!'

I took Chamu to look at the houses during our next lunch break. But Chamu was not to be persuaded. He found the street cramped and took one look at the row of houses before he shook his head and said, 'Let's move along down the street.' At the end of Ramayya Reddy Layout Street, we turned right. I didn't know which street we were on, so I stopped outside one of the gracious old bungalows with an overgrown garden and, rather hesitantly, knocked on the front door. An elderly Parsi lady came to the door, and I explained that I was lost. She answered, 'This is the Parsi Dharamsala and you are on Benson Cross Road near the Cantonment Railway Station. If you follow the road, you will reach the railway lines.' I did drive down the road to the railway lines and to the Bore Bank Road where Benson Cross Road ended. Several short lanes took off from the Benson Cross Road, and I explored them. Chamu questioningly looked at me, 'What are you up to? And where are you going?' I told him, 'I don't know where I am going but I am just looking around.' He didn't have the time for a lengthy exploration of the area. So, I dropped him back at ISEC and returned to Benson Cross Road. I was simply enchanted by the old single-storey bungalows with wide skirting verandahs, tiled roofs and well-tended gardens. Many of the bungalows had two gates at either end of a curved semi-circular driveway. As a schoolgirl, I had read stories wherein sahibs and memsahibs would be dropped off by their drivers in such driveways. That was gracious living!

Old Bungalow

I wished I could live in a house like the ones I saw on that drive. I drove down Harris Road, past the Indian Social Institute, and was delighted to see a 'For Sale' sign. A dusty-looking dog was looking through the bars of a metal gate out onto the street. A metal chain and padlock on the gate were clear signs that trespassers would not be entertained. I rattled the gate for several minutes, the dog started barking, and after several long minutes, an elderly watchman came ambling up the driveway and informed me in Kannada, 'Madam will be coming soon.' Sure enough, the owner of the house soon returned. The dog jumped up to welcome her. I asked her if I could see the house. 'I like the area,' I explained. She invited me in, talking to me in Hindi, led me to the front portico and opened the heavy, ornate teak wood front door.

'There is no power today.' I looked at the house, with its spacious rooms: a large-sized room in the centre, with a living and dining room and bedrooms leading off on either side. At the back, there were a row of rooms and the lady waved in the direction of her watchman and said, 'Driver, watchman, khansama, aayah,' meaning the rooms were the living quarters for her household staff. She said, 'You talk to Mr Shroff.' I was delighted. I went back a week later with an old family friend who was an engineer and Mrs Hussain, the owner, was there. As we walked into the house, my friend said, 'Rukka, did you notice the structural crack from the foundation going up the wall? I would not advise you to buy this property unless you plan to demolish and rebuild it.' I was terribly disappointed but decided to give up on that property.

But Benson Cross Road kept haunting me. I went back again during my lunch hour at ISEC and drove down one of the lanes and this time, I turned left on Benson Cross Road. On my left, there was a really enormous property with a bungalow that faced Nandidurg Road and to my right were the solid, large Binny company* houses. The boards read 'Tipperary, Rother House and Chiddingstone'. I stopped opposite Rother House, admiring the beautiful stone building with the large garden surrounding it, bounded by a low stone wall. The houses reminded me of the Southern Command stone buildings in Poona, where I had lived as a child. Later, I drove down the street with Chamu to show him the locality. He said the houses and stone walls reminded him of Oxford.

*The Binny Mills—the Bangalore Woollen, Silk and Cotton Mills—was set up in 1884, one of the earliest steam mills in British India. It was taken over by the Chennai-based Buckingham and Carnatic Mills, which ran the mills for over a century.

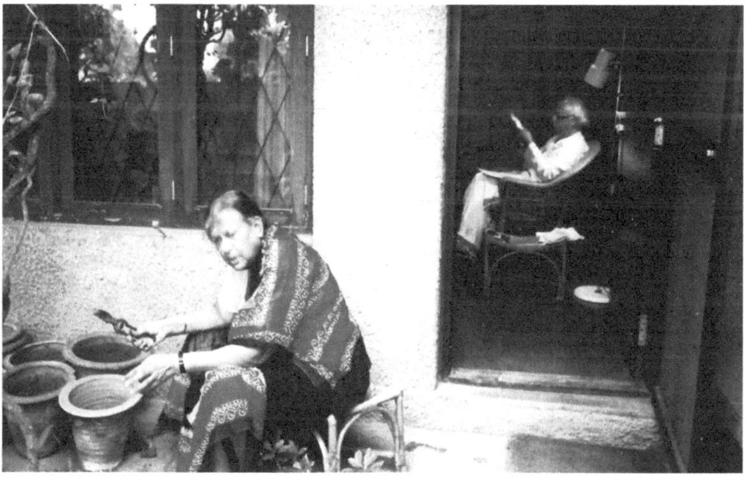

Evenings at Benson Cross

To the left and opposite Rother House was a vast empty lot! I stopped the car, looked over the short wall and spotted a mango tree and a jackfruit tree. That was the place I wanted. I found my way back to ISEC and that evening, I called Shroff and told him about my desire to live in that area. I described the site that I had seen. He immediately said, 'Oh! That is my friend Major General Bhatia's house and land. I'm not sure if that bit of property is for sale.' But he said he would talk to the Bhatias.

In a couple of days, Shroff came back to me with a very disappointing response: 'Well, Mrs Srinivas, Mrs Bhatia had carved out some plots of land facing Benson Cross Road, but unfortunately they have all been sold.' I didn't want to give up. So, I followed my nose and drove around the Jayamahal area near Benson Cross Road, and located a site facing the lake in the children's park. On informing Shroff about this, he said, 'Give me some time, I'll get back to you,' and he did. But the news was not to my liking. The lady who owned the land had been recently widowed and she was now dividing the site into three plots of 60 ft by 40 ft, and was asking for an exorbitant price for each.

A few weeks later, Shroff called me and said, 'You're in luck, Mrs Srinivas, the Benson Cross site has come up for sale by the new owner. He's suffered a heart attack and has been medically advised not to undertake a building project.' I then met Mr Talati, the owner, who, being a shrewd businessman, raised the price and insisted that I buy his architectural plan for which he said he had already paid the architect. I told Shroff that while I would consider the increase in price, I could not purchase the plan as it would not suit our family. We had to think of how to get the money. We did not have much savings and Chamu was hesitant to take a bank loan. But I persuaded him and when Shroff came back to us, we were ready. Much to my delight, the deal went through!

I was particularly happy about this site. We had managed to impress upon Mrs Bhatia that we would like the mango tree and the jackfruit tree to be included in the sale which was not part of the plot sold to Mr Talati. She charged what seemed to be an exorbitant price at the time for the two trees. Tara Chandavarkar, of the architects' firm Chandavarkar and Thacker, who had become a friend, entrusted a young and promising architect with drawing up a plan for our house. I supervised the building of the house, and went to the site practically every day just as I did with the building of my father's retirement home in Tanjore when I was in my late teens. The house took shape and within seven months, we moved in. It was 1976.

Chamu named the house 'Arakere' after his ancestral village near Srirangapatna. He said his family's roots were in that village. His father and mother had moved to Mysore for the sake of the education of their children. Selling the agricultural land in Arakere made it possible for Chamu and his brothers and sisters to go to university.

During this entire time, our site in Koramangala, which had been allotted to us in the mid-1970s, was lying vacant. I didn't want a repetition of the disastrous experience with our first CITB site and the Zamzama Hotel. Chamu's and my concern grew when the government enacted the Urban Land (Ceiling and Regulation) Act in 1976. Karnataka was among the first states to adopt the legislation that was intended to free up large parcels of land for housing the poor, by placing limits on the property an individual could own. This was the official reason given for the Act, but it led to a lot of chaos and did not achieve what it set out to. Instead, poor people and honest middle-class people lost their land. Though the Act was repealed in 1999, back in the 1970s we had no idea what the future held for the legislation.

So, in 1980, with the help of a local architect, we built a modest, two-bedroom house in Koramangala. It was a large site, 80 ft by 120 ft, and the single-storey bungalow stood with plenty of space for a garden. But we were never destined to live in it. The fear of losing the property with the enactment of the Urban Land (Ceiling and Regulation) Act and Chamu's argument that we did not need more than one house, as we would only live in one, led us to sell the house soon after we built it for the same price we bought the land for. When selling, I remembered what Chhaya Shastri, the astrologer in Ahmedabad, had foretold years ago that while we would own three houses we would only live in two of them.

A few years later, my hunger for land resurfaced. Coincidentally, the Futehally's, Zafar and Laeeq, invited us to their farmhouse in Hennur, on the outskirts of northern Bangalore—a drive of about an hour-and-a-half from Benson Cross Road. The Futehally's had moved from Bombay and made Bangalore their home. We fell in love with the well-planned and comfortable home Laeeq had constructed. And we learnt that Chandavarkar and Thacker were their architects too. The peace and quiet, the greenery and openness of the farm were so inviting. The house was in the midst of fields and groves of flowering trees. The only sounds we heard were birdcalls. Zafar showed us his horses, which he rode around the farm. He had built a study close to the house, where he would retire to write. Zafar, the naturalist and conservationist, was delighted that the area was ideal for bird-watching. He told us that he would go for long walks with his binoculars. Every visit to their home made me determined to buy some farmland. Zafar encouraged us to move there and be his neighbour.

As luck would have it, I located a six-acre plot of land for sale just down the road from where they lived. And we were able to buy it. We shared the land with a friend of ours. But Chamu was frequently travelling out of the country and I was teaching at Bishop Cotton Boys' School and had no time to build a farmhouse. At the time, the newspapers also reported a series of dacoities in that area, and one of the houses attacked were the Futehally's. We soon sold our land in Hennur, but I can't help thinking of what might have been.

The Street Where We Lived

Once we settled into our home on Benson Cross, Chamu and I resumed our routines. We explored our locality on our daily walks. As we walked down the street, we passed by the beautiful, single-storey bungalows with generous gardens around them, planted with shrubs and trees, creepers along the front verandahs, all of it looking a bit wild, not manicured, which we loved. I was told some of the bungalows were over a hundred years old. Many had built-in fireplaces but no ceiling fans, given the cool, hill-station climate Bangalore used to have. One of the bungalows to our right was the sprawling Parsi dharamsala, set back from the road. With tall trees surrounding it, it looked a bit spooky. Sometimes, we would see people sitting outside enjoying the evening air, sipping tea. Further down Benson Cross was the historic building of the YWCA that was later converted to an informal ladies' club. The road ended abruptly at the railway line.

Early morning, we would be woken up by the thudding of jackboots as a phalanx of 30–50 men in khaki shorts, singlets and metal-tipped boots would run in formation down our street. The one ahead would shout out orders and there would always be stragglers bringing up the rear. The men were on their morning exercise run from the grounds of the Territorial Army. Very often, a group of them would march to the beat of drums which would set off our dog, Kittu, who would rush to the gate and bark to defend us against the Territorial Army. The army also made its presence felt in the neighbourhood by playing music on loudspeakers. The music was an eclectic mix. Some mornings, we would be woken to the sound of 'Suprabhatam', the awakening prayer for Lord Venkateshwara, which would compete with the sounds of koels and barbets in the garden. In the afternoons, or for festival occasions—such as Diwali, Independence Day or Christmas—other kinds of music were blasted over the neighbourhood, including military marches, Christmas music and Hindi film songs. Residents complained of noise pollution, but it did not deter the Territorial Army.

Early residents of Benson Cross had purchased sizeable tracts of land next to the army grounds on which they had built small rental cottages. These dwellings really looked like they were from a bygone era. Cheek by jowl with these modest dwellings were the huge bungalows. Benson Cross Road was remarkable for its diversity as were many other localities around. You not only had people from different socio-economic backgrounds living close to one another but also people of different faiths and cultures—there were Coorgs, Mangaloreans, Bengalis, Malayalees, Parsis, Tamilians, and Muslim and Christian families.

Late in the afternoon, teatime at our home, the street would be taken over by schoolboys from the Quwathul Islam High School For Boys on Bore Bank Road. Also, in khaki uniform, they would walk in groups or cycle four abreast, ringing their cycle bells and blocking the road. Every few days, around 3.30 or four o'clock in the afternoon, I would find a few of these schoolboys in the front garden under the cherry tree, plucking the fruit. By the time I dashed out of the house to confront them, they would have jumped over the gate and sped off, sometimes leaving their school bags on the street for their friends to pick up.

Chamu would set out at six in the morning for a

contemplative walk. He would take a walking stick from his small collection. The stick also served to ward off stray dogs. On these morning walks, he would explore the adjoining locality of Jayamahal which would also give him a walk up a gentle incline. The houses in Jayamahal were larger and it was clearly a wealthier locality. We were told that one of the large properties belonged to a minor prince. Another had very high walls and we could only see the tops of trees inside the compound. Chamu once told me I must go and see the 'lake', an artificial water body in the Jayamahal Park. The park was a place where people would go for strolls in the evening and children would play. Some attempt at landscaping was evident. There was a grove of bamboo and a little wooden bridge over the water, in a Japanese garden style. In the afternoon, young boys would stone and torture the chameleons sunning themselves on the walls and Jayamahal ladies would walk round and round the park and then do 'deep breathing' together. There was a group that would laugh in unison, exercising their lungs.

Going for these walks, we became familiar with the denizens of Jayamahal and made many friends. A woman would regularly walk her Pomeranians, another, all dressed up as though going to a party, would walk briskly before her evening drink. We would invariably stop at Dr Bharatraj Singh's home near the park. He was an old friend of Chamu's, a retired professor of English from Mysore. Many an evening was spent recollecting their days in Mysore, including trips to the Bandipur forests and stories about the taxidermist brothers, the Van Ingens. I learnt much about Chamu's younger days in Mysore on these walks to Bharatraj Singh's home. Another deep friendship was forged with Mr C.S. Venkatachar, a retired official of Indian Civil Service. Mr Venkatachar also lived in Jayamahal and would meet us on our evening walks. Sometimes, he would walk down Benson Cross Road to our house. I would hear the clanking of our metal gate and a booming 'Hello Professor!' at exactly five in the evening. When I went out to meet him, he would ask, 'Are you ready? Is professor ready?' And we would set out for our walk. He became a very special friend.

Near the park was the Jayamahal Ladies Club. A number of events were organized yearly by the Club, including Durga Pooja celebrations by the Bengali Association that drew attendees from afar. The Ladies Club would also organize events with local schools and *balwadis**.

Returning from our walk, Chamu and I would stop briefly at the Hanuman Temple on Nandidurg Road. In the 1970s, when we moved to Benson Cross Road, it was a small and charming temple, almost like a woodland shrine nestled among the trees. The deity was hewn out of a large granite rock. The lone priest would offer us kumkum and do a simple aarathi. Dr Narasappa of the Cantonment Polyclinic, a Christian by faith, told me that the deity was his favourite and that he visited the shrine every morning before he went to work. Over the years, the prosperity of the temple transformed it. When I left Benson Cross in 2001, the temple was overbuilt with a hodge-podge of structures added to the compound. Devotees thronged the temple for elaborate morning and evening poojas. Sadly, the temple has lost its charm and the character that drew us to it years ago.

Our street, too, has undergone changes. On my travels, back and forth from the United States, I see dramatic changes during each visit. Many of the trees are now gone and mountains of garbage rot next to expensive homes. The bungalows with their surrounding gardens have been replaced by multi-storey

---

*Marathi term for preschools.

apartments. Rother House, Chiddingstone and Tipperary have been demolished and luxury apartments right next to the road have come up in their place. There are no backyards; indeed, hardly any space exists around these apartment blocks. One can tell the apartments that are occupied by the washing hanging out of windows and on balconies, but many remain empty.

It is treacherous to walk the streets these days. Traffic makes it difficult to cross Nandidurg Road and the pleasures of walking in the neighbourhood are lost. The elderly cannot go for a quiet constitutional and are trapped in their homes, invariably high-rise apartments, cut off from their friends and acquaintances in the neighbourhood. Gone too is the civility on the streets and the feeling that those whom you met on walks would greet you the next day. The feeling that we shared as a neighbourhood is now missing.

These changes began decades ago. Sometime during the early 1980s, Chamu's former student and colleague from the Sociology Department at Delhi School of Economics was invited to ISEC and he came home for early dinner. He had to take a morning flight back to Delhi and so a car from ISEC came to fetch him at 7.30 p.m. to take him to his hotel. It was a summer evening, so there was still natural light. We saw him to the gate and bid him goodbye as he got into the car.

Suddenly, a garish red car sped by on the narrow street and came to a screeching halt, the driver reversed at full speed and jammed the brakes within a few feet of where Chamu and I were standing. A youngish heavy man got down, raised his fist in the air, looked at Chamu and shouted, '*Aye Budda, khabardar* (Watch out, old man)!' Before we realized what he was trying to convey, he got into his car and sped away. Our guest was stupefied and shaken and urged Chamu, 'Professor, please go in. Bangalore has changed.'

When I married Chamu, we would regularly stop in

Bangalore for a few days on the way to visit his mother in Mysore. I would notice how different the Bangalore–Mysore region was compared to what I was used to in Madras and Delhi. It seemed to me that Mysoreans and Bangaloreans were gentle of speech and accommodating. '*Swalpa adjust madi* (Let's adjust)', seemed to be a guiding principle. In public settings, people were civil, even friendly. Over the years, the city has grown exponentially. Workers from all over India, as also people looking to invest in the city and the booming IT industry, have transformed it. Land values have skyrocketed. The beautiful old bungalows, that I once admired, have been razed to the ground to make way for multi-storeyed apartments that loom over the narrow streets. The beautiful city, where Gustav Hermann Krumbiegel planted thousands of blooming trees, is becoming treeless. The Bangalore I knew has certainly changed.

'Good Manners', sketch by Paul Fernandes

Doctor Murthy's Free Clinic

Dr V.K.R.V. Rao had introduced us to a family doctor in Jayanagar. Dr Anupama Niranjana was an unusual doctor, as she was also a Kannada novelist. Once we moved to Benson Cross Road in the Cantonment, a considerable distance from Jayanagar, I was keen (if not somewhat anxious) that we find a good family doctor in our new neighbourhood.

On one of our walks near our new home, I discovered a doctor's clinic just two streets away. I decided to go and see if the doctor would be suitable for our family. Around nine o' clock the following morning, I walked over and found a crowd: men and women of different ages, a few seated on the chairs in the verandah, others sitting on their haunches in the driveway and more standing inside the compound, with a few standing on the street. Most of the men wore veshti and a shirt, with a shawl thrown over their shoulders, for it was wintertime. What struck me was that almost all the women wore burqas. I went up to one of them and asked, 'What is happening here?' 'We are waiting for the doctor,' she replied in Hindi. One elderly patient standing near the entrance assumed the role of 'in charge' and asked those assembled, 'What number are you?' Each one had a square piece of cardboard with a number handwritten in green ink. It took me a while to understand him. 'First come first served,' he added. He was making sure that no one jumped the queue.

At nine o'clock sharp, the front door to the clinic, which

was one of the front rooms in the house, was thrown open by the doctor himself. Without looking at anyone in particular and with a movement of his head towards the inner room, he beckoned the first patient to enter. Inside a sparsely-furnished medium-sized room with windows opening onto the front of the house, Dr Murthy examined his patients. The furniture seemed identical to what I had seen in Dr Sabnis' clinic all those years ago. In addition to his desk, chair and an examining table, there was a tall stool with a metal washbasin and a jug of water next to it, a soap dish with a pink Lifebuoy soap and a hand towel.

Unlike Dr Mitra and Dr Sabnis, Dr Murthy wrote out prescriptions for medicines to be collected at the nearest pharmacy. His was a step above being a doctor and compounder.

Dr Murthy's appearance was unprepossessing and so was his voice, which was thin. In a gathering, you could pass him by without noticing him. What I did notice, though, the very first time I went in as a patient were two smears of sandalwood paste over his temples and when I mentioned my observation to Chamu, he identified the doctor as a Madhwa Brahmin, adding, 'In all probability, he is a practicing, orthodox Madhwa Brahmin.' This translated to Dr Murthy being very devout and a vegetarian. Hats off to him, I said to myself. He practices his religion and also Western medicine treating the ailments of patients that come from various castes, religious backgrounds and faiths.

I could tell the man by his garden—a space 25 ft by 20 ft in front of his house and where his clinic was located. A healthy tulsi plant used for worship occupied pride of place in front of the entrance. I recognized hibiscus, the original non-hybrid variety, bearing an abundance of bright red blooms; a few rose bushes; an oleander plant with pink flowers; a couple of jasmine bushes; and a *parijatam* (night-blooming jasmine). All these plants provided flowers for Dr Murthy's daily domestic altar and marked the man as the pious, uncompromising Brahmin I came to know. In the middle of one of the flowerbeds, a sign, 'Do Not Spit in the Garden', cautioned patients and tradespeople.

I figured out how Dr Murthy's system worked when, the following week, we as a family adopted him as our doctor. And he remained our doctor for the next 23 years. His methods worked smoothly and fairly. According to his longtime patient, Joseph, a bus driver from the neighbouring Chinnappa Garden, 'Every person gets to be examined by Dr Murthy. Where else will we get free treatment?'

When Chamu learnt that Dr Murthy offered free services, he became concerned for him. I was present when he gently explained to Dr Murthy that there was more than one reason why he should charge at least a 'nominal' fee for his services. His patients and the community at large may value his services more if he charged them, and then, he had three young children to educate! Chamu started leaving an envelope on Dr Murthy's table after every appointment. After a few years, Dr Murthy learned to charge a fee.

Scarlett Epstein, a well-known British anthropologist, stayed with us as our house guest whenever she came to Karnataka to do fieldwork. Once she arrived with a bad cold that developed into a flu the next day. I drove her to Dr Murthy's clinic. On being introduced, Scarlett reached out to shake hands with the doctor who very politely acknowledged her presence with a 'namaste'. He told me the next time I met him, 'I don't shake hands, I only examine.' He felt a namaste was preferable to shaking hands, as you don't have physical contact with people and therefore don't contract germs. In those days, there were no hand sanitizers, which created problems of resistant bacteria, or paper towels that contributed to trash. Dr Murthy would frequently dip his fingers in a basin of strong Dettol water placed on a tripod in his examination room and shake them dry. I was reminded of temple priests who would dip their fingers in sacred tulsi water before performing any ritual.

Dr Murthy also made house calls. He was a general practitioner who truly believed in the Hippocratic Oath. Many a time, he has responded to my midnight calls for help, arriving at our home on his two-wheeler moped. When his practice grew, he made house calls only to his older patients.

Over the years, Dr Murthy became a friend and we invited him to our daughter Tulasi's wedding and to the festive wedding lunch. He did come, in spite of his busy schedule in the hospital, but did not stay for lunch. When I met him the next time, he apologized saying, 'I don't eat out; neither at functions nor at restaurants.' At another time he told me he preferred South Indian rice meals. The reason he left Delhi, where he had a good and satisfactory job soon after graduating, was the 'chapatti culture'. For Dr Murthy, this meant both the food and what he saw as the aggressive culture of Delhi-ites.

Dr Murthy's sensibilities seem prescient today, when there is greater awareness of wheat (gluten) allergies and the safety of no-contact following the Covid-19 pandemic when even members of the British royal family were seen favouring namaste over handshakes.

On my visit to Bangalore in the winter of 2016 with Lakshmi, I had hoped to meet Dr Murthy, but was disappointed to learn he had left the area. We asked around but could not trace him. I was sorry I didn't get to say a proper goodbye. I took for granted he would be in the same house, continuing with his profession and way of life.

On that same trip, I fell ill and went for a consultation with Dr Charit Bhograj, a cardiologist. I found him to be a very caring and thoughtful human being and an excellent diagnostician. He got straight to the heart of the matter. Dr Charit had a way with words. When he learnt that I was due to travel back to Boston within a week, he smiled and said, 'Mrs Srinivas, may I invite you to be my guest at the hospital for just one night?' I am grateful for his timely care that made me travel-worthy.

These musings on family doctors lead me to dwell on the current status of medical care and its evolution, wherein hospitals are replacing the neighbourhood family doctor. Dr Murthy was not lacking in his sensibilities to the play of forces on the human body and I do believe that if necessary, he would have advised a consultation with a specialist. Today, I consult over a dozen doctors who are all super-specialists in their fields.

Morning Coffee

One evening, at dusk when I was in the kitchen making the dinner, I heard a weak knock on the side door. It was raining heavily, and I waited for a few minutes to see if indeed I had heard something, and when I heard the sound again, I opened the door slightly and turned on the outside light. A young girl was standing there. '*Yaaru Amma* (Who is there)?' I called out. She hesitantly stepped in, carrying a small bundle of clothes. She stood there in a cotton sari, soaked and shivering, her disheveled hair in a single plait down to her waist. She must have been in her late teens.

I asked her what she wanted and she fell at my feet crying, 'Please let me stay here.' I was a bit unnerved at the suddenness of it. I had never set eyes on her before. What was her story? And could I believe her?

I asked her how she found her way to my house. She said, 'I scaled the back wall and jumped in.' That was surprising because she would have needed some help to scale that high a wall. As her story unfolded, I learnt that the gardener of the big bungalow behind us was a well-wisher of hers. He knew all about her tragic situation and had helped her.

She said she was a live-in household help in one of the neighbouring houses where she looked after the cleaning and housekeeping. She told me she came from the Malnad area. The families there, for several generations, had been working on a coffee plantation of a senior planter who owned several hundred acres of coffee estates. She then told me her sad story.

Neither of us slept that night.

> You will not believe my story but my parents, grandparents and my sisters and brothers have no freedom of any kind. We have grown up being told that we are indebted to the *dodda mane sahibru* [master of the big house] and everything that we are and have is due to his kindness and generosity. But really, we have no freedom to live our lives and have to do the bidding of *Doddu Sahibru* [the Master]. None of us can leave the plantation because he and his family own all the bus services. So, all our movements are tracked and reported to him. I was brought from the estate to their house in Bangalore at the age of 15 when I was already engaged to be married to my cousin.
>
> I do all the housework and I help with the cooking. In the morning, I get up and make coffee. Madam will be in bed and I serve coffee to her downstairs and, on her orders, I take the master's coffee to him in his room upstairs. The first day I took the coffee up to the master, he asked me to close the door and said, 'Leave the coffee on the table.' Then he forced himself on me. I went downstairs but couldn't tell anyone. This happened frequently over the next few months.
>
> I found to my horror that I was pregnant and told the lady of the house. All she said was 'Oh, no matter. Come with me', and we walked down the street to the private nursing home. She went in first to meet the doctor and came out a few minutes later and told me, 'You stay here. In the evening, I'll come and take you home.'
>
> The lady doctor took me to a room and gave me an injection. I don't remember anything after that. When I opened my eyes, I found myself lying on a bench in the corridor. My mistress took me home in the car and

> ordered me to go and lie down in my room. I spent the next two to three days resting but was in pain. After that, I got back to doing all the housework. For a few months after, I was not asked to take coffee upstairs to the master. But I am now again expected to make coffee and take it to him.

Prema looked exhausted. She suddenly fell asleep on the floor of the living room. I left her alone to sleep off her exhaustion. It was early morning so there was no point in my going to bed. I made myself a cup of coffee and waited for Prema to get up. I was confused and wondered what to do with this young woman whom I felt very sorry for and who clearly needed help. I was debating whether to inform my friends down the road and ask for suggestions and help. In the meantime, Prema woke up and I gave her coffee.

Suddenly, there was a loud knock at the front door. I found two policemen in uniform standing on the doorstep and they handed me a warrant that ordered me to report to the police station nearby for 'harbouring a fugitive'. On seeing Prema, the two constables walked into the house without my permission and grabbed her. She yelled and screamed and held on to my sari. As they dragged her to the front door, her grip was so tight that my sari tore. They then asked me to hurry up and report to the police station. The policemen had come on a motorcycle, so I told them we would follow them in my car. The police station was not too far from the house, it took just a few minutes and as I parked my car, I noticed a blue sports car parked in front of the station taking up much of the space on the road. So, I parked on the side in the lane. The two police constables held Prema by the arm and led her into the sub-inspector's office.

I climbed a steep flight of stairs into a windowless room

where the sub-inspector was seated at a wooden table. He was facing the entrance and opposite him were seated two men—an elderly man with pitch-black hair and a younger, thin man with greying hair and a moustache. The elderly man, without even looking in my direction, said, 'Oh, this madam?! She is well known for enticing young girls in the area and has a girl-running business.' I was stupefied. In my naivete, I tried to explain that I was a respectable citizen of the area and to give them my credentials, I said I was a teacher at a well-known school. I also said I was horrified to hear of such accusations. But the police were strangely disinterested and did not seem to want to get to the bottom of this. It occurred to me that the constable had been compensated amply by the two men and he was willing to go along with their story. With a casual wave of his baton, the sub-inspector pointed to a hard wooden chair and said to me, '*Koothkolli* (Sit down).' He didn't seem very interested to hear what I had to say. He took notes in Kannada and I really don't know what information he was jotting down and what became of those notes.

At some point, he cut me short with a nod and told me I could go. Prema started sobbing loudly and clung to my waist. The constables took her away to an anteroom. I asked the sub-inspector what was going on. The explanation given was that she had run away from the gentleman's house and they were responsible for her since she was from outside Bangalore. I asked them what was going to happen to the girl. He said she would be sent to a 'destitutes' correction home' in Wilson Garden. I extracted the address from them. After my repeated questioning, the sub-inspector replied that Prema would be kept there for some time, after which she could return to her parents' home.

I went home feeling very upset, my nerves all jangled.

I was in a state of shock. I would never have imagined that such crimes were happening in my neighbourhood and that the police were allowing them to happen. The next morning, I left for the correction home in Wilson Garden to check if Prema had indeed been sent there. The address given by the police sub-inspector was non-existent. I drove around in the area. After many hours, I came across a small, nondescript hovel of a place on one of the side streets.

The superintendent there, an elderly woman, checked the name and said, 'Yes, she is here,' and then asked me, 'Who are you?' There were four or five women in that dark room. They were nameless, faceless shadows moving in the bare space. When I asked how long Prema would be kept there, the superintendent said she would not be able to tell me and explained the bureaucracy of the court system. When I went back there a couple of days later, I was told that the girl had been released and her employer had taken her. I do not know what happened to Prema.

The gardener from the big bungalow behind my house came over a few weeks later and told me Prema's story. It seemed to be a public secret in the neighbourhood that she was being held captive, in a sense, by her employers. According to the gardener, one of my acquaintances who lived on the same street knew what was going on in that house, yet did not want to involve herself. Instead, she told the gardener that I needed a maid. So, the gardener thinking he would help Prema, encouraged her to jump into my garden. He thought I would be a good employer for this poor girl.

The corrupt guardians of the law left me feeling defeated.

Street Vendors

Throughout the day, a number of vendors and those providing a variety of services for the household would walk or cycle down Benson Cross Road. On summer afternoons, the men who fluff cotton for mattresses would stop by the house. I would recognize them by the thrumming sound made by their single-stringed equipment. These were the days before foam mattresses. Cotton was said to be healthier as synthetic materials give off heat. Another very welcome service was the restoration of grinding stones in the kitchen—both the traditional *ammi kal* (stone) and the larger mortar and pestle. All that was needed in the way of equipment was a bag slung across the shoulder carrying two or three hammers of different sizes, metal chisels and a box of grease. After covering their eyes with some kind of protection, the men would deftly position their chisels and, using the right size of hammer, chisel grooves into the hard granite to make the stones rough again. After they finished, one could see the pattern they had carved in the stone. This was really an art. Both the men who did the work of fluffing cotton mattresses and those who restored grinding stones were from Tamil Nadu. You rarely find them walking in residential areas today.

Not all the vendors on Benson Cross Road would stop at our house or expect custom. In the forenoon, the fish seller would cycle down the street ringing the cycle bell and shouting, '*Meeeennnn* (Fish)!' He had his own clientele and would stop routinely at our neighbour's bungalow where transactions would take place at the front gate.

On summer nights, after our dinner, we would hear the call of '*nungu*'—the palmyra fruit that had travelled from Tamil Nadu to Bangalore and which would arrive by the evening train. The young men selling nungu would walk down our street at night calling out their wares, an invitation to come and enjoy this very special seasonal treat. The large palmyra fruit, encased in a fibrous husk, is wonderfully fragrant and gelatinous with a liquid inside like the coconut. On warm nights, it would serve as a welcome and refreshing end to a meal.

In the heat of the afternoon sun, the bicycle repair and shoe repair men would call out in a sing-song voice—'Shoe repairi! Cycle repairi!'—as they moved down the street. We could hear them wherever we were in the house. Sometimes, they would go by so quickly that we would miss them, and I would have to send the young woman who worked in our house, to run after them to call them back. The shoe-repair man was a handyman who also repaired leather belts, straps of school bags, wallets and leather spectacle cases. He carried a few basic colours of polish: black, brown and tan. He would offer to polish the items to make them look like new, and that too for free. Many of the leather workers came from the town of Vaniyambadi in Tamil Nadu and had been doing this work for generations. Shoe repair vendors vanished after a time and we then took shoes for repair to Rubin Moses on Commercial Street and invariably come back with a pair of new shoes for our daughters.

Other household activities like ironing clothes were also farmed out. As I remember, there was a time when the *dhobi* or washerman would come home once a week and collect our clothes—one set for washing and the other set for ironing. The dhobi would be instructed to bring back the ironed clothes the following day. He would usually come on a Saturday to our house, so that we would have freshly laundered and ironed clothes, including school uniforms, for the week. Today, the dhobi doesn't perform such an important function. In many homes, domestic help wash clothes on granite washing stones at the back of the house or in washing machines. Ironing can still be farmed out to mobile ironing services provided at street corners, mostly by men. The equipment consists of a wheeled wooden cart with a flat surface, a stone or slate slab to rest the hot iron and a hessian bag of charcoal. The men who did such ironing for households also carried a small pail for water to wet the clothes. In our neighbourhood there were a few men who did the ironing work. They each had their beat and took care not to encroach on another person's area. I would see Balu on Tirumal Rao Garden Road and Mani on Benson Cross Road and Binny Crescent. There was another man who stationed himself opposite the Hanuman Temple on Nandidurg Road. The convenience of that location was that he could sit on the steps of the house that opened onto the street.

Mani or Balu would take their positions in the morning by the roadside under a tree. Once they were spotted, household help would be seen depositing bundles of clothes with them. The ironed clothes would be ready for collection later that very day. On those rare occasions when someones else's shirts appeared among ironed clothes and a bed linen of yours went to a neighbour's house, they were quickly brought back. I wasn't conscious of it at the time, but the roadside ironing saved energy as a small bag of coal would iron the clothes for many households. Of course, it was coal and therefore not good to use, but the ironing services provided by Balu and Mani were more reliable, given the frequent electricity cuts.

The bangle seller was a draw for women and girls around the festival season and whenever there was a special function at home. In those days, bangles were mainly made of glass, and the bangle seller would carry them in large cloth bags slung on his shoulder. Inside the bag, the bangles were carried strung on long pieces of cloth or tape that were knotted into garlands. A couple of these 'garlands' slung across the shoulder served as advertising. In our neighbourhood, the bangle seller would announce his arrival with a song.

Roadside ironing

Strangely, the bangle sellers I remember were all elderly men. Once the bangle seller sat down with a crowd, more and more people would gather around. Sometimes, I would find him resting against the compound wall of a house with a group of women and children around him, blocking the road, enchanted by the beautiful colours of the bangles and their designs. There were many attractive varieties, some for everyday wear and some for special occasions. Some bangles would be of solid colours, even black. Green and red were in great demand, as they are thought to be auspicious colours. Other bangles would have specks of gold, or be striped or ridged, some would have spirals of two colours intertwined.

Some days would be good sale days and there would be a lot of bargaining and haggling over prices. The bangle seller would also fit bangles, gently pressing the women's hands, sliding the bangles onto the wrist two at a time to prevent breakage. He would also spin the bangles to check for any damages.

In some communities, between the seventh and ninth month of pregnancy, a *valaikaapu* (bangle ceremony) is arranged for the daughter of the house. Women relatives, friends and girl children are invited home. The bangle seller, a special invitee on such occasions, would arrive with boxes of beautiful bangles of different sizes. He would have been told what styles to bring. There would be a display of metal, glass and even plastic bangles—the latter being a recent addition. The atmosphere in the house would be festive and joyous; sometimes music played as the women, dressed in silk saris, crowded around the bangle seller. Everyone would be fitted with bangles, usually a minimum of four pairs. The mother-to-be would receive not only special gold bracelets as a gift from her mother but also at least a dozen glass bangles on each wrist.

What I missed on Benson Cross Road were flower sellers. Their absence was heightened when my friends from Malleshwaram visited me and brought strands of intoxicating jasmine, bright yellow chrysanthemums, salmon pink and orange kanakambaram (firecracker flowers), along with bunches of fragrant *maru* (marjoram) and tulsi—all the flowers and fragrant herbs used for worship by Hindus. Whenever I passed by the Hanuman Temple on Nandidurg Road, a short distance from our house, I invariably succumbed to the temptation of buying strands of jasmine from the flower seller stationed outside the temple. The flowers were strung on threads made from banana stem fibre and the seller would deftly snap the strand and use it to make a square packet with the banana leaf or a paper bag made from recycled newspaper. Those were the days when packaging was sustainable, though we never thought much about it then.

The Hand of Grace

By 7.30 in the morning, Lalitha, the vegetable vendor, would be at the gate at my parents' house, Number 8, Rajappa Nagar, in Tanjore. I would be woken up with a rattle of the metal gate and a shrill '*boni pannamma*' as she would call out to my mother to be her first customer for the day. If my aunt, Annam Athai, went carrying a wicker basket in her hand to buy the vegetables, she would be sent back with a request to call 'Periamma' (my mother) instead.

Lalitha lived with her three young children and her husband who, I learnt later from my mother, worked in a cycle repair shop not far from our house. Lalitha was convinced that her first customer of the day should be my mother, who had '*boni kai*'or the gift of good fortune—literally, 'the hand that bestows good fortune'. Our house was further down the street, yet Lalitha would not stop at any of the houses she passed by before she came to ours. After making sure she sold something to my mother, she would retrace her steps and go back to the houses she had skipped. Lalitha believed that my mother being her first customer would mean a good day for her with all her vegetables sold.

Buying vegetables from the street vendor was a morning routine. It was unheard of for a household in Tanjore to have a refrigerator in those days and so buying fresh vegetables for the day's meals was a regular practice. One summer in the 1950s, when I was home on vacation, I followed my mother to the gate and found this frail, young woman with an infant strapped to her hip with her sari, pushing a wooden cart piled high with an assortment of seasonal vegetables: orange pumpkins, white and green pumpkins, root vegetables like potatoes, elephant yam, banana flowers in a huge pod, banana stems, green raw bananas, ridge gourd, bitter gourd, along with 'English' vegetables like tomatoes, beetroot, carrots, cabbage, cauliflower and green beans. Sometimes there would be fresh peas in their pods, and Lalitha would draw my mother's attention to this 'Ooty' vegetable. A hessian bag slung on the handle of the cart carried lemons, chillies, ginger root, curry leaves and bunches of coriander leaves. This was a veritable market on wheels.

Lalitha could not afford a weighing scale, but she would gauge their weight by picking up the vegetables in her hand. After a quick mental count, she would say in Tamil, 'That will be 12 rupees, Amma.' Accepting the money, Lalitha would gratefully touch her eyes and forehead with it. She would then proceed to swiftly touch all the vegetables in her cart with the money given by my mother before putting it under a layer of gunnysack over which she had arranged the vegetables.

There were certain conventions that governed the transaction. Along with the vegetables my mother bought, Lalitha would add a handful of green chillies, a piece of ginger root, some curry and coriander leaves and a lemon, and say, '*Inda kosuru* (Take this gift)'—a free addition important for building a relationship with the customer.

In Bangalore, too, vegetable and fruit sellers would push their wheel-carts down the street early in the morning. Some would be on bicycles. Mornings were a busy time for me, as I would be in a rush to get ready for work like many other working women, but I would take the time to see what vegetables and fruits were in the cart, and which would save me a trip to the market. Some vendors would specialize in one or two items: bananas, guavas or tender coconut. Others would have a variety of greens and spinach.

Vegetable vendor

In the 1970s, when I lived on Benson Cross Road, there was a repeat of what I had encountered every morning in my mother's home in 1950s Tanjore. A Tamil-speaking woman would bring vegetables in a cart and knock on our gate, impatiently calling out to give her boni. I would walk out with a basket to help her make her first sale. Little by little, I learnt her life story and her daily routine. Every morning at four, she would push her cart to the City Market to buy vegetables at a wholesale rate and walk back with a laden cart to the Cantonment, her beat for selling the vegetables. Even if I told her that I didn't need vegetables that day, she would refuse to leave and keep clanking the metal gate insisting that I buy something, 'maybe a quarter kilo of tomatoes', anything to satisfy the boni. At times, this would become a problem, as I had to rush to work. But the woman would plead with me, saying, 'At least buy some lemons. I need your boni.'

The belief that the first transaction of the day is important and that certain people, their 'hands' or custom would bestow good fortune on the seller, is inherent in such negotiations. Some customers have 'the hand of grace' evidence of magic in commercial transactions.

Customers who are so identified by the seller may feel obligated to purchase something. I certainly felt so whether I needed vegetables or not. Boni also meant that you couldn't pay later, money had to exchange hands, even though it may not be the entire amount. Some households had monthly accounts with the vegetable vendor, but with me, the vendor would insist that I pay some amount in cash every single day, even if it was a few coins. I had to make sure I had a few rupees handy every day for her.

In spite of all the changes that have occurred in Bangalore, including its demographics, its information technology and corporate culture, the practice and belief in boni remains. On a recent visit to Bangalore, I was staying with friends near Benson Cross Road, and I clearly recognized the voice of the woman who used to sell me vegetables as she called out '*Vaa maa, boni pannamma* (Come and give me boni).' She was tracking down her favourite clients who would bring her profits for the day. I was both surprised and pleased that she remembered me as she asked me in Tamil, 'What Amma, where had you gone?'

Now when I think back, I wonder if Annam Athai's personality and other traits had anything to do with the vegetable sellers not approaching her for boni. Annam Athai was brusque in speech and she was not gentle by nature. And as I mentioned before, there was talk among women relatives that Annam should be discouraged from making pickles because 'her body was heaty', evident in the pickles she made, as they would develop fungus. Again, if Annam Athai ground batter for dosai, it would over-ferment and there would be a bitter taste to the batter; curd she set would go sour. Even the vegetable seller who was not privy to such information seemed to sense that Annam Athai did not have the hand of grace.

One morning, in 1972, a short while after we moved to Bangalore, I walked into Bhagatram's sweet shop on Commercial Street. I happened to be his first customer for the day. He waved the few rupees that I gave him reverentially in front of two framed photographs, one of an ancestor who may have been his father and the other of a spiritual leader, before he dropped the money into a metal box. I smiled saying, '*Boni, kya*?' He responded with his friendly smile.

I can recollect many such instances. For example, in the Malleshwaram Market on Sampige Road—and this was in the 1970s when many of the fruit and vegetable stall-owners were Hindus—if I stopped by a stall even momentarily and moved on, a banana or a bunch of curry leaves would be thrust in my hand with a '*boni maa*?' and I would feel compelled to buy it.

Boni is not confined to the sale and purchase of vegetables or food alone. At a shoe store in Karol Bagh in Delhi, I saw the principle of boni in practice. The daily fortunes of the store were linked, by pure chance, to the first customer whom store clerks would try and persuade to buy 'something, at least buy a pair of socks'—socks being a minor expense of a few rupees, but good enough for the boni. Clothing stores subscribed to the same belief. But I tend to believe this was truer of stores owned by Hindu proprietors.

Back to Bangalore, and to our friends' home where I was staying. At breakfast time, we heard the familiar voice calling out to clients to 'make boni'. My friend smiled knowingly and said, 'This is her ruse, she succeeds in making each housewife feel *she* is special.' Maybe, but it is a winning strategy and perhaps that is why it has withstood the passage of time.

Living by Bread Alone

Early evening brought the bread man. In our area of Benson Town, both Koshy's department store on St Mark's Road and the Nilgiris Bakery on Brigade Road had door-to-door delivery of bread every day of the week, except Sundays. Freshly baked loaves, the brown inviting crust smelling yeasty and warm, along with soft, spongy buns would be delivered home. I recognized the click of the gate and the ring of the bicycle bell and the breadman's call 'Bread!' It was such a familiar and welcoming call each day. I would choose as many loaves as I needed and, with a 'Thank you, Madam', the bread man would cycle away. He carried a little diary in which a page was devoted to each customer, where he would keep track of the dates of sale and the number of loaves sold at each house. Health-conscious families would order 'brown bread', which was dark brown in colour and supposedly made of whole wheat. Another variety of bread that was popular with children was the 'milk bread', slightly sweeter in taste and spongy soft.

My childhood friend from Poona, Paru, and her mother, Jaane, lived on Lavelle Road, which was close to Bishop Cotton Boys' School where I taught, making it easy to drop by and visit them frequently. One afternoon when I was visiting, their cook, Kitty, responded to the doorbell and came back with a high-dome loaf of bread. As she passed me by, I smelt a one-of-a-kind warm, fresh loaf. I remarked on how wonderful it smelt, and Jaane, who must have been well into her 70s, offered me a slice toasted with ghee. It was heavenly! The bread was full of holes and was very soft, the texture unlike other commercial breads available at the time. The high dome crust was an added bonus.

After that, every time I visited Jaane she would make sure to give me a loaf to take home. Realizing what a chore it must be for her, I asked her if I could also get the bread delivered home. One evening, I just happened to be at Jaane's when the bread was delivered. The breadman was on a cycle, a lean, middle-aged Muslim, tanned from all the time he spent on the road. He had two large cotton bags filled with loaves dangling from either handlebar. When I requested that he deliver the bread to Benson Cross, he refused at first, saying it was not part of his circuit. I learnt that he was the proprietor of Raffles Bakery and it was pretty much a one-man show. The bread would be baked in the morning and ready by about 3.00 p.m., after which he would start his rounds on the cycle to distribute it.

After I met him a couple more times at Jaane's place, I persuaded him, promising him that it would not be just one or two loaves, but many more if he came beyond the Cantonment railway station. He reluctantly agreed and started delivering the bread to us. In order to keep my promise, I used to buy three to four loaves, keep a couple for my family and distribute the rest to my friends in the neighbourhood who became hooked on the bread. In fact, the bread has even made its way to Mysore, to Chamu's sister's home, and to Delhi when his nephew visited us and took a couple of loaves with him.

Raffles Bakery was located behind the Russell Market in a predominantly Muslim area. It was next to the Taj Hotel and Restaurant, famous for its biryani. Wheelbarrows, cows and delivery tempos blocked the narrow lanes. The area had many old furniture shops, cane shops, cheek by jowl with kebab and biryani stalls, with an adjoining wholesale fruit market. There were many other treasures hidden there, if only one had the time to browse and explore.

Some years later, the proprietor of Raffles Bakery suddenly arrived home one weekend on a moped and stood at my front door with a very pretty young girl whom he introduced as his daughter. He wanted her to be admitted to a particular school for which her proficiency in English was not yet up to the mark. He said Paru had suggested that he ask me to give her tuition in English. I did not have much time due to my commitments at Bishop Cotton, but I did not have the heart to refuse him, and so I said I could teach her on weekends. After that, he would drop her off on Friday evenings and Saturday and Sunday afternoons. I did my best to help her. I was happy that she wanted to continue with her education. She must have been all of 13, but she was a determined young girl.

Suddenly our breadman disappeared and there was no response from his workplace. This was after I had tutored his daughter, so I couldn't ask her what had happened. I had a telephone number for him, but there was no response. After some months, he came by on a two-wheeler scooter that he had purchased second-hand. It was a weekend. He showed us the scars on his body and said that he had had an accident. He was unable to ride his bicycle anymore. He told us he had taken a loan to buy the scooter and very hesitantly asked us if we could help him clear part of his loan. He was a genuine person and so Chamu immediately wrote him a cheque and told him that he hoped he would recover soon. Although friends over the years have asked about him, we were sorry to have lost touch with him.

The Veteran

One Sunday morning, five-year-old Dhanam, our domestic worker's little girl, came running in from the front garden, where she was playing, and announced, 'Amma, Kurchi Thatha has come!' At the gate, I found my friend waiting to be let in. Seated in a wheelchair, high up on a pile of newspapers and with stacks of papers on either side of his seat and another pile on his lap, he was one from a group of *raddi paperwala* or *kabadiwala*—men who were self-employed and would take away old newspapers, books, empty bottles, cans, broken pots and pans and other unwanted items families would have thrown away.

Kabadiwalas were a crucial link in the process of cleaning out one's home and getting rid of unwanted goods. They facilitated the reuse or repurposing of these items and performed an important role in recycling. On our street, kabadiwalas would go by either on foot or on cycles, shouting '*raddi paper wala*'. My neighbours warned me not to let them in. There was a growing suspicion attached to kabadiwalas as stories circulated of such individuals breaking into homes.

One day, when I was returning home from Bishop Cotton Boys' School, I saw a man in a wheelchair going down the street. He had stacks of newspapers all around him. I braked the Fiat abruptly. When I asked if he would come home to collect my old newspapers, he nodded and promised to come the following Sunday. I gave him my address. This brief and chance encounter led to many years of our association.

True to his word, he turned up mid-morning the following Sunday, with a good-looking young man pushing his wheelchair, whom he introduced as his nephew. He spoke fluent English and seemed educated. I brought out all the newspapers—*The Hindu*, *The Times of India* and *The Indian Express*; exercise books that my daughters had set aside to be given away; empty glass bottles, some with lids, some without; empty tin cans; and other broken pots and pans. He reached for the weighing scales dangling on the side of his wheelchair and his nephew helped to bundle the papers into neat manageable stacks, which he then tied with twine. These bundles were then weighed. He produced a little diary in which he jotted down the final weight and the cash he owed. Calculations were done mentally, after which he told me how much he would give for each category of item—school books, newspapers, bottles and cans. Then he reached into a cotton satchel slung across his chest and handed the money to me. This became a routine. He was very regular in his visits. We would chat in English or Tamil, both of which he spoke fluently. Sometimes I offered him tea, which he would sometimes accept. I was delighted to find he also took old garden hoses, broken bits of pipe, bits of wire, metal buckets and so on. But he did not take clothing, rope, shoes or old spectacles.

He may have looked older than his age, but I thought of him as being in his early 50s. He had a thick walrus moustache and the wisps of grey hair on his balding pate were protected with a cotton cap with visor. He wore a black cotton waistcoat with many pockets, over his faded shirt. His knees were covered with a black-and-yellow checked blanket. I noticed that he sat very upright in his wheelchair and gave the impression of being in command of any situation. He had an undeniable presence.

His was an unusual story. Once, he told me he was born

a Hindu, but at the Red Cross Society the padre gave him a metallic cross which he wore ever since. I never learnt his name despite my asking him.

After I met him a few times, I picked up courage to ask him how he got into this work. He replied in Tamil, 'There was no other option,' as he slightly moved aside the blanket covering his knees, and I saw that his legs in grey shorts ended in stumps. He told me he was a war veteran. One day, he suddenly found himself at the Red Cross Society in Ulsoor, recovering from the amputation of both legs. He asked to be discharged and was thinking of various ways of being self-employed. He added that he had been doing the work of collecting newspapers and household junk for over 15 years and knew every street in the Cantonment, where there were many patrons who had helped him over the years. He now lived in a room on Narayan Pillai Street with his nephew, not far from the newspaper depot, the wholesale godown, where he sold all his day's collections. I admired his independence and his spirit in the face of adversity. He is an inspiration.

The Uninvited Guest

When I taught at Bishop Cotton Boys' School, I would leave home at seven in the morning, which was too early for me to have breakfast with Chamu. I would pack either a sandwich or an *aalu parotha* or some other dry snack in a sandwich box and place it carefully with some fruit in the glove compartment of my Fiat, MEQ6816. During the short break around 11.00 a.m., I'd have a bite of something I had packed while sitting in my car in the school grounds. I would then rush back to class, and eat the rest of my snack at lunchtime. My colleagues at school wondered why I didn't have lunch with them in the staffroom. But my habit was to do a little reading before class and to collect my thoughts before I faced my students. This was my routine for all the 10 years I was at Bishop Cotton. In the evening, on returning home, I would clean out the glove compartment.

On one occasion, though, a meeting regarding the end of the academic term dragged on till late in the evening. Later, I had to rush home to prepare dinner for Chamu and myself. In those days, Lakshmi and Tulasi were at university in the United States. Chamu, as usual, was waiting for me. Over dinner, I told him about the happenings at school in great detail. He was, as always, a very interested listener. He not only appreciated my interest in my students, but, I think, he also admired my enthusiasm and the diligence with which I prepared for school, though he would joke about it and ask, 'Is the schoolgirl ready?' when he came downstairs for breakfast.

My car needed attention and I had planned to take it to the service station on Benson Cross a few days after school closed. There was some delay—perhaps I was slightly under the weather, perhaps we were preoccupied with other things, I don't remember the details, but I didn't take the car to the service station for some time. Since school was closed for the holidays, I didn't open the glove compartment. When I decided to take the car for repairs and reached into the glove compartment to retrieve my driver's licence and car insurance papers, I found, to my horror, a small pile of finely shredded paper. The leather wallet, which contained the car papers, looked like it had been chewed through and what remained were bits of leather. What had happened and what was I to do?

I called Mr Seth, the garage owner, to come and pick up the car and told him about the damage done to car papers in the glove compartment. I had removed the shredded bits of paper and put them in a plastic bag, which I showed him. When he inspected the car, he found that wires that came into the glove compartment from the engine had been chewed through and there were mice droppings in the glove compartment and in the car. He smiled and said, 'Oh, this happens frequently with mice, I will seal it.' It appeared that mice had been regularly visiting my car, perhaps even living in it and may have been riding around in the car with me!

Our roomy garage was a refuge for rodents and insects. We had stored old newspapers, boxes, empty bottles, cans and pieces of wood. The mice must have found it a hospitable place, where they could carry on with their activities undisturbed.

The mystery of the glove compartment was solved, but how could I ever drive without my licence and insurance papers? Mr Seth offered to drive me to the Regional Transport Office (RTO) in Indiranagar. I took the shredded papers with me as evidence. The official at the RTO summarily dismissed me saying, 'Come back after a week.' On the way back to Benson Cross, Mr Seth explained to me that if only I had offered the official some 'compensation', he would have issued fresh papers.

Now the problem was I had no photocopy of my papers, so I knew neither my licence number nor the date on which it was issued. When I went back to the RTO and asked if they had a record, the official sent me to a godown—a big storeroom behind the office. He placed a big pile of books on the table and said if I looked through them, I should be able to find my name and licence details. So, I combed through the dusty volumes and located my name and licence information. Fortunately, at the end of the day, I could breathe a sigh of relief that I had succeeded. But when I went back, I was told I had to take another driving test. I had no option but to comply. At the time, I also applied for an international driver's licence. When I came home waving the fresh papers, Chamu smiled and remarked that what we think of as something so small can cause such havoc.

The Champion

There was a void in our lives when our beloved Kittu passed on. Chamu and I could see that Lakshmi and Tulasi missed his companionship.

Kittu's doctor was Dr Kapur, a veterinarian who had retired from the army. He lived in Defence Colony in Indiranagar. Dr Kapur had branched into dog breeding post his retirement, and his Dachshunds and Alsatians would have a few litters every year. Chamu and I decided to get a Dachshund puppy for the girls and when Dr Kapur's dog had a litter, he invited us to select a puppy. It was a sunny day and all the puppies were out, playing in the yard. Lakshmi liked the tiniest, the runt of the litter, as she found him the most entrepreneurial and adventurous.

Dr Kapur had already given names to the puppies. He told us they were pedigreed and the sire was bought from Germany. Cherokee, which was the puppy's name on the pedigree certificate, came home curled up in Chamu's beret. He was an adorable little fellow with a will of iron. He would twist us around his little paw and have things done his way. He started out with his bed in the girls' room upstairs but would be wide awake at midnight and start yelping. He missed his siblings and mother. So, I would go and run up and down the room with him, to play with him and try to keep him occupied in the hope that I would tire him out. Soon, Cherokee realized that there was a more comfortable bed in the next bedroom and we suddenly found him jumping on Chamu's and my bed, where he pushed his way between us and slept with his head on the pillow.

Cherokee understood several words and sentences and would infer a lot from the tone of voice. By observing our actions, he could anticipate what would follow. He loved his evening walk and we had to be careful and spell out the word because if we uttered it, he would start jumping up and down in a frenzy of anticipation, bark excitedly and run to the front door and back, waiting to be put on a leash. While Kittu was fed on a mostly vegetarian diet, Dr Kapur told us what he fed his dogs. So, I religiously went to the meat stalls in Russell Market and got the choicest cuts of mutton with the fat trimmed off and mutton bones. I would boil the meat and bones with rice and vegetables. Cherokee loved this stew! When Dr Kapur came to see him, he warned us against a rice diet, which would lead to obesity problems in later life.

When Cherokee was about two years old, Dr Kapur encouraged us to enter him in the Bangalore dog show held at the Rajendra Singhji Stadium in the army grounds. Chamu and I were not keen, but we thought it might be an interesting experience for the girls. I went there with Lakshmi and Tulasi and of course Cherokee, who was initially nervous about this new experience. Lakshmi was equally nervous for Cherokee, but Tulasi was brave enough to walk him in the show. As Cherokee went by the judges' table, one of them remarked to her, 'Young lady, you are not leading him, he is leading you!' To our complete surprise, he was judged 'Best of Opposite Sex', narrowly missing 'Best of Show', and was awarded a silver cup.

Cherokee

What we didn't anticipate was the immediate interest dog breeders showed in Cherokee. We were plagued by many phone calls. We said we would leave it to Dr Kapur, who talked us into entertaining one such caller. The caller brought his female Dachshund to meet Cherokee. But Cherokee barked and barked and viewed the intruder with suspicion. He then ran round and round the garden and hid under the car in the driveway. The dog owner was disappointed and left. Cherokee appeared relieved and went about his routines.

Two Markets

When we moved to Bangalore, walking on the streets was a pleasure. It was a safe city and the climate was moderate. Winters used to be chilly, but it was never too cold to go for a walk. Many of the streets were tree-lined avenues. Every time we drove along these avenues or went for a walk and saw the magnificent canopies, Chamu would remember Krumbiegel's plan for the city and remark upon his planting for 'serial blooming', which kept the trees in bloom for a good part of the year.

Gustav Hermann Krumbiegel, a German botanist, garden designer and one of the chief architects of the Lalbagh Botanical Garden, introduced thousands of trees and flowering plants in Bangalore. He was responsible for planting serially blooming trees along the main arterial roads. The spreading canopies of Gulmohar with its flame-coloured flowers, rain trees (or as children used to call them, 'powder puff' trees for their delicate pink flowers), the African tulip tree, bluish-purple jacaranda, wild fig, varieties of acacia, fragrant champak and others, shaded the streets and cooled them while providing shelter and food for birds, bats and insects. In fact, Krumbiegel was instrumental in Bangalore getting the name 'Garden City'.

In the 1970s, the city corporation would be busy monitoring the planting of saplings along the streets in suburbs and residential extensions or layouts (as they are called in Bangalore). The open spaces and vegetation increased biodiversity in the city. They attracted many birds whose calls were a welcome sound every morning and evening. On Nandidurg Road, the wild fig trees attracted both birds and bats. Only later did we learn that bats were important for controlling the insect population, especially mosquitos, which had created many health problems in Bangalore.

As I've said, the first locality we lived in after moving to Bangalore was Jayanagar in South Bangalore. In the 1970s, Jayanagar had gained worldwide recognition as the largest (covering the most area) residential suburb in Asia and one that was 'modern' and very well-planned. Many of our neighbours and friends told us that it was a very self-contained suburb with all the amenities and that we wouldn't have to go to the centre of the town for any shopping needs or medical care. There were even movie theatres nearby, the Nanda Theatre being one of them.

As a family, we would walk from our home in ninth block Jayanagar to the commercial section of fourth block for our marketing and this would be at least thrice a week. Sometimes we would take Kittu, who enjoyed the walk. Jayanagar had a new and very well-laid-out fruit and vegetable market. It was clean, orderly and safe, and a pleasure to spend time strolling through it. One of Chamu's relaxations was a walk to the market. He often told friends that such pastimes would take away the stress of his work.

When we moved from Jayanagar to Benson Town in North Bangalore, neither I nor my daughters knew the area. Chamu, of course, had relatives in the suburb of Malleshwaram, whom he would visit from Mysore when he was still a student. His aunt, Srirangamma, was a well-known public figure in Malleshwaram and she lived on 18th Cross Street. But at the time, we didn't know other parts of North Bangalore, including the area called the Cantonment.

After living in Benson Town for a while, we realized we

were located between two very different markets. Nearby, there was the Russell Market off Infantry Road, about 10 minutes by car from our home. Further away was the Malleshwaram Market, and each had its own distinct character and clientele.

Russell Market

Named after the municipal commissioner T.B. Russell and dating back to 1927, Russell Market was a wonderful place to explore. I would drive to the market in my Fiat, usually on a Saturday when Chamu was home, and park opposite the tonga stand. Sunday trips were to be avoided, as on Sunday mornings churchgoers would throng the St Mary's Basilica opposite the tonga stand and it would then become impossible to navigate the area and find a parking spot.

Russell Market

Even before people entered Russell Market, they would come across vendors on the pavement in front of it, selling lemons, jasmine and newly-hatched chickens, even puppies—a heart-wrenching sight. One of our friends bought a puppy from Russell Market, determined to give a loving home to a street dog rather than opt for the status symbol of owning a pedigree. That is how Russell K. Russell—'K' for '*katnai*' (street dog)—we were told, came to lord over a large property in the Cantonment.

Russell Market had close to 400 stalls. On either side of the main entrance were flower stalls with colourful and fragrant blooms in metal buckets. The intoxicating fragrance of roses, chrysanthemums, carnations and tuberose enticed shoppers to splurge. Whenever I went to the market, I would come home with bunches of flowers and especially tuberose for Chamu. The flower market was a different olfactory zone from the tonga stand, with its strong smell of horse dung, that was just outside, a few feet away on the street.

Sketch of Russell Market by Paul Fernandes

Unlike markets in Jayanagar, in those days Russell Market had a greater variety of vegetables, including 'English vegetables'—

celery, lettuce, red radish and avocados. Shopping there meant we would occasionally have a Western salad, after carefully washing the lettuce leaves in potassium permanganate solution and saline. I would also make soups with celery and carrot, and serve it with garlic bread croutons and bake a vegetable-cheese casserole. This was a welcome change from the usual Indian menu.

The fruit section at Russell Market had a large variety of local tropical fruits: mango, *chickoo*, jackfruit, different types of bananas, papaya as well as custard apple, pomegranate, guava, *mosambi* (sweet lime), oranges, grapes and pineapple. It also had seasonal peaches, cherries and the plums called 'Ooty plums'. Chamu liked pears more than apples and we found a variety of pears that he was fond of from his Oxford days. In later years, kiwi from Australia and New Zealand, durian from Southeast Asia or Malaysia, and dragon fruit from Thailand found their way to the market. Like the Jayanagar Market, here, too, the vendors were very civil and visiting the market also meant a chat with them. What I found remarkable was that vendors remembered a shopper's or a family's favourites. Upon seeing me or Chamu, they would hold out pomegranate, pears or chickoo, and the vegetable sellers would tempt us with shiny double beans, all of which were our favourites. Dry fruits were also available and would go into the shopping basket for Chamu, who liked to snack on them while working.

Not satisfied with wandering around the vegetable and fruit markets, I would walk across to Richard's Square and Old Poorhouse Road. Richard's Square adjoined the Russell Market and there I would very often chance upon light English crockery, teacups and saucers, baking dishes made of glass, ice cream cups and so on. There were open-air stalls, selling chandeliers from Chettinadu, even old lamps and furniture. From Richard's Square, I would walk to Old Poorhouse Road and stop by at the wicker furniture stalls. In fact, we ordered many of the pieces of furniture we have in our Benson Town home from these stalls.

Old Poorhouse Road was like a scene from a Charles Dickens novel. The dilapidated stalls and shops on the street were a surprising treasure trove of grandfather clocks, antique cuckoo clocks, pocket watches from a bygone era, metal spittoons and old medical kits. Wooden and cardboard boxes that smelt of dust and mould held faded photographs of the freedom struggles, of Gandhiji, Nehru, scenes from the Satyagraha Movement and other images of British India. I was tempted to buy some of these photographs, but when I asked the price, the shopkeeper was evasive and asked me to return the following day. Of course, that was not possible. When I did return with Chamu a week later, he said that those had been sold but there were others to buy if I was interested. The prices had increased, actually skyrocketed, and I couldn't afford to buy any. So sadly, I went home empty-handed. While browsing, I dug up coloured portraits of British men and women in formal dresses, along with Tanjore paintings, all of which evoked other times and places. My spending time in these shops was unplanned and I couldn't afford many of the treasures there, but at least I got to hold them and admire them, albeit briefly.

Over the months, I became a familiar figure to many of the shopkeepers. They would call out to me, 'Madam! Come!', inviting me to their shops. One of my discoveries was Mani's Frameworks, where I spotted two young lads putting frames together. Fascinated by their skill and artwork, I stopped to watch. These handmade and painted frames would enhance the beauty of whatever they framed.

Chamu had two precious photographs of Gandhiji taken by Margaret Bourke-White. He wanted to get these framed and I thought Mani's Frameworks would be the right place. I went back with the photographs the following day. Chamu had advised not to leave the photographs at the shop and so I sat on the steps of the shop while they were framed.

On the way back from Russell Market and Richard's Square, two of my favourite stops were the Chinese noodle shop and one that sold varieties of loose tea—both on Broadway. The tea stall offered a choice of Darjeeling, Nilgiri or Assam teas. I wonder now whether there was really any difference between one and the other but we found the tea fragrant, and it made for a nice cup in the afternoon which Chamu would make with meticulous attention. The noodle shop, run by a migrant Chinese family, was a very interesting place and unusual in Bangalore of those days. As you climbed up the steep steps, you were faced with strands of freshly-made noodles hanging like garlands from wooden frames. Inside the shop there were rows and rows of noodles hanging on these frames in various stages of readiness and cases of packed noodles ready for sale. As one climbed the steps to the entrance, a bell would ring inside and someone would emerge from the depths of the shop. I would take a few cases of the freshly-made noodles and cook them for dinner when I felt the need for variety. Noodles with vegetables and a soup would be a welcome change at dinnertime for the family.

Malleshwaram Market

For a different experience of marketing, we would go to Malleshwaram. Chamu and I would leave after three o'clock in the afternoon when he took a break from his writing. One route I took went through the residential suburb of Palace Orchards and past the Sankey Tank. At that time in the afternoon, schoolchildren would be on their way home.

Seeing me at the wheel, they would stop and point, 'Look, look, *Ajji* (grandmother) is driving the car!' Even in the 1980s, it was rare to see women drivers on the roads.

Sampige Road was the main commercial street we visited when in Malleshwaram. What a beautiful name for a street, I thought, that was once lined with sampige (*magnolia champaca*) trees. Parallel to Sampige Road was the more residential Margosa Road, with towering neem trees that cast a cool shadow. The streets in Malleshwaram were well laid out in a grid. Traffic was orderly and we enjoyed our drive there.

At the entrance to the Malleshwaram Market was a shrine of Lord Ganesha. A priest would perform pooja every morning and evening and light the lamp. Devotees would stop for a moment and then move on to their daily activities.

Rukka and Chamu at Malleshwaram market

Parking our Fiat near the 8th Cross in Ganesha Temple Square, we would walk up the gentle incline of Sampige Road to the vegetable market, bustling and seemingly chaotic—simply a visual and aromatic delight! Some of the vegetable stalls were on the inclined area, others were in the main market at the lower level. On one side of the market were the dry goods stalls, where one could find stalls selling bangles, trinkets, items for the many temples nearby, like incense, cotton, camphor, kumkum and rhizomes of dried turmeric, heaped in trays and baskets. This was quite a contrast to Russell Market, which had none of this.

Malleshwaram market stalls

On the other side of the market were the stalls of fresh vegetables. Each stall was devoted to a few vegetables, sometimes specializing in one kind: different kinds of greens and spinach; varieties of pumpkin and squash; or ginger, chillies, coriander and curry leaves. There was one lady who only sold raw plantains, plantain flowers and the white stems of banana plants. Up a small incline was a fruit stall. It was always brightly lit after dusk. The heat of the afternoon would bring out bees and wasps that buzzed over the baskets of ripe fruit.

Seasonal specialties were a treat for the eyes. During the

Hindu harvest festival of Pongal or Makar Sankranti, celebrated around the same time, one could buy fresh turmeric with its leaves and the sod clinging to the rhizomes; fresh ginger; *yellanda pazham* (a kind of berry); and sugarcane stacked with its leaves, 10 ft high. At dusk, small lamps and kerosene lanterns were lit, as the market was not electrified. Each stall had its own light, some brighter than others.

Sankranti festival at Malleshwaram market

What I remember about the shoppers was that they each carried their own shopping bags, made of cloth, a tarpaulin-like material or woven plastic. These were durable bags and taken on every shopping trip. There was no sign of disposable plastic bags anywhere. Vendors would deftly package a handful of chillies or turmeric in newspaper and tie it up with a string. Small paper bags were also used—they were made from the pages of old exercise books and magazines recycled by the kabadiwala, and a cottage industry employing women and girls. All the packaging was recycled and biodegradable. All that has changed and now shoppers demand plastic bags as a right.

Flower stalls at Malleshwaram market

Chamu befriended many of the stall keepers and entered into conversation with them. Even a visit to the market was an opportunity for him to do fieldwork and hear the stories of people there. A bangle seller told him that he came from Andhra Pradesh. Chamu asked why he had come all the way to Karnataka. He replied that his wife was from Karnataka, so he moved in with his in-laws and set up a bangle stall.

An elderly man with his young teenage son managed a stall with a variety of green chillies, lime and lemon. The stall also carried fresh ginger, mango ginger, fresh green peppercorns, sarsaparilla, amla, green mango and fresh, tender tamarind pods—all for pickling and not available throughout the year. I once bought some sarsaparilla and put it in gin. The fragrant drink was a hit with dinner guests who tried to guess the flavour.

When we returned to the stall a few times at dusk, the elderly father was not there, and the teenage son was in charge.

He would be poring over his homework in the dim light of the oil lamp. Chamu admired his determination. 'Dogged does it!' he would say. He gifted the young boy a torch to see better. Chamu passed on in 1999 and a few years later, I visited the stall. The old man greeted me and asked in Kannada, 'Where is *buddiyouru* [Sir]?' When I told him about my loss, he expressed his regrets and said, 'If he was around, he would have been very happy. My son is in Delhi now, working for Satyam [the computer firm].' He was sorry he could not convey this to Chamu.

The Frymaster

Chamu had a way with words. He would sum up situations—get at the heart of things and of people, what they were about—with a word or two. He also had a wicked sense of humour and was witty to boot. When we stayed at a hotel called the Palm Grove and were disappointed with the service and tired of being badgered for tips, Chamu named it 'Palm Grease'. Once, when he returned from his morning walk, he announced he had met 'Fako' at the corner store. She was an acquaintance of mine. I leave my readers to use their imagination to get a sense of what kind of person fits this description. He christened another acquaintance of ours who was employed at the Forestry Department as 'Woodlouse' and would ask me, 'Oh, did you run into Woodlouse?' The gentleman did look like a burrowing beetle of sorts.

'Frymaster' was another term Chamu coined. This time, the name expressed his admiration and wholehearted approval. After buying vegetables, fruits and flowers at the Malleshwaram Market, he and I would amble along up the street. The pavement was made up of uneven granite slabs that would turn slick on rainy evenings and trees often obscured the street lights. Our path would be lit by the kerosene lanterns and some tubelights from shops. We would be drawn by the whiff of onions being fried and would come upon the Frymaster, the vendor who made piping hot bajjis and *bonda*s at a street stall. The stall started out with a stove and a kerosene lamp on the granite sidewalk. The Frymaster would be there only after dusk, when people were returning home or going about their evening rounds to stores or to the many temples in the area.

The Frymaster
Photo credit: Richa Bhavanam

There would always be a crowd around the Frymaster's stall. Many of the customers were men who stopped to have a quick, hot bite on their way from work or take a packet of freshly made bajjis home. I would push my way through the throng to place my order for the chilli bajjis, potato bondas and the excellent *masalvadai*. Seated on a low stool in front of a huge metal *bandli* (wok)—about 2 ft in diameter—about 2 ft in diameter bubbling with hot oil, was the master fryer. Heavy and bare-chested, he had a towel thrown over his shoulders and would always be dressed in a veshti. I remember him with a white ash and red kumkum dot on his forehead, signifying he was a Hindu. There was a big platter of prepared vegetables near his stool: chillies slit down the middle, rectangles of raw plantain, rounds of raw onion, a tray of small potato spheres that were the bondas and a bowl of chickpea batter. Next to his right hand, the Frymaster would have a medium-sized pail of water into which he would dip his hands every now and then, and dry them on the towel. With quick, deft movements, he would drop the battered chillies into the hot oil with his fingers.

Business was brisk. There was no time for relaxed conversations. Orders were shouted out, hollered, and responses were brusque. '*Mesankai bekku* (I want chillies)!' The Frymaster would respond with, '*Mensankai illa, only irulli* (No chillies, only onion).' The chillies went fast! A little boy sitting next to the Frymaster would take the orders. We would get little paper cones of chilli bajjis and potato bondas wrapped in newspapers and tied with strings, and take them home to have with drinks. Whenever I remembered to carry my thermos with me, I would fill it with a couple of glasses of *badam halu*, the sweet almond milk drink, flavoured with cardamom that is beloved by Kannadigas.

When we knew friends were about to drop in, we would make a dash to the Frymaster and get some hot bajjis. When we had to make unplanned trips and didn't have much time, I would drive on Chowdaiah Road, park the car near the Kadu Malleshwara Temple and walk to the Frymaster.

Our friends, Dr Raja Rammana, Navaratna Sreenivasa Rao, Chamu's colleagues and students have all enjoyed the Frymaster's delights. Scarlett Epstein, who visited Bangalore from Sussex, would eagerly look forward to her sundowner and the Frymaster's bondas. It was an addiction. We would also distribute them to our friends and neighbours. Mrs Seetharam, our neighbour, would always welcome an evening snack. The Frymaster would never disappoint.

Vadai Day at NIAS

Dr Raja Ramanna came home one evening and over a couple of whiskies and homemade snacks, he outlined his vision for the National Institute of Advanced Study (NIAS). He was keen that Chamu join as a Fellow.

Dr Ramanna was a highly respected nuclear scientist who had worked on the early stages of India's nuclear programme and later became the director of the Bhabha Atomic Research Centre, in 1972. He had led a team of scientists in testing the nuclear device under the code name, Smiling Buddha. Besides his achievements in physics and nuclear science, he was trained in classical music and I learnt from Chamu that he was a student of Western classical music. I even heard him play classical piano at his home in R.T. Nagar. On one or two occasions, his daughter Nirupa joined him.

When I was teaching at Bishop Cotton Boys' School, Dr Ramanna was invited on many occasions as one of the illustrious 'Old Boys', and he was very gracious and generous with his time, talking to the students and the staff. I felt I had known him for a long time because he was easy to talk to and was not formal.

One other reason I felt close to him was because of his appreciation of home-cooked food. In a very informal manner, he would say, 'Srinivas, are you and Rukmini free? I'll come over for the evening.' And over a drink and cheese pakodas, Chamu and he would talk about a range of matters—politics, history, education and, more importantly, the direction in which NIAS should go.

Dr Ramanna was very charming and he had a talent for bringing together people who would help him in his vision for making the NIAS a centre of excellence. We had frequent dinners at the Institute, which was on the campus of the Indian Institute of Science. At these dinners, faculty would bring their families and were free to invite a guest. Major General Paul would be in charge of all the arrangements and, being a retired army person, he made sure everything worked like clockwork.

In a smallish room on the second floor, staff and their families and guests would gather for drinks and dinner. There would be music and dance performances and lectures, and Dr Ramanna would never miss these evenings. He introduced us to an army drink—rum with a slit green chilli in it—and popularized it at the Institute. He regaled us one evening with a piano recital. The atmosphere created was so informal that everyone loosened up and enjoyed themselves. On one occasion, Dr Ravi Kapur, who was the joint director of the Institute at the time, got onto the stage and gave an impromptu performance of a Punjabi song and dance.

The Institute gardens were the pride of the campus. Here again, Major General Paul gave his all for the maintenance of the gardens. It was his idea that dinners be moved from the small room upstairs to a space in the garden. I remember when Rajmohan Gandhi gave a lecture at the Institute, he joined us for dinner in the garden.

The Institute was a welcoming place. Dr Ramanna would arrive accompanied by his Lhasa Apso, Chinchin, who would follow him around the Institute and take naps in the sun-filled corridor. On weekdays, lunch was served to all staff and Fellows and anyone could invite a guest for lunch. Mid-morning and late afternoon, there would be tea and coffee with biscuits. Some days, students and faculty would take a break from their work and play cricket. Sundar Sarukkai, one of the research fellows at the time, organized a 'limited overs' (one day) match, 'The Maddur Vadai International' (Maddur Vade is a crisp, disc-shaped savoury snack, a speciality of the town of Maddur, on the way to Mysore). Chamu and I were once invited as chief guests and Chamu bowled leg spins and googlies.

Dr Ramanna had a sudden brainwave for a mid-week special snack day. On Wednesdays, he declared, tea and coffee would be served with vadai, not biscuits. And each Wednesday, there would be a different kind of vadai: uddina vadai, masala vadai, maddur vadai, aama vadai, potato bonda, along with accompaniments of spicy, sweet and sour sauces and coconut chutney. Nowhere did we see bottles of tomato ketchup. Vadai Day became an important institution and people would look forward to chatting over hot vadais and coffee. It was the day to invite scholarly guests to meet faculty and students. Dr Ramanna knew the importance of creating such occasions for scholars to talk to each other, exchange views and ideas.

Although there was a lot of camaraderie, small talk and happy hours, the Institute was a place for serious research in a wide variety of fields. Apart from the pure sciences, social sciences and humanities were encouraged. And there was a sense that young people would attend the lectures and participate.

When Lakshmi and I visited NIAS in the winter of 2015, the head gardener proudly showed us two healthy coconut palms and reminded us that one was planted by Dr Ramanna 'Sir' and the other by Srinivas 'Sir'.

The Bangalore of those days, just a few decades ago, seems another world altogether in very many ways.

Treasures in Kalasipaliyam

I was introduced to the area of Bangalore known as Kalasipaliyam after I married Chamu in 1955. And at first, it was in passing—as Kalasipaliyam, the depot for long-distance buses and taxis, featured on our yearly trip to Mysore in the summer. Knowing that I was born in Bangalore, Chamu would teasingly say, 'Here Bangalore girl, let me show you your Bangalore.'

I never had the time on those trips to explore Kalasipaliyam and its surroundings, but I did some years later. When we lived on the campus of Delhi University, I met Mrs Doraiswamy, my friend Uma Chakravarty's mother. Mrs Doraiswamy was a very outgoing person, very friendly and with an encyclopaedic mind. We were both pleased to learn that we had something in common—Bangalore, the city where I was born. Mrs Doraiswamy had lived in Bangalore and knew the city well. She was a person who I think was in search of new experiences and had many interesting stories to tell. When she learnt that I spent every summer in Mysore, she enquired if I had ever spent any time in Bangalore on my way. I said I did, in Malleshwaram, with Chamu's cousin. She asked if I had ever taken a bus ride or a taxi ride from Kalasipaliyam. I said I had done so quite a few times. She said, 'That is also my favourite haunt for shopping.' I wondered what she meant. What kind of shopping would a middle-class woman like Mrs Doraiswamy want to do in the crowded area that was Kalasipaliyam, with rows and rows of nondescript shops that looked a bit tumbledown? She said, 'Go to the street behind the bus station and you will see a stall. It opens after 12 noon and you will know what I mean when I say it is a treasure house.' Years later, when we moved to Bangalore in 1972, I went in search of the stall she had mentioned, behind the bus stop. I went after midday as she had instructed me to. The stall was raised from the ground, propped on four legs. A flight of wooden stairs took me into the little shop.

Inside, there were rectangular wooden planks lined up against the side. A middle-aged man was sitting cross-legged in front of a small wooden desk. He greeted me, asked me to sit down on the wooden floor over which was spread a quilted coverlet. There were old steel cupboards against the three walls and there was a small metal box. A noisy fan whirred above my head. The man asked me in Kannada, 'What do you want?' I told him: 'My friend Mrs Doraiswamy sent me to your shop.' His face brightened at the sound of her name and we immediately became friends. I learnt he was from the Marwari community and that his family had lived in Bangalore for generations.

Without knowing or asking what I was there for, because I myself didn't know, he opened some of the steel cupboards and very carefully and gently took out some heavily embroidered gold-lace silk saris. I had never seen the likes of those textiles before. I asked him in Kannada, 'What are these?' He said they were called temple saris and many were bought at auction from big temples, like Tirupati, where devotees offered these to deities. The saris were like museum pieces and I was simply stunned by the workmanship, the excellent condition of the gold-lace woven saris and the bright colours.

The shop owner, who was also a pawnbroker, seemed to know a lot about these textiles. He told me these were not chemical dyes; vegetable dyes had been used instead. And the price he quoted was not exorbitant for the kind of treasures they were. When he saw I was seriously interested in buying a couple of saris, he opened a couple of more cupboards and showed me many more beautiful saris and shawls. Thanks to Mrs Doraiswamy, I found myself in a world of textile treasures. I remember I bought a pink one and another that was bright blue in colour with kingfisher checks. The saris had elaborate borders and even more elaborate pallus. The man in the shop said that he did not accept cheques, only cash. He then opened the little box on which he was resting his left thigh and showed me some beautiful pieces of what he called old jewellery. I didn't have the cash for these, and I was content to buy two saris. When I went home and showed Chamu the saris and told him about the shop, it piqued his interest. He also liked the saris. The anthropologist in him appreciated not only the aesthetics of the saris but their history too. He was pleased that I had bought two and said, 'Why don't you model them for me?', which I did. These were one-of-a-kind saris and with Chamu's encouragement, I went back some months later and bought a couple more—this time, one with no gold lace at all and the other with delicately woven gold motifs in the body of the material.

When my sisters visited me, they fell in love with the saris and each one of them wanted a treasure piece as a keepsake, but by that time, my pawnbroker friend had sold almost all of his saris. He told me, 'There are just one or two pieces left. I don't get anymore. They are not being woven anymore. And foreigners come and buy from me.' My younger sister in Bombay pleaded with me to get her one, which I did. Her relative in Canada, on one of his visits to Bombay, saw her sari and demanded that she get one for his daughter in Canada. So, I got her another one. By that time, the price had increased tenfold. Even so, it was a very small price to pay for this extraordinarily beautiful piece of art.

Annual Pilgrimage to Mysore

Between 1960 and 1972, when Chamu and I were at Delhi University, we would start planning for our trip down south every April. And we were happy to get away from the searing heat of Delhi. Chamu would look forward to the summer holiday, to the trip to Mysore to see his mother and siblings, and I would spend some time with my parents in Tanjore before joining him in Mysore. Our lives in Delhi were hectic with teaching, and as Chair of the Sociology Department, Chamu would be immersed in departmental duties and his research. I looked forward to spending a relaxed time with relatives and without the responsibilities of running a household and the children's school.

The last few weeks in April, I would shop for gifts to take for our relatives, something I loved doing. I knew that family members back home would expect gifts and also, they would have lovingly bought gifts for me and my family. One of the valued gifts from Delhi were the light wicker baskets from the Kashmiri state emporium. I took Lucknow chikan-work saris for my sisters and sisters-in-law, little bead necklaces, kolhapuri chappals, which were not available in the South at that time, and not to forget various kinds of sweets—*pedas, revadi* and *sohan papdi*—for my brother-in-law. On the train journey, Chamu never failed to buy Nagpur oranges, the juiciest and sweetest that I have ever tasted, and when we crossed Andhra Pradesh he would always buy a basket of sitaphal—his mother's favourite fruit.

As I said earlier, from Bangalore there were two ways to get to Mysore. When we took the train, the Grand Trunk Express took us to Madras, from where we boarded the Night Mail to Bangalore. It was indeed a long journey across the subcontinent. After a few hours' halt and breakfast in Bangalore, we either took the train to Mysore or one of the taxis that plied between Bangalore and Mysore. If we hired a taxi, we would be in Mysore in three hours. We often chose the latter to avoid changing trains in Bangalore in the early predawn hours.

To get to the taxis, we had to go from the City Station in Bangalore to the Kalasipaliyam area in the city, where the mofussil bus station was located. Here, we would find buses to Mysore. From a distance, one could hear touts shouting the destination of long-distance buses, 'Mysuru-Mysuru, Mandya, Chickballapur, Kodagu', and so on, all over Karnataka state. The area around the bus station was very busy with lots of small eateries and hotels and hole-in-the-wall lodges where travellers could stay cheaply.

Before dawn, the bus station was lit with petromax lanterns and the bus conductors would carry torches to help passengers climb aboard the buses—very thoughtful indeed. There wasn't an inch of space to move around. I saw crowds of men and women with children in tow boarding the buses. Some men stood around drinking tea or coffee or smoking, waiting for their buses, and women sat on their haunches with wailing infants in their arms. Stray cattle wandered around and stray dogs looked for scraps to eat. In fact, to me, it seemed total confusion.

In the predawn hours barbers plied their trade—giving men seated on low stools a shave and removing their earwax. The many tea and coffee stalls did brisk business. Young boys carried trays of steaming hot coffee and tea in glass tumblers to travellers in the buses and passed the glasses through the windows. One had to gulp the hot coffee before the bus left, as the glass had to be returned. There were no disposable plastic cups those days.

There would also be a large number of black-and-yellow Ambassador taxis in another section of the bus stand where touts would shout the destinations of individual cabs through a megaphone. Teenage boys in shorts would be employed by the taxi owners for this job. They would also come and seek prospective passengers by grabbing them by the arm and asking, in Kannada, 'Where do you want to go, Sir?' and then lead people to where the taxis were waiting. Since we would have several pieces of luggage, the porters at the railway station would pounce upon us and even before we could say anything, they would grab pieces of luggage and haul them off to the waiting taxis. Since the railway station was so close to the bus station, the porters would rush from one station to the other and we would have to run to keep up with them.

The first time I got into a taxi with Chamu, I expected the driver to right away start on our road journey to Mysore. But he was nowhere to be seen. The same tout who brought us there continued shouting, '*Mysuru Saar, banni, banni* (Please come, Sir, going to Mysore).' The arrangement—which I didn't know of then—was to share a taxi and the charges of long-distance travel. The Ambassador taxis could comfortably take four other passengers besides the driver, with one or two children on the passengers' laps. We waited till the taxi filled up with three other passengers, while the tout continued to shout in Kannada, 'One seat available to Mysuru.' The driver would then stroll up to the cab leisurely after his coffee and hot idlis, smelling of beedi.

Sharing a taxi meant going for a long ride with strangers in close proximity. Chamu and I were already tired after a long train journey, and fellow passengers' body odour, the smell of their food and their travel habits made the journey tedious. There was always at least one person who would fall asleep and snore loudly or lean on another heavily. I remember a passenger insisting on frequent stops to light his beedi, ordering the driver, '*Nillisi, Nillisi* (Stop, Stop)!' The other passengers would share a smoke on the side of the road. It was a source of irritation to me that no one thought of the inconvenience to others or considered that there were children in the car.

After a couple of years travelling this way, we would go directly to a taxi. Chamu would honk the horn till the driver appeared, and then tell him that we would pay the entire taxi's fare and that he should start right away. One thing the drivers seemed to understand was 'I have an important meeting in Mysore'. Chamu used this reasoning to start on our journey and leave the cacophony in the bus station behind us.

If we went by taxi during the day, Chamu would eagerly look out at the fields of coconut and paddy waving in the breeze, a landscape he loved and felt connected to. If we took the slow night train to Mysore after spending the day in Bangalore, we would fall asleep in our compartment to wake up early morning, as the train rolled into Mysore station. Chamu would wait for Maddur station, where we would sometimes get the specialty snack—crisp Maddur Vadai—to savour with hot coffee. Passing Srirangapatna, the train would near Mysore and as it took the bend, Chamu would excitedly point to the Chamundi *Betta* (Hills) and say, 'We've arrived.' Living in the flat plains of Delhi, he longed for this landscape and scenery. I could sense the excitement in him every year as we travelled to Mysore.

In those days, Mysore was a very green town—the number of trees with broad canopies sheltered many birds. There were hardly any high-rise buildings. Many houses had big gardens, with flowering plants and fruit trees—coconut, guava, chickoo, papaya and mango. Chamu's family lived in a cosy but sprawling bungalow with wooden shutters and monkey tops. The coolness of the evening would require a quilt or blanket at bedtime.

Life would suddenly change for us in Mysore. We often travelled within the city by tonga and I associate Mysore with tonga rides on wide avenues lined with blooming jacaranda and gulmohar trees, under overcast skies and with the smell of damp earth on the breeze. We would go for long walks, visit friends and come home to a sumptuous meal of local delicacies prepared by the cook Sheshadri. Rainy afternoons would be spent at home, chatting or reading with steaming hot tumblers of coffee in the semicircular verandah. Often, pakodas and jalebis, Mysore pak and halwa from Indra Bhavan or Guru Sweets would accompany the afternoon coffee if we did not have homemade sweets like *cobri obattu*. For me, this would be a carefree time free of all household responsibilities, and the leisurely pace of life was like a tonic.

I loved roaming around the KR (Krishna Rajendra) vegetable and fruit market, looking for the special tender green brinjal and the umpteen varieties of greens that always seemed to be available. Never in Delhi had I bought baskets of Raspuri mangoes as I did in Mysore. It was sheer gluttony. The mangoes would be finished in no time by my nieces and nephews, and visitors to the home. For a few days, dessert would be *mango shrikarne*, a rich mango pudding with cardamom and almonds.

My sister-in-law, Thanga, known as 'Thangu' at home and to her friends, on her return from the university where she was a lecturer, would hurriedly have her tiffin and a cup of tea and set out on her social visits, to return home at dinner time. She was an enthusiastic walker and I have accompanied her on walks to the homes of her friends and colleagues, and a few times to Manasa Gangotri and to Crawford Hall on the university campus. Walking to the market would be quite a stretch for me and when I passed a tonga stand, I would suggest that we take a tonga. Thangu would smile and agree to that. But left to herself, she would walk the distance. Walking on the wide tree-lined streets, and in perfect weather, was a great pleasure. And one would come across people walking in groups—it was a social activity.

Rukka with Thangu

Chamu's mother did not go out of the house much. She would occasionally visit the temple. But I do remember going to the sari shops with her every summer. She would insist on buying me a few silk saris and we would walk into two or three of her favourite stores on the main market street. She was an esteemed customer—from the moment she would walk in, the store manager would clear the carpets, put some bolsters and cushions for her to sit down and, knowing her preference for old styles and old designs, the salesmen would exhibit some exquisite saris. Chamu, too, liked to look around the shops and markets some afternoons and on one of those afternoons, he came home with three beautiful silk saris—maroon with delicate gold lace, for his two sisters and for me. He had got them at the Karnataka state-run Cauvery Emporium for just a few hundred rupees each.

Chamu with his mother

Summer vacation in Mysore also meant many trips for the family. Nearer home, we would go to the Chamundi Hills. I remember walking up the many steps cut into the hillside. It was wild and beautiful in those days and we were even warned about wild animals. When we drove up the hillside, our daughters would look out for the statue of Mahishasura, the 'buffalo demon', and ask Chamu to tell them the story. At the foot of Chamundi Hills was the Mysore Zoo, another place on our itinerary. But we stopped going there after a couple of years

Chamu's mother and Lakshmi

because we could not stomach the conditions in which the animals were kept. Visitors too—both children and adults—would tease the caged animals. The entire experience became more painful than pleasurable. What a contrast to the wild jungles of Bandipur.

Another mandatory summer outing was the Krishna Raja Sagara Dam and Brindavan Gardens. Chamu's mother would pack a meal of varieties of mixed rice with accompaniments and a dessert of coconut *cobri mitai.* My nieces and nephews would sometime go boating in the small lake. We would stroll around, admiring the fountains that were lit at night and which transformed the garden into a magical place.

There were few places where we would eat out. A treat for adults and children was Kitty's Squash, where one could have fresh fruit juice made on the premises or ice cream—just two flavours, chocolate and vanilla. Chamu introduced me to 'set dosai' at Raju's Hotel, which was called 'Raju Hotlu' by locals. It was a very small, hole-in-the-wall eatery that specialized in Mysore-style 'set dosai'. The delectable dosai were small and spongy, served with a pat of fresh homemade butter and coconut chutney. Even without our ordering it, steaming hot filter coffee in a metal tumbler would appear at the table. Raju Hotlu was an institution that drew people even from faraway Bangalore, and customers came from all walks of life.

The house that I walked into when I was engaged to Chamu was his family home on Venkata Krishnaiah Road, renamed College Road. It was a narrow street with semi-detached houses on both sides. Most of the houses had their own wells. The houses were built in the old style of a street house, with the front room facing the street and an inner courtyard with a couple of fruit trees and plants for worship, such as tulsi and jasmine. There was a small patch of garden at the back. Chamu's mother told me that she and her husband had built the house themselves. She showed me her hands when she explained that she had placed the bricks herself. I have many pleasant memories of visiting Chamu's traditional family home. Years later, when I visited Mysore, I visited College Road out of sheer nostalgia. I found that Chamu's parents' house stood as it was, even though it was no longer owned by the family. Many houses on that street had been remodelled.

Home Visits and Social Calls in Mysore

The first time I met Dr Sanjeev Rao was the day after I arrived in Mysore, a couple of months before Chamu and I got married. The doctor was on a home visit to check up on Chamu's mother. He was an amiable and friendly person, a garrulous visitor, and would bring in all the news about the town. He quizzed me about my parentage and my education and wanted details of my meeting with Chamu, almost to the point of intrusion. But that was just his way of being friendly, I thought.

Dr Sanjeev came home every evening at the same time. Nearing five o'clock, he would announce his arrival by hollering at the door, 'Amma!' I learnt he had been the family doctor for decades. He brought with him his little doctor's kit, a small thermometer and an instrument for measuring blood pressure. Chamu's mother would stop whatever she was doing—usually at that time in the evening she would be in her chair in the living room, reading the newspaper *The Star of Mysore*. Dr Sanjeev would first take her temperature, then he would take her blood pressure, check her lungs and heart with his stethoscope, prod and poke her in the abdomen, examine her legs for any edema, and would say, 'Okay, you're good.' Then he would wait for his cup of steaming hot filter coffee and with a 'see you tomorrow', he would get into his car. As I learnt a few days later, it was an arrangement made decades earlier that he would visit Amma every evening to keep a tab on her health and be paid on an annual basis; also he would take care of every family member. Anyone with a cough or cold would be treated when he came home.

This was my first experience of a professional doctor visiting his patient's house on a daily basis. I am sure Amma felt well just being assured of his unfailing daily visits and the news he brought with him. I learnt from Chamu that Dr Sanjeev was also family doctor to R.K. Narayan, and their home was also on his round of daily visits.

Plant Mania

From the 1950s through the 1980s, most houses in Mysore and Bangalore, even those with very limited space for a garden, had a few plants and flowering shrubs. Flowers one used to see in gardens were orange *kanakambaram*, hibiscus, roses, chrysanthemum, yellow and orange marigold, December flower, *arali* (oleander), champak and so on, which were also used for worship in Hindu homes. Rock roses or *kallu roja*, with yellow or pink flowers, grew on middle-sized shrubs. The fragrant blooms would be strung into garlands. One rarely sees rock rose plants now. The 'pooja garden' was a sacred space and women would decorate the ground around the tulsi plant with kolam made of rice flour. A lamp and incense would be lit in the alcove in the evenings. Aside from plants used for worship, crotons were a popular plant to grow in pots, so also varieties of ferns and what used to be called geraniums (actually pelargoniums) with their bright flowers, which were also easily propagated from cuttings. Succulents were also popular house plants, as were 'money plants'—vines grown both outside in gardens and also brought indoors—as they would grow lushly in a vase of water.

Thangu, Chamu's sister, was a psychologist by training, but a horticulturist and plant enthusiast at heart. Thangu's deep interest in plants was evident at our first meeting. On my first visit to Mysore, Chamu took me to his mother's home and I saw a youngish woman watering potted plants on the terrace. On being introduced to her, she didn't turn to look

Thangu

at me but just nodded her head absently and continued watering the plants. 'How very strange,' I thought. But I soon realized that Thangu's passion for plants overrode all other considerations.

When Thangu built her own house on a large site in an upper middle-class suburb of Mysore, she could indulge her love of plants. The house was set in the middle of the plot with space for garden all around. We would stay with Thangu every summer when Chamu, our daughters and I would visit Mysore from Delhi and so, over the years we saw the garden take shape. Thangu had divided the space into a kitchen garden at the back and a front garden of flowering shrubs. On the side of the house, there were a few fruit trees: three mango trees, one sapota, an *amla* tree and one of bitter orange. I mustn't forget the pomelo tree. There were also banana plants, moringa and curry leaf in the kitchen garden, as there were in many kitchen gardens in South India.

In her kitchen garden, Thangu grew a variety of greens—French beans and a special type of slender, pale-green brinjal that is a Mysore variety. This section of the garden was irrigated with the waste water from the kitchen. In those days, no detergent or soap was used to wash the dishes. Instead, ash from the wood fire, tamarind, soapnut and sand would be used. So, plants flourished with all the nutrients from the run-off.

Flowering shrubs, like hibiscus, rose, chrysanthemum, tuberose and several varieties of jasmine, were planted mainly for Chamu's mother's daily worship. There was a large collection of scented geraniums (a favourite plant of Thangu's) and different varieties of tulsi. The jasmine bush near the front entrance of the house would be covered with fragrant blooms in summer. In a corner of the garden was a *Parijatham* tree—the fragrant white flowers with their short orange stems were also used for worship.

I was amazed at the care Thangu gave each and every plant. Except for her mother's ritual worship and pooja needs, Thangu did not believe in cutting flowers. Once, anticipating visitors to the house, her niece cut a couple of roses and placed them in a vase to arrange the front room for visitors. Thangu chided her, 'Why did you cut the flowers?'

One evening, when Chamu and I returned from a visit to the market, we found Thangu sitting on the doorstep, sobbing. On seeing us, she said, 'Chamu, *hoyitu, hoyitu* (It's gone).' Not knowing what she meant, Chamu, concerned, sat down next to her on the front step. It turned out that the jasmine plant near the front gate had died a slow death because of termites. Thangu felt guilty that she had not noticed; she said she could have prevented it. Chamu promised to get her a plant of her choice for the entry space, but that didn't seem to lessen her sorrow.

Thangu was god-fearing; she would visit temples and pray for the well-being of her family and friends. In most areas of her life, she played by the rules. But where plants were concerned, the rules went out the window. She would gleefully swipe plants from friends' and neighbours' gardens, pinch off succulents from gardens she visited, and strip dried seed pods from plant to plant in her garden. She would put the purloined plants in her handbag to take home. They thrived in her garden because she had a green thumb.

Thangu's friend, Rajanna, on one of his visits home, took a walk around the garden, and pointing to some orchids asked her, 'Where did you get these from, Thangamma? Which nursery? Is it in Mysore?' He had lost his orchids of the same kind and said he didn't know what had happened to them. He wanted to replace them. She answered, 'I really don't remember, Raju.'

Rajanna had a beautiful home in another part of Mysore and he, too, was an enthusiastic and competitive gardener. He had collected plants from far and wide and would make trips to Lalbagh in Bangalore especially to buy plants at the plant exhibitions. A good family friend, he would hospitably invite us home for Bournvita, his favourite drink. Once when we visited him, he proudly showed us a Jersey cow he had bought and some new plants in the garden that he knew would spark Thangu's interest and envy. Thangu was very interested. As we were leaving, she quickly grabbed a couple of potted plants—a croton and a scented geranium, and surreptitiously put them in the boot of the car. Taken aback, we tried to ask her what she was doing but she hushed us up. After we said our goodbyes, in the car on the way home, she said, 'So what, he has taken many of my plants!' It seemed this was the foundation of the relationship between many plant fanatics.

Thangu visited us when we lived in Delhi on 14 Cavalry Lane. This was in the early 1960s. She requested me to take her to a nursery. I took her to a favourite nursery of mine, Sundar Nagar Nursery. As we were getting out of the car, Chamu took her aside and said, 'Don't try your tricks here.'

Recently, I happened to see one of the television shows hosted by Monty Don, the British horticulturist. The show was titled 'The Secret History of the British Garden' and in it Monty Don describes the enthusiasm of Victorian era plant collectors. Their obsession with plants drove them to collect plants from all over the world, by fair means or foul. In her own way, with her meagre resources, Thangu, like the intrepid

Victorian plant collectors, would devise ways and means of collecting and transporting plants. She would arrive home with her bags full of soil, leaves and earthworms. Her enthusiasm and interest in plants and her desire to have them all in her garden matched the desire and enthusiasm of the collectors who established the Kew Gardens.

The Healing Tree

I would sometimes accompany Chamu on his evening walks, a more leisurely stroll than the brisk morning walk he was accustomed to. We would set out from Benson Cross Road towards the Jayamahal Park. The road leading up to the park was a slight incline and though we walked slowly, I would frequently feel out of breath and experience some pressure in the chest. When this happened, I would stop for a few minutes and then we would continue on our walk. When the road plateaued, the pressure I felt would disappear.

The discomfort became a regular feature of our daily walk and it caused some concern. It was at this time that the Wockhardt Hospital on Cunningham Road opened its doors to the public. It was mainly a cardiac care hospital. I felt fortunate and registered myself as a patient of Dr Khanolkar. He diagnosed me with a mild heart condition and said it might need some surgical intervention. He prescribed some medicines and told me to see him after a couple of months.

The Ashoka Pharmacy was just around the corner from the hospital. I used to stop there to get prescriptions filled. I became a familiar face to the proprietor, a young man who was a Bangalorean by birth, and he would greet me with a friendly 'Auntie, how are you?' He was not just a store manager but also a pharmacologist by training, so I could ask him about the medicines when he filled out the prescription. On this visit he gestured towards the front of the store, 'Auntie, do you see those plants growing in the drain outside? Do you know what they are?' I, of course, recognized the Peepal leaf plant. He said, 'It's a remedy for all heart ailments. Before you go in for surgery, take these leaves and see how you feel.'

He then disappeared to the backroom of the store and brought out a booklet, from which he read in Sanskrit, 'Take 20 of these leaves every day. Wash them, cut off the stem and tip, steep them in three glasses of water, boil the water with the leaves till the concoction reduces to one glass. Remove the leaves, cool the decoction and take one-third of it thrice a day, morning, noon and evening.' Then he explained the process in case I had missed anything. The course of treatment was for two weeks and during that time, I was not to eat any rice or rice products. He assured me confidently, 'You wait and see, when you go back for your appointment, the heart picture will be very different.'

From then on, I delegated the job of bringing me fresh leaves everyday to my gardener, who would forage the leaves from various places. The majestic Peepal tree (*Ficus religiosa*) is native to the Indian subcontinent, where it grows wild like the banyan. They are not domestic garden trees but are found on roadsides, in open ground and in temple compounds. The Peepal is sacred to Hindus and has been worshipped for centuries. A member of the mulberry family, it is one of the oldest trees known to humankind, and is referenced in the Bhagavad Gita as the eternal Asvattha tree. It is believed that every Saturday, Goddess Lakshmi sits under the Peepal tree and that gods both live in the tree and hold council under it. Even Jains and Buddhists worship the Peepal—the Mahabodhi, under which Gautama Buddha gained enlightenment, was a Peepal.

I came to know from my Dr Chitappa in Tanjore that women who wanted children would worship the tree, which was said to confer fertility. But worship of the Peepal tree was also recommended for a host of other troubles and ailments. In the Ayurvedic system of medicine, the Peepal tree has scores of medicinal properties. I learnt that it could be a remedy not only for ailments of the heart but also for blood purification, kidney and liver issues, constipation, diarrhoea, eczema, cough, bronchitis, eye pain and inflammation of various kinds.

Chamu was quite concerned about my diagnosis, as was I. He told me worriedly, 'You have to take care of yourself.' I didn't see what I could do differently. I didn't eat much fat and had a fairly balanced diet. But I religiously followed the treatment prescribed by my friendly pharmacist: drinking one dose of the concoction in the morning, taking one with me to work for the afternoon, and downing the evening dose on returning home. I didn't miss a single dose.

I consulted an astrologer, Gayathri Devi Vasudev, who had her office in Seshadripuram, a 20-minute drive from where we lived. B.V. Raman Associates was a family firm and Mrs Vasudev's father was the renowned astrologer B.V. Raman. Gayathri Devi worked out of the same office as her father, helping him with publishing an astrological magazine and bringing out a few issues in the year. We would sometimes see Dr Raman in his tennis whites on his way to a game. We got to know Gayathri Devi Vasudev—or GDV, as she was called in our family, and over the years she became a friend.

Chamu took an appointment with GDV, who was also known for her expertise in medical astrology. That evening, she studied my horoscope chart and the placement of planets, and we told her about my upcoming appointment and possible surgery with Dr Khanolkar. She listened to us, then categorically said, 'I see no intervention with the knife. You can go and see him, don't cancel the appointment, but there will be no surgery.' We left thanking her, feeling both relieved and bewildered, wondering how I could possibly avoid surgery when Dr Khanolkar had advised it.

I returned to Wockhardt for my appointment. Dr Khanolkar ran some tests and reported that the blockages had disappeared and, therefore, no surgical intervention was necessary at the time. He was very surprised as to how this could happen. I didn't tell him about the Peepal leaf or the astrologer, for that matter. But I continued with my treatment with the Peepal leaves for a good many years.

A few weeks later, an acquaintance of Chamu from Mysore who was passing through Bangalore stopped and had a bite with us. It so happened that he came home on the day I was to have had the surgery. So, we were talking about it. He said his mother had had a heart attack and he was rushing to Mangalore by car to go see her. We told him about the Peepal leaf treatment and he was very interested. Some weeks later, he called Chamu excitedly and told him how the treatment had worked, and that his mother's heart condition had improved. Thereafter, I told my colleagues at school about this miraculous remedy for heart blockages and some of them also followed the treatment for their family members.

Peepal tree

Photo credit: Richa Bhavanam

After that, I started noticing Peepal trees wherever I went in the city. There was a row of mature trees on either side of Nandidurg Road, on the way to Mekhri Circle. I also noticed the magnificent Peepal tree in the Ganesha Temple compound in Malleshwaram. It is surprising that I hadn't noticed them before and that I had no idea about how important they are.

Acknowledgements

We would like to thank family, friends and colleagues for their help and support—Krishna and Aruna Chidambi, Michael Fisher, Hamsa Kalyani, Prem Rao, Paula Richman, Sundar Sarukkai and Jyoti Thyagarajan.

Our gratitude to Paul Fernandes for generously giving us permission to use his sketches of Bangalore and for his sketch of Rukka's childhood home in Bangalore, made for the book; Ricabeth Steiger for allowing us to use her photo of Rukka for the cover; and Athreya Chidambi and Richa Bhavanam for use of their photographs of Bangalore.

Many others gave us their support in a variety of ways, and we thank them all.

Our special thanks to Tulasi Srinivas and Popsi Narasimhan who supported this project from start to finish in innumerable ways, and to Monster and Carnie Williams who helped in every way they could and kept our spirits up. We could not have completed the book without them.

Rukmini Srinivas would like to acknowledge the readers of *Tiffin*, whose letters encouraged her to write this second book of reminiscences.